OBJECTIVELY ENGAGED JOURNALISM

McGILL-QUEEN'S STUDIES IN THE HISTORY OF IDEAS
Series Editor: Philip J. Cercone

1 Problems of Cartesianism
Edited by Thomas M. Lennon, John M. Nicholas, and John W. Davis

2 The Development of the Idea of History in Antiquity
Gerald A. Press

3 Claude Buffier and Thomas Reid: Two Common-Sense Philosophers
Louise Marcil-Lacoste

4 Schiller, Hegel, and Marx: State, Society, and the Aesthetic Ideal of Ancient Greece
Philip J. Kain

5 John Case and Aristotelianism in Renaissance England
Charles B. Schmitt

6 Beyond Liberty and Property: The Process of Self-Recognition in Eighteenth-Century Political Thought
J.A.W. Gunn

7 John Toland: His Methods, Manners, and Mind
Stephen H. Daniel

8 Coleridge and the Inspired Word
Anthony John Harding

9 The Jena System, 1804–5: Logic and Metaphysics
G.W.F. Hegel
Translation edited by John W. Burbidge and George di Giovanni
Introduction and notes by H.S. Harris

10 Consent, Coercion, and Limit: The Medieval Origins of Parliamentary Democracy
Arthur P. Monahan

11 Scottish Common Sense in Germany, 1768–1800: A Contribution to the History of Critical Philosophy
Manfred Kuehn

12 Paine and Cobbett: The Transatlantic Connection
David A. Wilson

13 Descartes and the Enlightenment
Peter A. Schouls

14 Greek Scepticism: Anti-Realist Trends in Ancient Thought
Leo Groarke

15 The Irony of Theology and the Nature of Religious Thought
Donald Wiebe

16 Form and Transformation: A Study in the Philosophy of Plotinus
Frederic M. Schroeder

17 From Personal Duties towards Personal Rights: Late Medieval and Early Modern Political Thought, c. 1300–c. 1650
Arthur P. Monahan

18 The Main Philosophical Writings and the Novel *Allwill*
Friedrich Heinrich Jacobi
Translated and edited by George di Giovanni

19 Kierkegaard as Humanist: Discovering My Self
Arnold B. Come

20 Durkheim, Morals, and Modernity
W. Watts Miller

21 The Career of Toleration: John Locke, Jonas Proast, and After
Richard Vernon

22 Dialectic of Love: Platonism in Schiller's Aesthetics
David Pugh

23 History and Memory in Ancient Greece
Gordon Shrimpton

24 Kierkegaard as Theologian: Recovering My Self
Arnold B. Come

25 Enlightenment and Conservatism in Victorian Scotland: The Career of Sir Archibald Alison
Michael Michie

26 The Road to Egdon Heath: The Aesthetics of the Great in Nature
Richard Bevis

27 Jena Romanticism and Its Appropriation of Jakob Böhme: Theosophy – Hagiography – Literature
Paola Mayer

28 Enlightenment and Community: Lessing, Abbt, Herder, and the Quest for a German Public
Benjamin W. Redekop

29 Jacob Burckhardt and the Crisis of Modernity
John R. Hinde

30 The Distant Relation: Time and Identity in Spanish-American Fiction
Eoin S. Thomson

31 Mr Simson's Knotty Case: Divinity, Politics, and Due Process in Early Eighteenth-Century Scotland
Anne Skoczylas

32 Orthodoxy and Enlightenment: George Campbell in the Eighteenth Century
Jeffrey M. Suderman

33 Contemplation and Incarnation: The Theology of Marie-Dominique Chenu
Christophe F. Potworowski

34 Democratic Legitimacy: Plural Values and Political Power
F.M. Barnard

35 Herder on Nationality, Humanity, and History
F.M. Barnard

36 Labeling People: French Scholars on Society, Race, and Empire, 1815–1849
Martin S. Staum

37 The Subaltern Appeal to Experience: Self-Identity, Late Modernity, and the Politics of Immediacy
Craig Ireland

38 The Invention of Journalism Ethics: The Path to Objectivity and Beyond, Second Edition
Stephen J.A. Ward

39 The Recovery of Wonder: The New Freedom and the Asceticism of Power
Kenneth L. Schmitz

40 Reason and Self-Enactment in History and Politics: Themes and Voices of Modernity
F.M. Barnard

41 The More Moderate Side of Joseph de Maistre: Views on Political Liberty and Political Economy
Cara Camcastle

42 Democratic Society and Human Needs
Jeff Noonan

43 The Circle of Rights Expands: Modern Political Thought after the Reformation, 1521 (Luther) to 1762 (Rousseau)
Arthur P. Monahan

44 The Canadian Founding: John Locke and Parliament
Janet Ajzenstat

45 Finding Freedom: Hegel's Philosophy and the Emancipation of Women
Sara MacDonald

46 When the French Tried to Be British: Party, Opposition, and the Quest for Civil Disagreement, 1814–1848
J.A.W. Gunn

47 Under Conrad's Eyes: The Novel as Criticism
Michael John DiSanto

48 Media, Memory, and the First World War
David Williams

49 An Aristotelian Account of Induction: Creating Something from Nothing
Louis Groarke

50 Social and Political Bonds: A Mosaic of Contrast and Convergence
F.M. Barnard

51 Archives and the Event of God: The Impact of Michel Foucault on Philosophical Theology
David Galston

52 Between the Queen and the Cabby: Olympe de Gouges's Rights of Women
John R. Cole

53 Nature and Nurture in French Social Sciences, 1859–1914 and Beyond
Martin S. Staum

54 Public Passion: Rethinking the Grounds for Political Justice
Rebecca Kingston

55 Rethinking the Political: The Sacred, Aesthetic Politics, and the Collège de Sociologie
Simonetta Falasca-Zamponi

56 Materialist Ethics and Life-Value
Jeff Noonan

57 Hegel's *Phenomenology*: The Dialectical Justification of Philosophy's First Principles
Ardis B. Collins

58 The Social History of Ideas in Quebec, 1760–1896
Yvan Lamonde
Translated by Phyllis Aronoff and Howard Scott

59 Ideas, Concepts, and Reality
John W. Burbidge

60 The Enigma of Perception
D.L.C. Maclachlan

61 Nietzsche's Justice: Naturalism in Search of an Ethics
Peter R. Sedgwick

62 The Idea of Liberty in Canada during the Age of Atlantic Revolutions, 1776–1838
Michel Ducharme
Translated by Peter Feldstein

63 From White to Yellow: The Japanese in European Racial Thought, 1300–1735
Rotem Kowner

64 The Crisis of Modernity
Augusto Del Noce
Edited and translated by Carlo Lancellotti

65 Imprinting Britain: Newspapers, Sociability, and the Shaping of British North America
Michael Eamon

66 The Form of Politics: Aristotle and Plato on Friendship
John von Heyking

67 War as Paradox: Clausewitz and Hegel on Fighting Doctrines and Ethics
Youri Cormier

68 Network Democracy: Conservative Politics and the Violence of the Liberal Age
Jared Giesbrecht

69 A Singular Case: Debating China's Political Economy in the European Enlightenment
Ashley Eva Millar

70 Not Even a God Can Save Us Now: Reading Machiavelli after Heidegger
Brian Harding

71 Before Copernicus: The Cultures and Contexts of Scientific Learning in the Fifteenth Century
Edited by Rivka Feldhay and F. Jamil Ragep

72 The Culturalist Challenge to Liberal Republicanism
Michael Lusztig

OBJECTIVELY ENGAGED JOURNALISM

An Ethic

Stephen J.A. Ward

McGill-Queen's University Press
Montreal & Kingston • London • Chicago

ISBN 978-0-2280-0188-1 (cloth)
ISBN 978-0-2280-0214-7 (ePDF)
ISBN 978-0-2280-0215-4 (ePUB)

Legal deposit second quarter 2020
Bibliothèque nationale du Québec

Printed in Canada on acid-free paper that is 100% ancient forest free (100% post-consumer recycled), processed chlorine free

This book has been published with the help of a grant from the Canadian Federation for the Humanities and Social Sciences, through the Awards to Scholarly Publications Program, using funds provided by the Social Sciences and Humanities Research Council of Canada.

Funded by the Government of Canada | Financé par le gouvernement du Canada | Canada | Canada Council for the Arts | Conseil des arts du Canada

We acknowledge the support of the Canada Council for the Arts.

Nous remercions le Conseil des arts du Canada de son soutien.

Library and Archives Canada Cataloguing in Publication

Title: Objectively engaged journalism: an ethic / Stephen J.A. Ward.

Names: Ward, Stephen J.A. (Stephen John Anthony), 1951– author.

Series: McGill-Queen's studies in the history of ideas; 78.

Description: Series statement: McGill-Queen's studies in the history of ideas; 78 | Includes bibliographical references and index.

Identifiers: Canadiana (print) 20190239042 | Canadiana (ebook) 20190239093 | ISBN 9780228001881 (cloth) | ISBN 9780228002147 (ePDF) | ISBN 9780228002154 (ePUB)

Subjects: LCSH: Journalistic ethics. | LCSH: Journalism—Objectivity.

Classification: LCC PN4756.W378 2020 | DDC 174/.907—dc23

This book was typeset by Marquis Interscript in 10/12 New Baskerville.

For Nadia Francavilla, my musical muse.
Every day, and always.

Contents

Acknowledgments

No author works alone, even if they write in solitude. No idea is entirely a fresh invention of our mind, a creation *ex nihilo.* We work amid community and tradition. Some members of my family and community are no longer with us. But their advice, encouragement, and invaluable criticisms still ring in my inner ear.

So I owe a debt to all of you, named and unnamed, who have continued to support my mental labours and my life: my family, Glenda, generous academic friends, close musical comrades, publishers, and, strangely enough, those philosophers who stare down on me from my overburdened bookshelves, as I write.

I owe a special debt to Nadia, who reignited the flame of love and life and would not let my passion for writing and thinking be extinguished.

I thank you all passionately and, yes, objectively.

PART ONE

Deconstructing

1

Introduction: History, Holism, and Dualism

Lack of an historical sense is the hereditary defect of philosophers … So what is needed now is historical philosophizing, and with it the virtue of modesty.

Friedrich Nietzsche, *Human, All Too Human*, 2

CONCEIVING ETHICS

Ethics as Practical

Ethics is inherently practical. It is the analysis, evaluation, and promotion of correct conduct and virtuous character in light of the best available principles. Ethics asks how we should live in goodness and in right relation with each other, a task that may require us to forgo personal benefits, to carry out duties, or to endure persecution. This stress on the practical assures us that "the problems we have followed into the clouds are, even intellectually, genuine not spurious."[1]

Our ethical principles are practical proposals on what rules we should follow so as to promote fair social cooperation. Ethical reasoning is an essential means to evaluating such proposals. We constantly reinterpret and balance principles so as to respond to new problems, new facts, new technology, and new social conditions. Even the boundaries of ethics change. In our time, ethics has come to include such issues as animal cruelty, violence against women, pollution of the environment, and the oppression of gay and transgender individuals. Ethical reflection is *normative reason in social practice.* Ethics is the never-completed project of inventing and critiquing norms that guide interaction, define roles, and justify institutions.

Ethics is typically divided into a theoretical and an applied part, although in reality both parts are involved in ethical thinking.[2] Theoretical ethics refers to philosophical theories such as realism, relativism, and emotivism.

1 Dworkin, *Sovereign Virtue*, 4.

2 See Ward, *Ethics and the Media*, 16–51.

The theories ask about the meaning of "good" and "right" and they debate the status of ethical statements. Are ethical statements objective? How do we justify ethical claims?

Applied ethics is less concerned with the meaning of "good" or "right." It wants to know *what* things are good or right, and *what* are the ethical principles that should guide conduct. How do our ethical principles apply to concrete issues, from abortion to ending the life of a terminally ill patient? Applied ethics is also the study of social practices, such as the principles of corporate governance, the ethics of scientific research, and the responsibilities of professional practice. Historically, applied ethics has been a debate between dominant approaches such as an ethic of utility (or utilitarianism), a deontic ethic of rights and duties, an ethic of virtue, and an ethic of community and care.

Objective Engagement

This book provides an ethical theory for a digital, global journalism that is increasingly interpretive, emotive, and engaged in the world. A theory is needed because much of journalism ethics, constructed a century ago for a pre-digital and non-global media, struggles to be relevant to emerging forms of journalism and non-mainstream practitioners. Traditional journalism ethics, with its narrow notion of objectivity and its opposition to interpretation and attachment, lacks the conceptual tools to guide digital news media.[3]

The central empirical thesis of this book is that journalism is a form of social engagement that interprets culture and promotes certain public values and political goals. The central ethical thesis is that journalism should be a form of objective social engagement that, ideally, is responsible and open to dialogue and change. It should be *objective engagement* in the service of democracy and human flourishing, globally.[4]

The two most important concepts are "objectivity" and "engagement," and the most important question is how they are related. Engagement in journalism can take on questionable forms. This prompts people to argue against *any* relationship between objectivity and engagement. They argue that to avoid partisanship and parochial bias journalists should be completely

3 In this book, for stylistic variation, I treat "journalism" and "media" as synonymous. Media will mean "news media." I alternate between "journalism ethics" and "media ethics." I am aware of the blurring of the distinction between journalism, as professionally practised, and other forms of media practice. Today, we all struggle with the ubiquitous, vague term "media."

4 I explored what this engagement means when dealing with racism and extreme populism in *Ethical Journalism in a Populist Age.*

neutral. They call this ideal of detachment "objectivity" and embellish it with narrow, overly restrictive rules and standards. Therefore, many traditions in journalism ethics are solidly *against* regarding journalism as engagement, let alone as some hybrid called "objective engagement." Nonetheless, if we insist on understanding journalism as engagement, the crucial question is what form of engagement is best. I will support the idea that journalists are advocates of a special kind with a specific social role. Journalists are objective advocates for plural, egalitarian democracy within the larger ethical goal of global, human flourishing. Journalism needs an explicit and philosophically grounded ethics of democratic engagement that is neither a biased, partisan form of engagement nor a mincing neutral journalism.

The purpose of this book is to define and defend this type of objective engagement and to show why it is better than other approaches to journalism and its ethics. To do so, the book will put forward a distinct conception of objectivity, an objectivity with a human face, as the preferred objectivity of practice.

The main rival conception is what I call the professional objective ethic which has dominated Western journalism ethics for over a century, especially in North America. It is strongly opposed to thinking about journalists as advocates and journalism as engagement. In this view, journalists should be neutral (or disengaged) reporters of "just the facts." They report on the clash of views among lobby and advocacy groups in the public sphere, but journalists are not themselves advocates. They report on advocates; they do not advocate. To be engaged or to advocate anything is to express a bias or a point of view, which means going beyond the facts. To go beyond facts is to violate the ideal of non-engaged journalism.

This framework of professional objectivity still influences journalism debate despite widespread skepticism about objectivity. The influence is mainly negative. As a rigid and outdated conception, disengaged objectivity limits our capacity to think creatively about alternatives. It has become a tradition to be overcome. Overcoming requires that we come to clearly understand the framework, and why it is outdated and questionable. In particular, we need to reject two dualisms that define the framework. The first is a cognitive dualism that draws a hard line between reporting and interpreting the world; and the second is a social dualism that draws a hard line between reporting for Us (our nation) and reporting on Them (the rest of the world). This is a form of moral tribalism, of Us versus Them. It thinks that journalists have a duty to serve the public of their nation, not the humanity that exists outside its borders. The cognitive and social dualisms prevent us from constructing a new ethic for digital and global media.

The language in this book is deliberately "odd sounding" and anti-dualistic. I think in a hybrid and holistic manner, mixing elements that are separated in other theorizing. My thinking integrates reason and emotion, value and facts, observing and interpreting, objectivity and purposive activity, human construction and human nature. For some, this way of speaking is paradoxical or contradictory. I speak of an objectively engaged journalism, despite the presumption that objective journalism cannot be engaged. I aim at an ethics that is interpretive yet factual, rational yet inclusive of emotions, value-laden yet impartial in method, advocatory and committed yet not narrowly partisan. One reason for this terminological quirkiness is to transcend the dualisms embedded in our discourse, to make conceptual space for a holistic framework of ethical thought. A second and related reason is to provoke a fresh examination of accepted distinctions that have become what Mill called "dead dogma."[5]

Philosophy of Journalism

To achieve this synthesis of concepts, I had to do philosophy of journalism. But one may ask: Why delve into philosophy, psychology, and value theory when the topic is something as concrete as how to make editorial decisions in journalism? Because to make well-justified editorial decisions presumes a viable philosophy of journalism, for two reasons. First, there is the argument of inescapability. Philosophy, inescapably, is at the bottom of our concrete ethical judgments in journalism, whether we are aware of it or not. Philosophical assumptions, in the form of notions of fact, knowledge, justified belief, and the ultimate aims of activity, are embedded in our concrete ethical decisions in life and in journalism. They influence us, even if our assumptions are implicit and not brought to consciousness for examination. In making ethical judgments, or in disagreeing with someone on what actions to take, you are "doing" philosophy, if only in the minimalist sense of working implicitly from philosophical assumptions. You do not have to be a philosopher to employ philosophical notions.

Second, these presumptions come to the surface when we are challenged to justify our judgments. Call this the "ladder of justification." For every reason we give, we may be asked to give a more general reason for *that* reason, and then a more general reason for *that* reason. We climb step-by-step until we reach abstract philosophical principles. Sometimes, we end in a philosophical fog. We realize our conceptions are unclear, and therefore we lose some confidence in judgments that contain these concepts. We may *not* know what we think we know. Socrates was a master of inducing philosophical fog to persuade people to reflect on their beliefs.

5 Mill, *On Liberty and The Subjection of Women*, 42.

Our judgments about journalism practice face the same inescapability of philosophy and the ladder of justification. Imagine that I form a positive assessment of a news report that embarrasses the government because the report is accurate and informs the public. Both accuracy and informing the public are standards. But why, you may ask, are they so important? Well, I reply, because accuracy falls under the more general standard of truth-telling in public communications. And because citizens need truthful and factual reports to make decisions and to judge their government. But you persist. Why are informed citizens important? I reply with a more general reason: Because it aids democracy. But why aim at democracy? And so on. By climbing the ladder of justification, I realize that my judgments are grounded in general social and political values. Change those philosophical assumptions – for example, presume an authoritarian view of media as state "mouthpieces" – and you will not judge the report to be good. You may consider the report dangerous because it undermines confidence in the state. There is, then, *no such thing* as a stand-alone practical ethics consisting only of judgments tied tightly to specific situations in journalism.

As Lyotard said, to ask "Why philosophize?" is to ask a philosophical question. It is the fate of humans to philosophize because of the creatures we are – with consciousness, desire, language, and a critical ability to question what is and to wonder what might be. Philosophy's mission is to recall humans back to their inherent capacity to philosophize, and to ask questions that "irritate everybody."[6] As McIntyre wrote, a central task of the moral philosopher is "to articulate the convictions of the society in which he or she lives so that these convictions become available for rational scrutiny."[7] The philosopher that best expresses my view of philosophy is John Dewey, who thought that philosophy could overcome its historical "craving" for theoretical, infallible truths and become a socially engaged, but fallible, form of inquiry into our most serious problems. He wrote: "Philosophy recovers itself when it ceases to be a device for dealing with the problems of philosophers and becomes a method, cultivated by philosophers, for dealing with the problems of men."[8] Ethics ceases to be a philosopher's quest for the one supreme moral principle, or the promotion of one singular interest (e.g., increasing utility). It becomes a quest for the intelligent and sensitive solution of human problems, based on a "motley" of different but supporting concerns, such as our freedoms and duties.[9]

6 Lyotard, *Why Philosophize?*, 13.

7 McIntyre, "Is Patriotism a Virtue?," 3.

8 Dewey, "The Need for Reform in Philosophy," 94.

9 Wittgenstein uses "motley" to describe the techniques of proof in mathematics. In *Remarks on the Foundations of Mathematics*, 84.

If this view is correct, then making sure we have the best available philosophy for evaluating our ethical beliefs and practices is important, theoretically and practically. Incorrect assumptions lead to fruitless or incorrect approaches to important problems. In journalism, we end up with faulty and restrictive conceptions of what one is doing, or should be doing, in journalism.

Ethics as History

An important (and faulty) philosophical assumption about ethics is that it is, or ought to be, a static set of moral beliefs. Ethics is defined in terms of its content – a set of rules of conduct for some group or domain of life. Any dictionary will tell you that. Reform of journalism ethics runs up against this view because reformists typically adopt a historical perspective that explains how we arrived at some juncture. They regard ethics as a non-static, evolving enterprise. However, "adopt a historical perspective" can be misunderstood and trivialized. To regard ethics historically is to do more than construct a chronology of moral philosophers and major works in the history of ethics. Historically viewing ethics is not like viewing, in a detached mood, a film on a previous era. A historical approach takes the history of ethics seriously. Current conceptions are seen as shaped by the history of their development. Time and situation are intrinsic to ethics. Ethical thinking is thinking *in* time, occurring in a particular historical moment, with a past and a future. It is a thinking that could have turned out differently, and could change tomorrow. We think *now* from within conceptual schemes shaped by the past. We think from some tradition, some cultural heritage. Our ethics, like all social activities, is a contingent cultural product of converging lines of development – developments in society, in culture, in ideas, and in practice. We have arrived at this moment, for better or worse, equipped with these mental tools to address the issues that swirl around our lives.

Ethics as history is a theme in contemporary ethics and philosophy. Nietzsche warned about the philosopher's penchant to "dehistoricize" things, to adopt an "Egyptianism" that turns an idea into an unchanging "mummy."[10] Jose Ortega y Gasset talked about the ethical good itself as a process that is "like nature, an immense landscape in which man advances through centuries of exploration."[11] I am not certain that people heed these philosophical insights when doing ethics. Too often, we regard ethics

10 Nietzsche, *Twilight of the Idols*, 45.
11 Ortega y Gasset, *Meditations on Quixote*, 37.

as an arena of established principles, and disregard (or are suspicious of) talk of history, change, and invention in ethics.

What are the implications of taking history seriously?[12] The first implication is that we need to cast a critical eye on existing principles. These guides are the outcomes of past thinking and experience. We need to be sure we are operating with the best tools available to address the issues of an ever-challenging world. History shows us that our current ethical beliefs and practices are *revisable* outcomes. They have been useful in the past but there is no guarantee they will remain useful.

The second implication is that ethics is humanly created, proposed, and socially approved. It does not consist in moral facts discovered in the world; it is not composed of norms imposed on humans by a higher authority, such as God. Our norms are not *discovered* as existing independently from the historical thinking, the way we might discover a new planet, or a new scientific law. Discovery is a favorite idea of a realist approach to ethics, of moral facts existing in nature.[13] For the historical view, ethics is grounded in nothing more, and nothing less, than groups of people using logic, facts, and experience to agree on reasonable rules of conduct for mutual benefit.

The historical ethicist replaces discovering with proposing. She talks about practically reasonable rules of conduct. What is proposed is thoroughly the work of the human mind embedded in society: conceptual inventions that involve choices and alternatives at every turn. In ethics, it is choice, proposal, and persuasion – all the way down. Ethics is not the attempt to fit our ethical thinking to pre-existing, external principles. Rather, we are trying to organize our conduct and the world to fulfill our ideals and goals.[14]

Third, the historical approach shifts the emphasis away from content (propositions of thought) to intersubjective reasoning and dialogue (processes of thought among persons). The historical approach, instead of thinking of ethics as pre-established content, regards ethics as the *activity* of constructing and applying the best possible standards for responsible practice.

Fourth, historicism in ethics means that our rules of conduct and ethical values are not absolute principles; they are not uniquely correct standards,

12 I provide a detailed account of this historical approach to ethics and meta-ethics in chapter 1 of *Radical Media Ethics.*

13 See Shafer-Landau, *Moral Realism: A Defence.*

14 Philosopher John Searle makes a similar distinction in contrasting factual statements, which are true if they "fit" the world as it is (a word-to-world direction of fit), and ethical statements, which try to make the world fit our promises and ideals (a world-to-word direction of fit). Searle, *The Social Construction of Reality,* 216–17.

austerely existing outside of history and social change. They are imperfect, contingent, fallible, value affirmations. Absolutists think of ethics as a set of unbending prescriptions, established by God or some other authority. Moral systems are called "codes" or "commandments." In its strongest form, absolutism views ethics as an austere code of inflexible rules to be applied similarly in all circumstances by all people. Reasoning and learning in ethics amounts to learning how to recognize actions as cases of lying, stealing, and other conduct prohibited by the rules. An action is either right or wrong, good or evil. It falls under a principle, or it doesn't.

Not all people who think of ethics as primarily content are absolutists. But a "content approach" to ethics, in any of its forms, has a central limitation: it minimizes the *activity* of thinking ethically, especially in concrete situations – and all the uncertainty and difficulty such activity involves. It ignores how rules do, and must, change to meet new conditions. It deemphasizes dialogue and critically challenging presumed absolutes. It leads many people to see variability, disagreement, and change in ethics as signs that our reasoning has gone astray, that moral truths are being undermined, or that ethics is "merely" subjective.

The idea of ethical rules as pragmatic, reflective responses to complex problems strikes me as the correct approach to journalism and communication ethics in a changing world. If we see ethics as inherently involved in addressing new issues with mental tools inherited from the past, we are inclined to ask about the tools, and whether we should revamp our thinking. The historical approach opens the door to reform.

Deconstructing and Reconstructing

Developing an alternate ethical framework for journalism requires major reform. The task is not to add to, or extend, an existing framework. If we are attuned properly to our media revolution, to its deep implications for humanity and communication, our ethics work will, perforce, have a sharp edge. We recognize the need to disrupt journalism ethics as traditionally conceived. We will disrupt habitual, entrenched, and limited ways of thinking about journalism ethics that we inherited from a specific culture of journalism, ages ago.[15]

The traditional objective model has become one of those entrenched and limited ways of ethical thinking. It was constructed for another news media in another news media era. The fashioners, most of them senior newsroom journalists, provided normative guidance for a restricted,

15 On the role of disruption in journalism ethics, see my *Disrupting Journalism Ethics.*

emerging class of professional journalists working mainly for newspapers in a non-global world. They could not envisage the issues that would face today's responsible practice. They did not write norms for a hybrid journalism of professionals and citizens, and their evolving forms of journalism. And now the model is in deep trouble. Tinkering with old ideas, or trying to protect them from the winds of change, will not do. Journalist ethicists cannot put Humpty Dumpty back together again.

We need to do radical ethics.[16] Not radical in the political sense, but radical in the philosophical sense – a reformulation of how we *think* about journalism and its ethics. The first entry for "radical" in *The New Shorter Oxford English Dictionary* says that the word means "going to the root or origin ... affecting what is fundamental; far-reaching; thorough." I am concerned with a fundamental rethink of the ethical framework that is used to direct journalism. Being radical has two conjoined parts, like the opposite sides of a coin: deconstruction and reconstruction. Deconstruction is the critical task of literally "taking apart" existing frameworks idea by idea, noting their meanings and their history. The aim is to determine what principles, practices, and ways of thinking about journalism ethics remain valid. What ideas should be abandoned or reformulated? The second part is the positive reconstruction of a new ethic with reinterpreted ideas, and new aims and norms.

In journalism ethics, there is a plurality of journalism frameworks and traditions. I focus on deconstructing the professional objective ethic because it has been an important and influential model, and it is the tradition most responsible for skepticism about engaged journalism. It principles, and its way of thinking about the principles, are common to many approaches to journalism ethics and many codes of journalism ethics. Even though its principles have been subjected to criticism, and new forms of journalism reject some of its precepts, the model remains a force in journalism ethics.

It is not enough to criticize in a superficial manner the traditional objective model. We need to dig down to its conceptual roots in philosophy to understand their force on us. Until we know, explicitly and in detail, *why* the model is incorrect and *how* it limits our ethical thinking, we will not be liberated from its seeming plausibility. Until we do some hard philosophical work, journalism ethics will struggle to overcome its trouble-making heritage.

Progress in journalism ethics depends on developing a philosophical perspective and a corresponding framework to guide a journalism that no longer draws a hard line between fact and value, and reporting and

16 For my full view, see *Radical Media Ethics.*

interpreting; and no longer insists on a strict neutrality. We need a new philosophy of journalism. If I had to choose a word to describe what I am doing in reconstructing the ethics of objectivity, I would choose the word "palimpsest": the idea of something altered but still bearing traces of its original form. Like a house is a palimpsest of the taste of previous owners, objectivity is a palimpsest of previous conceptions and previous users of the term. My task is to identify traces of the original meaning of objectivity and how it has changed over time.

My historical critique leans heavily on the contingency of all things in life, including our intellectual life. My approach is compatible with Nietzsche's use of "genealogy" in studying ideas. I also see some similarities in approach with Foucault's attempt, in *The Archeology of Knowledge* and elsewhere, to show how the systems of thought unearthed by his "archaeology" were accidents of history. However, I am closest in spirit to philosopher Bernard Williams's notion of genealogy as a kind of explanation, a narrative that "tries to explain a cultural phenomenon by describing a way in which it came about, or could have come about, or might be imagined to have come about."[17] Also, I am close to philosopher of scientist Ian Hacking, who examines the role of "construction" in defining multiple personality disorder and other topics. Of special interest is Hacking's notion of "sharp mutations in systems of thought and [the idea] that these redistributions of ideas establish what later seems inevitable, unquestionable, necessary."[18] I hope to show how the development of modern objectivity, as neutral, isolated (and pure) fact, was once a sharp mutation that now, at least to some people, seems inevitable. What else could objectivity be?

DUALISMS AND DISTINCTIONS

My reinterpretation of journalism ethics takes aim at the restrictive and outdated dualisms of thought embedded in Western thinking in general and in journalism ethics in particular. The dualisms in journalism are applications of broad, philosophical dualisms to journalism and its ethics. But, first, what is a dualism?

What Is a Dualism?

The etymology of dualism is simple. It comes from "dual" or "duo" which is derived from the Latin and French words for two. Sometimes, dualisms are

17 Williams, *Truth and Truthfulness*, 20.
18 Hacking, *Rewriting the Soul*, 4.

called dichotomies, which comes from the Greek word *dikhotomos,* to cut something into two parts. So, a married couple is a duo. My car has "dual" traction, meaning two tires (not one) are used to move the vehicle.

These mundane duos are not dualisms in the intended sense. "Dualism," as used in this book, is a technical philosophical term. The "ism" in "*x* is a dualism" could indicate (1) a conceptual dualism – that is, a way of thinking about worldly phenomena. Conceptual dualisms come in two forms: a striking contrast between two concepts (e.g., love or hate, good or evil), or a dualistic theory that explains some phenomenon (e.g., a theory of the human mind as divided into an unconscious and a conscious component). Alternatively, the "ism" in "*x* is a dualism" could indicate (2) an ontological dualism: a fundamental division in nature, such as the difference between mind and matter. A conceptual dualism usually implies an ontological dualism. The duelling concepts refer to a dualism among objects. For instance, the conceptual division between love and hate refers to two emotions existing in the world. In philosophy, dualism often means Cartesian dualism – Descartes's theory of humans as consisting of two ontologically different substances, mind and matter.[19]

When Is a Distinction a Dualism?

Our mind, by necessity and by evolution, is an avid distinction maker. We distinguish between colors, shapes, sensations, human faces, voices, animal species, and concepts. We distinguish between animate and inanimate objects; between objects moving toward us and objects stationary; between the idea of a triangle and the idea of a square. We can distinguish between bitter and sweet, between Merlot and Shiraz wine.

Not all distinctions are dualisms. Often, distinctions are informal ways of registering differences in everyday experience. They are informal because we do not formally (or philosophically) define the differences. Nor do we set the differences apart as quite separate things. Dualisms, however, are formal. They are the products of philosophizing about differences in experience. They place objects into separate, defined, categories. In many cases, a dualism turns an informal distinction useful in everyday life, such as a distinction between the mental and the physical, into a philosophical dualism, such as that between mind and matter.

Many distinctions are not about the relationship of two separate and entirely different objects. Instead, they register a difference in degree of

19 For example, the entry for dualism in Honderich, *The Oxford Guide to Philosophy* (221), is devoted entirely to the theory that mind and body are two distinct things, and it attributes the most famous expression of this dualism to Descartes.

some property among objects. We perceive the world analogically, not digitally, as differences of degree. For example, a difference in the amount of body weight (or mass) distinguishes a thin and a plump man. Sensations come in degrees. I distinguish between the light blue colour of my automobile and the deep blue of my neighbour's car. I perceive the different degrees of heat that arise from the electric baseboards that heat my home. Conceptually, we place the gradations of colour or heat on a continuum that represents degrees of difference in the property in question. Recall the shades of colour on the colour charts found at any paint shop. The charts are continua. A continuum is a set of gradual distinctions; it is *not* a dualism.

When, then, does a distinction become a dualism?

When we make a firm and defined distinction (or division) between two things, whether the things are properties, substances, forces, faculties, or principles, and when we use the division to understand some phenomenon. Two things are said to be clearly different in kind and stand on the opposite sides of a wide division. Dualisms have no degrees. Good is not evil and evil is not good. Life is not death. Yin is not yang. For Descartes, there is nothing "in the middle" between mental and physical substance. No continuum runs from the highly physical to the highly mental. There are no degrees of being mental or physical. Something is either a mental substance or a physical substance.

In a revealing passage, Hilary Putnam recounts a conversation with Noam Chomsky wherein the latter suggested that philosophers often "take a perfectly sensible continua and get in trouble by trying to convert it into dichotomies."[20] When we consult our untutored intuitions, we tend to agree on whether something is relatively subjective or objective on a continuum from highly subjective to highly objective. For instance, we consider the judgment that something is funny or amusing as relatively subjective compared with the judgment that something is soluble. However, when we try to impose a hard line between these differences, we tend to disagree on what is subjective or objective and quarrel over the category in which examples should be placed.

Antagonistic Dualisms

Dualisms allow for a relationship between their two components. For instance, Descartes postulated, implausibly, that mental and physical substance (mind and body) interact in the pineal gland in the centre of our brain to

20 Putnam, *The Many Faces of Realism*, 27.

produce human motion. One type of dualistic relationship dominates this book. It is the relationship of rivalry or tension. I call dualisms that display this relationship "antagonistic dualisms."

Antagonistic (and other) dualisms abound in religion, ethics, art, psychology, and everyday life. In religion, there are dualisms of saint and sinner, sacred and profane. For example, Zoroastrianism, one of the world's oldest monotheistic religions, was founded by the prophet Zoroaster in Persia (ancient Iran) about 3,500 years ago. Dualism in Zoroastrianism is the complete separation of good and evil in two ways: a cosmic dualism and a moral dualism. Cosmic dualism in Zoroastrianism is the belief that there are two opposing forces in the universe. There is an ongoing battle between Good (the Wise Lord and creator, Ahura Mazda) and Evil (Angra Mainyu) within the universe. This cosmic dualism explains the existence of other dualisms such as life and death, and day and night. Moral dualism in Zoroastrianism is the belief that the human mind is torn between the two opposing forces of good and evil. God gave man a free will to choose between good or evil.

Antagonistic dualisms pervade the Bible. St Paul, in Romans 13:11–14, speaks of being ready for death and salvation. He vividly contrasts dark and light, being awake and being asleep, and the antagonistic relationship of soul and flesh. "Now it is high time to awake out of sleep … The night is far spent, the day is at hand: let us therefore cast off the works of darkness, and let us put on the armor of light … and make not provision for the flesh, to fulfil the lusts thereof." The antagonistic moral dualisms of the Bible filter into the history of ethics. Human attempts to be virtuous are portrayed dualistically as a field of battle between the selfish, myopic forces of desire and a rationality that looks to long-term consequences and the common good, and so acts as a restraint on impulse. Weakness of will (failing to do what you think is right) is explained as the overcoming of rationality by the forces of desire. Dualisms divide actions into good and bad, right and wrong, actions that bring pleasure or pain, actions that are my duty versus actions that promote my self-interest. Rival theories claim that human action is free (acting on one's will) or determined by physical and other forces.

In psychology we classify people as introverts or extroverts, with little in between.[21] We juxtapose impulse and thought, idea and object, rationality and irrationality. In biology, we are familiar with dualistic distinctions between life and death, life and non-life, male and female. In epistemology

21 The tendency to think dualistically about introversion and extroversion led Susan Cain to write *Quiet*, a book arguing that introversion and extroversion are matters of degree, and can be placed on a continuum.

and metaphysics, dualisms include firm divisions between observation and theory, fact and value, truth and falsity, the objective and subjective, the theoretical and practical, the real and unreal, matter and form, being and nothingness.

Talk of dualisms pervades discussions of art and music. Sometimes it refers to a striking contrast in the colours of a painting, such as bright objects on a black background. Sometimes it is a contrast or tension between types of sounds in music and the moods they evoke. Consider, for example, how a photographer, Michael Mead, described a piece of music by Luciano Berio, the "Sequenza I" for flute. Mead was asked to provide a photographic image for the piece, to be displayed when the music was performed on stage. He produced an image of a bubble floating vulnerably in what appears to be a liquid. Here is how a dualism that he perceived in the music led to his choice of image:[22]

> This piece (of music) was an ephemeral dichotomy for me: a dance between the manically playful, and the oppressively brooding. Dark and almost calming undertones left me both on the edge, and at peace. It reminded me of the fleeting life of a bubble. Fun, light and airy, yet evanescent: a stark reminder of the fragility of life itself.

We describe a Bach fugue, with its pricewise counterpoint and structure, as "rational" or logical when compared to a romantic piano concerto by Tchaikovsky. In design, the sleek and integrated modern designs of Scandinavian and Swiss artefacts and the works influenced by the Bauhaus school of art do seem to be more the work of the head than the heart, when contrasted with eighteenth-century Rococo exuberance.

Romance novels, soap operas, and countless literary works depend on antagonistic dualisms between heart, mind, desire, and repressive social attitudes. The conflicts make their topics interesting and add "depth" to the characters of a play or novel. Much of Shakespeare's plays are dualisms of heart and mind, rationality and impulse, love and obligation. Will Hamlet "listen to reason" or go mad in his fierce desire to revenge the death of his father? The gory, crazed ending to *Hamlet* testifies to the conflict between our desires for revenge, power, and greed, and our cognitive capacities to anticipate consequences and control powerful feelings.

22 The quote was included in the program for a concert that featured four sequenzas by Berio, with four accompanying images. The concert, organized by violinist Nadia Francavilla, musician-in-residence at the University of New Brunswick, Fredericton, was on 18 March 2017. I attended the concert.

Characters in tragic operas beat their breasts and insist that evil acts require revenge and desires require satisfaction no matter what rationality and logic say. In Puccini's *Turandot,* set in China, Prince Calaf falls in love with the cold Princess Turandot. To obtain permission to marry her, a suitor has to solve three riddles; any wrong answer results in death. Calaf passes the test, but Turandot still refuses to marry him. He offers her a way out: if she is able to learn his name before dawn the next day, then at daybreak he will die. Needless to say, Prince Calaf's friends and family are beside themselves and apply "logic" (read: reality-based cognition) in vain to dissuade the love-besotted prince. Clearly they feel his cognitive powers are overwhelmed. He has literally "lost his mind." The entire opera depends on a dualism of faculty: the cognitive powers of rationality and logic (based on considerations of self-interest and probability of death) are pitted against the non-cognitive powers of impulse and overwhelming feelings. Even where cognitions play a part in an opera, non-cognitions may rule the day. In *Romeo and Juliet,* the cognition-based actions – the plot to use a sleeping portion to feign death – are driven by acute passions, and the end is tragic.

Dualistic thinking has influenced recent popular books on psychology. Bloom, in *Against Empathy,* a book on the limits of empathy in morality, falls back at times on dualistic language that pits rationality against the presumed biased forces of empathy.[23] *Moral Tribes,* by Joshua Greene, argues that the world, divided into conflicting "tribes," needs a global metaethic that finds common ground among the tribes, a role he thinks is best fulfilled by utilitarianism. He divides morality into two, often rival, ways of thinking: an innate emotional way of responding to moral issues and a rational way of evaluating issues that corrects for the biases and limitations of the moral emotions. He refers to a "dual process" way of doing ethics. It is clear that he thinks the rational side should win out, especially when we are considering disputes between tribes. Morality is largely a problem of reason versus emotion.[24] Interestingly, Greene sees his dual process view as consistent with the distinction between "fast" (intuitive, emotive) and "slow" (rational, discursive) thinking in humans, in the work of Daniel Kahneman.[25]

Psychologist Jonathan Haidt, in *The Righteous Mind,* also employs a dualistic model of moral reasoning, where "emotion and reasoning are separate paths to moral judgment."[26] Haidt thinks emotions are the most

23 Bloom, *Against Empathy.* See, for example, chapter 6, "The Age of Reason," 214, where reason and emotion (and gut feelings) are discussed as "two opposing facets" of human nature.

24 Greene, *Moral Tribes,* 134–7, 148.

25 Kahneman, *Thinking Fast and Slow.*

26 Haidt, *The Righteous Mind,* 35.

influential factor in moral judgment although we may use reason to rationalize what we already feel is right. In a well-known paper in 2001, he described the relationship in the title: "The Emotional Dog and Its Rational Tail." One comes away from these books with the impression that the ancient reason-emotion dualism is still alive and well in Western thinking.

These dualistic tendencies prevail despite the fact that anti-dualism philosophers, such as the pragmatists John Dewey and Hilary Putnam, have warned about the negative influence of dualism in the history of thinking and in philosophy. They contend that philosophical dualisms are limited, distorting ways of thinking about humans and knowledge. Putnam noted that Dewey cautioned us, in philosophy, against the crucial slide from "an innocent distinction" (or "ordinary distinction") to a metaphysical, philosophical dualism."[27] Too often, philosophical dualisms become inflexible, contentious dogma.

A word of caution: Not all dualisms are false or misleading. Some things in the world can be legitimately, or usefully, viewed as made up of two different substances. Electricity can be a direct current (DC) that maintains polarity or direction; or it can be an alternating current (AC) that changes polarity or direction over time. I am either alive or dead, pregnant or not pregnant. My drink on the bar is a dualism: rum and Coke. Also, it *may* be the case that humans are made of mind and body, two quite different components; and it *may* be the case that life is best lived where reason imposes itself firmly on our desires. We cannot reject a dualism simply because it is a dualism. If a dualism is to be rejected, then we need to show its limitations and compare it with other, presumably better ways of thinking. While most dualisms are too simplistic for use in philosophy or science, we still need an *argument* against types of dualism, not an a priori dismissal of all dualisms.

Therefore, in this book, I am not saying the professional objective framework is weak *simply* because it contains dualistic thinking. I am saying, and hope to show by argument, that the particular dualisms in question are limiting, simplistic, unproductive, and out-of-date – and there are better ways to think about journalism ethics.

Embedded Dualisms

I have defined a dualism as a formal and explicit way of viewing a phenomenon, as consisting of two entirely separate parts, often in tension. However, in the professions and in life, dualisms, once established, can become

27 Putnam, *The Collapse of the Fact-Value Dichotomy and Other Essays*, 9–11.

implicit assumptions that escape scrutiny yet still affect practice. In this manner, cognitive and cultural dualisms are passed down from decade to decade. They are what I call "embedded dualisms."

Therefore, the problem of dualisms in journalism ethics is not necessarily on the surface of things. Journalists can follow norms without being aware of the dualisms that lurk beneath those norms. On the surface, a code of ethics may appear to *not* contain dualistic language or premises. A journalistic code may talk about accuracy, objectivity, and reporting the facts, but there is no mention of dualisms. My problem is deeper: *how,* conceptually and philosophically, frameworks of journalism ethics are grounded in dualisms. When I think of the strength of dualisms in our thinking, I recall how Wittgenstein endorsed philosophical "therapy," to show how we are captive to certain metaphors, dualisms, and other ways of thinking.[28] Journalism ethics also needs therapy. We are captive to embedded, dualistic conceptions and we must bring them to consciousness for critique.

Cognitive and Social Dualisms

I end this discussion on dualism with one more distinction – the distinction between cognitive and social dualisms.

"Cognitive dualism" refers to a way of explaining how cognition works, or should work. It is a dualism between two psychological functions or faculties. Cognitive dualisms come in two forms. There are external dualisms that contrast cognition as a whole with some other faculty, such as desire or emotion. And there are internal dualisms among the elements of cognition itself, such as between observing and theorizing, asserting a fact and drawing inferences from it. Many of these dualisms are embedded and antagonistic.

"Social dualism" refers to a way of viewing society, with implications for how the groups should be related and structured. Typically, a social dualism divides a collection of people, a nation for example, into two quite different kinds of inhabitants. Often, the dualism supports a negative view of people

28 Wittgenstein famously said that the purpose of philosophy is to show "the fly the way out of the fly bottle." The fly bottle represents pseudo-problems of philosophy that captivate philosophers and the fly is the philosophical thinker. He also said that philosophy does not have one method, but it does have methods or "different therapies." Wittgenstein, *Philosophical Investigations*, §133, §309. If this means we can leave philosophy behind, after therapy, I disagree. Philosophy is not a disease of which one can be, and should be, cured. It is an indispensable part of human thinking and flourishing. One can, and should, become aware of one's captivity by language, a conceptual scheme, or an inadequate philosophy (or set of problems). But that leaves us thinking from within another, hopefully more adequate, philosophy.

on one side of the divide, and a positive view of those on the other side. Examples are racial views that divide citizens into superior whites and inferior blacks; that divide a society into privileged males and subjected women; or that divide a collection of people into the original inhabitants of a land, who are the "real" citizens, and those who immigrated later, who are secondary citizens.

Across human history, there have been two dominant kinds of social dualism. One is the division in society between Me (the set of individuals) and Us (the group or nation to which the individuals belong); a second division is between Us (our group) and Them (other groups). Many moral problems require that we balance the rights of individuals against their duties to a group. Or, they ask us to consider: To what extent should we assist other groups? In Us versus Them, the groups are often nations in tension. Attachment to Us is a matter of group loyalty, a patriotism to a nation. It is a patriotic, moral tribalism that draws a firm line between what is good for the group and what is good for other groups. Moral tribalism is a form of parochialism that thinks that citizens' duties are primarily the advancement of their nation. At its worst, this tribalism becomes an extreme nationalism which justifies negative attitudes towards other groups and sanctions self-interested, aggressive conduct against other nations.

The cognitive dualism that interests me is a dualistic way of understanding objectivity. It takes the ordinary, and ubiquitous, distinction between what is objective and what is subjective and turns it into a philosophical dualism. This distinction is often a matter of degree, a matter of coming to understanding something *more* objectively than before; or, of thinking that some view is more objective than another. The social dualism that interests me is a moral tribalism that pits one nation against others. In this form, Us versus Them tribalism is a parochial loyalty. Both forms of cognitive and social dualism have shaped the cognitively narrow, and socially tribal nature of the traditional objective framework, where journalists' primary social duty is to promote the group to which they belong, typically their nation.

In sum, journalism ethics struggles with the legacy of two embedded dualisms: a fact-centric cognitive dualism and a patriotic social dualism of Us versus Them. Ironically, the demand for objective, neutral reports about domestic events is set aside when it comes to journalists supporting their nation, parochially, especially in times of war. Interestingly, the advocates of news objectivity see no inconsistency in arguing for objectivity within the boundaries of a nation, but relaxing the need for objectivity when journalists cover their nation on the world stage.

My argument is that these dualisms are the central ethical premises of traditional journalism ethics, and continue to negatively affect our thinking about journalism. I will show how these ideas were handed down to journalism from a long, empirical cum positivistic philosophy that was, itself, riddled with dualisms. When this philosophy of objectivity – of objectivity of pure fact – collapsed in the twentieth century, so did the plausibility of journalism's objectivity model. At least in theory. In practice, journalists continued to defend, reformulate, and reassert the ideas of this professional objective model, and still do today.

In the chapters ahead, I argue for three claims about dualisms in journalism ethics:

1 *Dualisms exist:* The professional objective framework, and other models of journalism, are based on philosophical dualisms, cognitive and social. The dualisms are deeply rooted, having a long history in our culture.
2 *The dualisms affect practice*: The dualisms influence, implicitly or explicitly, how journalists understand themselves and their practice.
3 *The dualisms are highly questionable and need replacement*: The dualisms should be replaced by non-dualistic understandings of objectivity and other norms of journalism. Journalism ethics needs new philosophical foundations.

CONCLUSION: THE STRUCTURE OF THIS BOOK

This book is, in part, the extension and culmination of previous work. It places my previous concepts in a new context, the context of engagement. Speaking musically, these notions are notes transposed into a new key. Those notions include my concept of pragmatic objectivity, my ideal of human flourishing, my global journalism principles, and my idea of radical media ethics. Yet the book is also original. It is my first serious attempt to spell out an ethic for non-neutral, interpretive journalism within my commitment to global ethics. To do so, I introduce new notions of objective engagement and democratically engaged journalism.

The book approaches objective engagement by showing how dominant notions of objectivity have failed. Then it redefines objectivity for engagement. The book depicts the history of objectivity in three giant steps:

1 *Objectivity as knowledge through reason*: the emergence of philosophical rationality in Greek antiquity as the means to objective knowledge of the world.
2 *Objectivity as knowledge of fact*: the rise of a fact-based notion of objectivity in the seventeeth century; this is empirical objectivity made possible by stressing *one* aspect of cognition – the discernment of fact.
3 *Objectivity as knowledge of pure fact*: the fact stripped of all interpretation and known in its empirical purity.

Many interesting developments occurred between these steps, and there are so many forms of objectivity that I cannot do justice to them all. Moreover, I am not going to have much to say about periods where there are few developments of direct significance to journalistic objectivity, such as the medieval period and the Renaissance.[29] However, I include developments during the Enlightenment. My purpose is an overview of the history of objectivity, from the standpoint of what was most important for the construction of journalism objectivity. The book is not a history of objectivity in all media cultures in the world, which would be an astoundingly large project. I am charting the rise of journalism objectivity in North American news media, and its origins in Western European news media. Nonetheless, it is evident that this Western tradition of journalism objectivity has influenced journalists in many other countries. One only has to look at the codes of journalism ethics in Asia and Africa. Therefore, I hope this discussion is of global interest, although the reader needs to remember the Western focus of the book.

There is one further qualification. I focus on those Western philosophies of greatest import for journalism, such as classical empiricism, analytical philosophy, pragmatism, and scientific empiricism. I do not spend a great deal of time in Part 1 on "continental" philosophy. However, in Part 2, my argument is influenced by the ideas of continental philosophers such as Husserl, Habermas, and Gadamer. Their work helps us to envisage journalism as interpretive inquiry and as a form of objective engagement.

My hope is that the book helps readers appreciate the important point that objectivity of fact and traditional journalism objectivity are only two of many possible conceptions of objectivity. I also hope that the book helps readers appreciate the complexity of objectivity as an idea. Despite this complexity, the study of the concept of objectivity retains its interest because, as an epistemological notion, it "organizes most of the knowledge projects of the past four centuries."[30] With an overview at hand, we are less likely to get lost in the maze of history.

The book consists of two parts. Part 1, over four chapters, studies the history of ancient objectivity and modern objectivity of fact. I show how, by the twentieth century, empirical objectivity of fact was in deep philosophical trouble, and there was a need to reconstruct objectivity. Part 2 begins the reconstruction by providing an alternate conception. Chapter 5 promotes a pragmatic conception of objectivity called "objectivity with a human face." It is an objectivity *in* time, situated, and yet a rational guide

29 For details, see my *The Invention of Journalism Ethics.*

30 Poovey, *A History of the Modern Fact,* xiii.

to thinking. In chapter 6, I show how objectivity with a human face is well suited to agents engaged in society. I define objective engagement. The rest of the book, chapters 7, 8, and the conclusion, applies objectivity with a human face to journalism.

2

Objectivity Naturalized

Truth, it is grounded in facts. Truth, it has no alternative.

Ad for the *New York Times*, April 2017

I have always had a high regard for those who defend grammar or logic. One realizes fifty years later that they have warded off great dangers.

Proust, *Remembrance of Things Past*, Vol. 1, 46

So many misunderstandings surround the notion of objectivity that we cannot avoid examining its component ideas and its relationship with other key terms. One cannot treat objectivity as a stand-alone concept. It makes sense only as part of a web of other terms such as rationality, truth, fact, correspondence with reality, and correct cognition. In this chapter, I explain objectivity as a natural capacity linked to other epistemic capacities.

COGNITION AND OBJECTIVITY

Cognition

Objectivity of belief is objectivity of cognition. But what is cognition?

Gregory provides what must be the shortest definition of cognition, as "the use or handling of knowledge."[1] A textbook adds the idea of a mental system: "All of our mental abilities are organized into a complex system the function of which is called cognition."[2] By "knowledge," researchers in cognition typically do not mean the highest cognitive achievements in science or art. They study everyday knowledge, which we often take for granted – information about the world that we gather, remember, and use. We know that eagles fly, water flows downhill, and fire causes heat and pain if touched.

1 Gregory, *The Oxford Companion to the Mind*, 149.

2 Glass, Holyoak, and Santa, *Cognition*, 2.

Remembrance of the past guides current activities. We speak a language whose complex rules we have internalized.

To say that cognition is the use of knowledge by a mental system is too broad to be informative. What is the nature of the system, what are its components, and how do they work together? How does cognition relate to the non-cognitive capacities of individuals, and how are cognitive functions realized by the brain and nervous system? To answer these questions, psychology analyzes cognition into an interrelated set of processes with distinct functions, such as conceptualization, memory, attention, belief formation, language, reasoning, problem solving, and planning. We sometimes think of these processes as the "higher" functions of primates.

Cognition can be defined broadly or narrowly. Cognition for medieval philosophers, such as Aquinas, was the operation of a subset of our mental capacities, those of the "intellect," which included perception, memory, conceptualization, and reasoning. But early modern psychology broadened cognition beyond intellect. It divided the mind into many "faculties," from sensation to the association of ideas. Today, some philosophers distinguish between cognition, such as perception, memory, and belief; and volition, such as desire, intention, emotions, and will.[3] Others place cognition, volition, and action under "cognition." Lately, the field of cognitive studies has moved toward an ever more inclusive set of disciplines. In the 1960s, cognitive psychology declined during the heyday of behaviourism, which ignored mental processes. However, by the 1970s the study of cognition was returning to favour because of the failure of behaviourism to explain complex behaviour and the rise of the all-purpose computer. Perhaps the mind is an internal, information-processing computer whose software is installed on our neuronal brain? The disciplines studying cognition came to include computer science and linguistics. In addition to cognitive psychology, there was now something broader called "cognitive science."[4]

The study of cognition includes the relationship of reason and emotion, cognition and moral judgments, and the role of cognition in making decisions, for example, "heuristics and biases"[5] and game theory. Sometimes, it appears that our ordinary cognitions are based on logical procedures. For example, researchers in artificial intelligence have used Bayesian statistics (which combines the strength of new evidence and existing hypotheses) to model how youngsters learn about cause and effect. Neurological research indicates that primate facial recognition is controlled by a complex multi-dimensional

3 See Searle, *Rationality in Action.*

4 See Gardner's *The Mind's New Science.*

5 Heuristics and biases research looks at the mental shortcuts and irrational mistakes (biases) that result from heuristic thinking.

coding of stimuli.[6] Researchers also study "controlled cognition" – how we "orchestrate" thoughts, emotions, and actions according to goals.[7] Cognition "controls" the interaction between processes, such as when the pursuit of a goal (e.g., maintaining information in mind) needs to be protected from interference (e.g., a distracting stimulus). Writing an academic article amid the noise of a coffee shop is a case of controlled cognition.

What gets on the list of cognitive components, and why? There are bodily and mental experiences that clearly do not fall into the category of cognition, including bodily sensations that cause shivering, stimuli that prompt reflexes, irrational fears, and unthinking impulses. But there are other capacities that raise questions. Historically, for example, emotion has not been considered part of cognition. However, in the past thirty years, research increasingly shows the interdependence of thinking, judging, and emotion. Some writers stress the intelligence of emotions.[8]

Maintaining clear distinctions between cognitive and non-cognitive components is difficult because almost any experience or any capacity can influence cognition. Exhaustion of the body can dull the mind. Emotions can bias my judgment. In Charles Dickens's *A Christmas Carol*, Scrooge wonders if the appearance of a ghost (Marley) is due to indigestion. Cognition is embedded in a complex organism where the brain brings it together with emotions and desires. We face many notions of cognition and many lists of cognitive elements. Therefore, what notion of cognition to use is not settled by surveying the linguistic usage of "cognition." We ask, instead: What concept *ought* we to adopt? We need to choose some conception of cognition that matches our intuitions, is consistent with our best theories, and serves current purposes. Here, philosophy can help.

Philosophers tend to view cognitive processes as having two distinctive features: (1) mental intentionality and (2) a representation of some state of the world.[9] Mental intentionality, as philosophers have long noted, is a defining feature of consciousness.[10] It does not mean intending to do

6 See Gopnik, "Artificial Intelligence Helps in Learning How Children Learn," and Chang and Tsao, "The Code for Facial Identity in the Primate Brain." Chang and Tsao develop a model representing each face as a vector in a fifty-dimensional "face-space." They show that the firing rate for each face-sensitive neuron represents the location along a single axis through this space. The model challenges exemplar-based models of face recognition.

7 Greene, *Moral Tribes*, 127–8.

8 Nussbaum, *Upheavals of Thought*.

9 Later in the book, I will question the representation of objects in the world as a necessary condition of some mental act being an instance of cognition. Some acts of cognition, such as ethical cognitions, are not best described in terms of a realism of external representation.

10 Aquila, *Intentionality*.

something. It means that acts of cognition, conscious or non-conscious, "intend" or aim at some object in the world beyond themselves. Intentionality uses the mind's powers of representation, through symbols, to present information on the world to the mind. Our cognitions can represent facts, objects with certain properties, cause-and-effect processes, other people, and other minds. Representational processes assist the organism to attend to the world, to plan. The results of this symbolization are concepts, propositions, meanings, conceptual schemes, beliefs, arguments, and evaluations. We record these apprehensions in texts, journalism reports, scientific theories, political interpretations, documentaries, novels, videos, and works of art. These products of symbolic cognition have cognitive meaning since they imply that the world exists in a particular way. Symbolic cognition is developed in society and in culture. Our first concepts, values, languages, and ways of reasoning are learned from others. Human cognition is cognition of an encultured human being. We know ourselves through our symbolic thinking and languages over time. Just as ethics is history, so are humans a history – the history of their cognitions in the world.[11] We do not experience in some pre-symbolic manner and then "add" meanings and symbols. Rather, we start and end with our cognitions, symbols, and meanings. We never escape the hermeneutical circle of meaning.[12]

This capacity to apprehend meaning – to symbolically represent the world – sets the stage for debates about the nature of objectivity and the objectivity of belief. Cognitions contain propositions that make claims about the world. They can be evaluated as true or false; as explanatory or not; as justified or not; as probable or not; as efficient and useful or not; as reasonable or not; as creative and beautiful, or not.

Naturalized Objectivity

Cognition is embedded in the world. It is what Merleau-Ponty called embodied or incarnate reason.[13] To view cognition as embodied is to reject the view that objectivity is primarily an abstract principle or ideal. It is, at bottom, a psychological capacity. Objectivity is a form of evaluative cognition.

11 This view of social and cultural cognition has been explored at length by contemporary philosophers of language and existence, often in the "continental philosophy" tradition, from Ernst Cassier, Martin Heidegger, and Wilhem Dilthey to Hans-Georg Gadamer.

12 In this circle, the meaning of a part depends on the meaning of the whole, and vice versa: e.g., the way the meaning of a sentence depends on the meaning of other sentences and vice versa. The idea has been used by philosophers such as Wilhelm Dilthey and Martin Heidegger.

13 Merleau-Ponty, *Phenomenology of Perception*, 40.

Humans, and other animals, exercise this capacity every day. Cognition, then, can be descriptive or evaluative, or both at the same time. We can describe Mary as having bronchitis or we can evaluate whether that belief is accurate. In coming to a belief (e.g., why Hitler did not invade England), we form a belief and evaluate its evidence. Evaluation occurs *within* the information-processing systems of cognition. Cognitions work to find some "fit" between the information available and the object of experience.

Sometimes the objects evaluated are unconscious sense data. For example, there are brain processes whose function is to represent accurately the edges and shapes of objects. They interpret the incoming stimuli from my smartphone and decide where the phone's edges are, allowing me to pick it up with my hand. None of this processing is conscious. This descriptive function ("accurately locate the edges of this object") contains evaluation by the perceptual system. Evaluation is evident in cases of ambiguity, for example in bad light, where I am unsure whether the edge of the phone is here or there. It is automatic, yet developed through experience. Open your eyes as an adult and it happens. You see a world.

To be concerned about objectivity is to ask evaluative questions: Which beliefs, reports, and theories are reliable representations of the world? Which ones should guide our decisions and actions? Does my belief that Muslims are terrorists fit the facts about Muslims? How objective is Darwin's theory of natural selection as an explanation of evolution? Is my fog-hampered, late-night perception that the highway is turning sharply to the right an accurate representation of the world, and should I steer my car accordingly? Objectivity is the cognitive desire to have cognitions "true to the world" or "true to the object" in question. Long before objectivity became a theoretical concept of philosophy and a term of derision by relativists, and long before people argued in academic books about the objectivity of moral belief, there was naturalized objectivity. Objectivity is a necessary, universal, evaluative part of cognition, guiding action. It is a cognitive function realized by the brain, as "real" as remembering or reasoning.

Humans would not have survived as a species if they did not have reliable experiences of the world and reliable means for evaluating the objectivity of these experiences. Fail to identify a tiger bolting out of the forest *as* a tiger and you are, well, dead. Our cognitive system does make mistakes in concrete cases. A pilot may misjudge the location of the runway, and cognition may fail to provide unequivocal answers in abstract areas, such as ethics. Objectivity as a psychological power may seem weak or subjective where it wanders from its roots in perception. But *some* capacity for evaluating experiences there must be.

We approach evaluation systematically. Given our capacity for self-reflection, humans ask more than "Is this belief objective?" They also ask two sorts of higher-level question. The first sort of question is about *kinds of belief*: How objective are beliefs of this kind? And how objective is my belief system as a whole? The second sort of question concerns *testing*: What are the ways that assure me that the belief is objective? What methods and criteria do I use? And equally importantly, what methods and criteria *should* I use? These two types of higher-order question give rise to the normative study of cognition that we call epistemology, with its examination of the "sources" of knowledge and methods of evaluation. The questioning is prompted by experience, by both the failure of some cognitions and the success of other cognitions, and by disagreement on what is true and reliable. And the two types of question, we will see, express two conceptions of objectivity: Objectivity as ontological – do beliefs map the world? – and epistemic – do beliefs have objective evidence?

Epistemology, as a common human practice, is cognition investigating cognition, a cognizing that uses evaluative criteria. Epistemology is second-order evaluation of first-order judgments about the world. Given our reflective abilities, we can question these second-order criteria, and question that questioning, and so on. When we organize our evaluative practices into an explicit doctrine, we have epistemology as a branch of philosophy. We create epistemologies, and divide into rival camps of rationalists, empiricists, naturalists, and skeptics. Epistemology as philosophy is derived from a natural impulse to make sure our cognitions fit the world. As a psychological capacity, objectivity is a permanent feature of organisms. But how we exercise that capacity has a history and multiple realizations.

Three Senses of Objectivity

Getting our cognitions "right," or to fit the world, means three things: Right means what is true, or ontological objectivity; right means what is well-evidenced, or epistemic objectivity; and right means what is correct conduct, or moral objectivity.[14]

ONTOLOGICAL OBJECTIVITY

Ontological objectivity is knowledge of the world as it exists. A belief is ontologically objective if it denotes an object, property, or state of affairs that exists independent of mind, such as Mount Everest, and it accurately describes Mount Everest. That is, the belief gets right its height, size, location, and so on. We also call the object objective because it is actually exists.

14 For a fuller discussion of these senses, see Megill, *Rethinking Objectivity*, 1–20, and Ward, *The Invention of Journalism Ethics*, 45–9.

Something is ontologically subjective if it is non-existent, such as a ghost, or exists only in the mind, such as a hallucination. Beliefs about such objects are subjective. Beliefs are also subjective if they inaccurately describe an object, such as the location of Mount Everest. Since philosophy in antiquity, ontological objectivity has been an ideal of inquiry. Objective beliefs are right because they are true, they map the world. Subjective beliefs fail to map. Ontological objectivity is inseparable from notions of truth and what is real.

In recent years, I have added a second sense to ontological objectivity, what I call post-facto objectivity.[15] This objectivity is post-facto in being after the fact of human creation. We can talk objectively about some objects even though they are mind-created and mind-dependent. Examples are social practices, institutions, functional objects such as screwdrivers, and society itself. The properties of such human-dependent objects are what Searle calls "observer-relative" properties.[16] Yet, despite such dependence, there is still an important sense of objectivity in play. We can make all manner of statements – objective or subjective, true or false – about them.

EPISTEMIC OBJECTIVITY

How to decide which beliefs map the world? There is only one way. We do epistemology. We examine *how* we formed a belief. We evaluate its reasons. We evaluate sources of knowledge and formulate standards of evidence. Objectivity becomes epistemological. Objective belief is belief well-supported by evidence. Subjective belief lacks such support. Or to put it more carefully: Beliefs are epistemically objective if they satisfy, to some acceptable degree, our best practices and standards. Otherwise they are epistemically subjective. There are many kinds of tests for beliefs. The most familiar modes of testing are the methods of science. But criteria for objective inquiry populate philosophy, logic, critical thinking, social science, law, and journalism.

Descartes embraced epistemic objectivity when he wrote that only correct method could lead to science's goal of "true and evident cognition." "By method," he explained, "I mean certain and simple rules, such that, if a man observe them accurately, he shall never assume what is false as true … but will gradually increase his knowledge and so arrive at a true understanding of all that does not surpass his powers."[17] Even if our epistemic norms and methods do not guarantee truth, they lead us closer to the truth of some matter. Scientific investigation into cancer presumably

15 Ward, *Radical Media Ethics*, chapter 1.
16 Searle, *The Construction of Social Reality*, 9.
17 Descartes, *Rules for the Direction of the Mind*, 1:7.

leads us closer to the truth about the causes of cancer. Why bother with the complex methods of science, if we could get adequate answers by consulting astrology?

MORAL OBJECTIVITY

A third sense of objectivity arises from the need for fair and objective rules for governing the interaction of people in society, and for a rational assessment of our goals. There are two key questions. One question is procedural: Is this process guided by objective guidelines, guidelines that are not undermined by subjective bias or personal interests? Is the procedure, in some sense, fair or neutral to the competing parties? This moral objectivity looms large in public debates where government policies are assessed. It also influences the procedures of social institutions and officials, such as when they hire employees, award contracts, mark exams, or judge court cases. In these cases, and many more, people insist that officials make decisions based on objective moral criteria in line with equality and fairness. They are not asking, ontologically, whether the judgments and processes somehow "fit" (describe) an independently existing object in society. They are asking whether the judgments and processes "fit" (or follow) some socially agreed-upon rules for good judgment. Despite the current skepticism about moral objectivity in theory, such skepticism fades away when concrete decisions must be made. During this process, people distinguish between objective reasons, such as hiring on the basis of merit, and subjective reasons, such as hiring on the basis of nepotism, racial prejudice, or self-interest.

In summary, the objective-subjective distinction arose from a concern to distinguish between reliable or true beliefs and unreliable or false beliefs, and to distinguish between fair and objective decisions and unfair and subjective decisions. True and reliable beliefs are called "objective" because they are true to the "object" in question, or true to established procedural rules. Behind the quest for objectivity is a dual "fear" or concern: the fact that humans make mistakes, and that the mistakes are due to the subject, or the self and its impulses.[18]

In each of these three forms of critique – ontological, epistemic, and moral – we express a desire for *good or faithful cognition* of things, and a desire to act accordingly. But we should not apply this tripartite categorization too rigidly. In practice, we bring all three senses into play. Journalists, for example, may defend a report as ontologically objective because they describe events as they occurred; epistemically objective because the report

18 Daston and Galison think that a concern for objectivity is motivated by a fear of the biases of the inquiring subject. It is a "morality of self-restraint." Daston and Galison, *Objectivity*, 185.

is backed by facts; and morally objective because the report met the moral standards of practice. Moreover, we use one form of objectivity to critique or support another form. Objective facts about a course of action, such as ending a government program that supports vulnerable citizens, help us to evaluate the moral objectivity of the action.

Some thinkers identify objectivity with the capacity to transcend one's partial and local perspective on some claim, issue, or action. Philosopher Thomas Nagel, in his influential *The View from Nowhere*, defined objectivity as follows: "A view or form of thought is more objective than another if it relies less on the specifics of the individual's makeup and position in the world, or on the character of the particular type of creature he is."[19] As I argue later, this is a misleading attempt to define objectivity as unsituated. There are better "situated" and "intersubjective" notions of objectivity where a strict Nagelian transcendence of one's subjectivity is not required. The key is not to abandon one's human situation and beliefs but to be willing to subject them to public scrutiny. Objectivity is an ever-evolving dialogue among "subjectivities" (situated people) mutually correcting, improving, and balancing each other. Later, I call this "objectivity with a human face," an objectivity developed *among* us. There is no objectivity from nowhere.[20]

REALISM AND OBJECTIVITY

Realism

Ontological objectivity is commonly associated with a philosophical form of realism, which leans toward absolutism – knowledge of reality not relative to viewpoints. This absolute realism is opposed to constructionism, a view of knowledge as human construction.[21]

19 Nagel, *The View from Nowhere*, 5.

20 See Sen's description of "positional objectivity" and "open impartiality" in his *The Idea of Justice*, especially chapter 7. Rawls argues that objectivity is always situated in some view of what counts as a rational and reasonable person. In his words, the objective view "must always be from somewhere." See Rawls, *Political Liberalism*, 116.

21 Realism is also contrasted with idealism and anti-realism in philosophy. Realism denies metaphysical idealism, that what exists is mental or spiritual. As such, realism is identified with materialism or naturalism, especially when the worldview of science is discussed. Anti-realism is skepticism about the existence of certain kinds of object. For example, I can be an anti-realist about the existence of "moral facts." No such facts exist. I can be an anti-realist about almost anything, e.g., the existence of God, the Freudian unconscious, Santa Claus, or ghosts. A realist is someone who affirms the opposite: that certain types of objects, like moral facts, exist.

This realism is an ancient view of truth and knowledge, and the mind's capacity to know what is real, or what exists independently of the mind.[22] Realism posits the existence of an external world, apart from our psychological experiences, feelings, representations, and desires. Humans are part of this reality, but ultimately the world exists independently of humans, human interests, and human minds. If all humans were to die, there would continue to be a world. This thesis is expressed by Searle: "The world (or alternatively, reality or the universe) exists independently of our representations of it." Or, "Realism is the view that there is a way that things are that is logically independent of all human representations."[23] Another formulation is provided by Alston: "For the realist, there exists an independent, external world containing an immense number of objects, properties, relations, facts, and law-like behavior which await correct description."[24] Alston's phrase, "await correct description," indicates realism's epistemological attitude: We have reached truth and knowledge only if our propositions accurately describe the world, or some part of it, as it exists, independently of human interests, viewpoints, and biases. Transcendence of limiting viewpoints to "discern" reality as it is – this is the achievement of knowledge. Otherwise, we are dealing with partial or biased belief about things.

Many realists have attempted to explain this achievement of knowledge by developing a "correspondence theory of truth," which holds that truth is the correspondence of belief to the object as it exists.[25] Often, the correspondence is said to be between propositions and the facts they describe. Facts are worldly states of affairs that exist apart from human conceptions and interpretations, the way that water is made of hydrogen and oxygen, and Mount Everest is so many meters high. Realists also think our categorization of worldly objects should be based on "natural kinds" – kinds created by nature, such as snow, molecules, stars, and bacteria. For example, in the nineteenth century, John Stuart Mill argued that nature created kinds, and humans named them: "The differences (between objects, in virtue of which they are or are not members of a kind) are made by nature

22 Realism is also an attitude in art, politics and other domains. In the Renaissance, Leonardo da Vinci urged painters to paint from nature. "It is safer to go direct to the works of nature," he wrote. "For he who has access to the fountain does not go to the water-pot." Quoted in Gottlieb, *The Dream of Reason*, 410.

23 Searle, *The Social Construction of Reality*, 150, 155.

24 Alston, *A Realist Conception of Truth*, 5–6.

25 Realism is compatible with other theories of truth, such as Alston's "minimalist" theory of realist truth. In *A Realist Conception of Truth*, Alston posits a relation of proposition and fact but leaves it open as to what that relationship is.

… while the recognition of those differences are grounds of classification and of naming which is, equally in both cases, the acts of man."[26]

Today, a major form of realism is scientific realism. This is the view that our best scientific theories (especially the natural sciences) achieve knowledge of reality in itself and describe natural processes as they exist apart from the human mind. The objects discovered and explained by science exist. The sciences are our best indicator of the way reality is. Our inventory of the furniture of the world is based on what science says exists, or must presuppose to exist to make sense of its theories. One version of scientific realism holds that while scientific theories evolve, nevertheless the sciences are converging on knowledge.

Hacking summarizes scientific realism as holding that: [27]

> The entities, states and processes described by correct theories really do exist. Protons, photons, fields of force, and black holes are as real as toe-nails, turbines, eddies in a stream, and volcanos … Theories about the structure of molecules that carry genetic codes are either true or false, and a genuinely correct theory would be a true one … Even when our theories are not exactly correct, we often get closer to the truth. Our aim is to discover the inner constitution of things and at knowing what inhabits the most distant reaches of the universe. No need to be too modest. We have already found out a good deal.

Constructivism

Constructivism views human knowledge as a psychological and social construction that cannot, in principle, map reality as it exists independently of human minds, perspectives, interests, concepts, and values. Realism's prescription to know reality as it exists is too demanding, or impossible. Why is it too demanding? Because what we can know about the world is *mediated* necessarily by the structure of our minds and the era in which we are situated. Mediation takes two forms. First, what we believe relies on concepts and conceptual schemes, whether innate or inherited from society. We literally see the world through our concepts. Second, what we believe is affected by our purposes and values. It is assumed that this combination of conceptual and interest-based mediation shapes all attempts to know reality. All knowledge is constructed from human "materials." This is tantamount to saying that there is no direct, non-mediated contact with the

26 Mill, *System of Logic*, 123.

27 Hacking, *Representing and Intervening*, 21. For a more recent introduction, see Dicken, *A Critical Introduction to Scientific Realism*, 1, which defines scientific realism as "the view that our scientific theories are approximately true."

world, so knowledge *cannot* be defined as truth about the world as it exists apart from mind. The question left to answer is: what is left of our notions of objectivity, truth, and even justification if belief formation and valuation is internal to conceptual schemes and interests?

Constructivism can be interpreted in ways that are consistent with skepticism, solipsism, relativism, and, in the social sciences, the social construction of knowledge. It should not be identified with the purely psychological thesis that the mind constructs complex ideas from simpler ideas. Early empiricists, like Locke, were psychological "constructivists" in a special sense. They explained how complex ideas were formed by the "association" of simpler ideas derived from sensations. But Locke, and many other empiricists, are realists. They believe that ideas can correspond to reality as it is, and they do not entertain the general thesis that the mind has no direct contact with reality. In Locke, for example, "primary" ideas of shape and mass *do* refer directly to real properties of the external world. Also, the idea of "association" is not some subjective and deliberate forming of belief. Rather, association is an innate and irrepressible tendency of the mind to combine ideas in certain ways, much as physical particles are prone to combine in certain ways. Locke does not say that we cannot know the world as it is because we see the world through our ideas and purposes.

Realists believe that the aim of inquiry is truth, or knowledge of what is real, beyond our minds. Truth exists even if, in various areas of life, we lack a process by which to know it. Are there mountains on some very remote planet? We cannot verify it presently one way or the other. But the statement is either true or false. If the mountains exist, they are "awaiting our correct description." There may be truths about the world – that is, complex truths about the universe – which will be forever beyond the power of the human mind to know. Yet, for the realists, such truths exist, whether any human knows them. We may stumble upon truths through luck or by taking a drug. Truth is not reducible to what can be justified or conclusively verified by strict method. Even our best-supported beliefs today may turn out to be false tomorrow. Hence, realists think ontological objectivity is prior to epistemic objectivity. Our methods of inquiry and evaluation are means to the pursuit of truth, even if the methods are imperfect. Truth that is absolute – truth that is not relative to conceptual scheme or social perspective – is the goal of inquiry.

In contrast, the constructivist thinks that notions of truth and ontological objectivity play a diminished role in inquiry; or they are rejected as empty notions. Some forms of constructionism are blunt: we cannot know the world, but only what we think about the world. Constructionism can lead people to become extreme skeptics or relativists about knowledge. Yet constructivists do not *have* to be extreme skeptics. They can aim, as I do, at epistemic objectivity. Mediated cognition can lead us to warranted beliefs and reasonable standards of evaluation.

The constructionist's central objection to absolute realism is often put like this: We cannot get outside our experience to see if our beliefs and standards somehow line up with reality. One never gets outside of one's beliefs and mental processes to confront naked reality, minus any human influence or perspective. Our epistemic standards are themselves constructed by humans, and are internal to worldviews, cultures, and practices. No conceptual scheme is uniquely and absolutely the correct scheme for evaluating belief. There is a plurality of schemes. What is true, known, and justified is defined internally within a system of thought and inquiry, which is a situated epistemology. All epistemologies are situated; objectivity is standard-based situated judgment.

Realism in absolute form has dominated much of the history of philosophy. So much so that Putnam observes that, before Kant, it is hard to find a philosopher who did not subscribe to the correspondence theory of truth. Plato sought to show that there were absolute truths that at least some people, philosophers or mathematicians, could know through philosophical reasoning. Later, the Stoics in Greece and Rome developed realism as a theory of natural law. Morality, virtue, and society consisted of universal laws of nature. Realism in the medieval era was a metaphysics that described the one true nature of the world, a divine artefact, plus disputes about the existence of certain objects, such as universals.

By the seventeeth and eighteenth centuries, realism was confronted with the modern idea of knowledge as a matter of internal, mental representation. Now the problem was how to determine when our ideas actually referred to real objects. The problem anticipated the aforementioned thesis of constructionism that there is no stepping outside of one's conceptual scheme. This is why Kant occupies such a pivotal place in modern philosophy. He devoted his philosophical energy to showing how we can still talk about knowledge even if we give up the realist premise that humans can know things as they absolutely are. Centuries later, Richard Rorty, in *Philosophy and the Mirror of Nature,* argued that the entire modern project of showing how our ideas can "mirror" the world as it truly is cannot be accomplished.

Across the twentieth century, constructivist doubts about realism and the correspondence theory of truth grew in strength. The idea of reality known by universal scientific methods and objectivity was under fire from several different directions. There were philosophical elaborations of the idea of conceptual relativity, or the role of conceptual schemes in inquiry; relativistic sociological theories of science that questioned the universality of science; empirical studies of how groups "make" knowledge; and historical views of scientific rationality. In the social sciences, the term "social constructionism" became popular. It refocused epistemology from abstract philosophical debates about knowing an external world to studies of the situated processes of knowing – the processes by which individuals and disciplines come to investigate problems and reach "knowledge claims." The scare quotes here are crucial. They indicate that many of these writers on knowledge were not presuming a realism of knowledge – that the inquirers being studied actually had reached knowledge in an absolute, ontological sense. Rather, the writers were interested in the psychological and sociological factors that lead people and groups to *believe* they have knowledge, or to assert *power* based on their claim have knowledge. The stress on the social and political aspects of knowledge led to the question: *Who* gets to define knowledge?

Rationality

Objectivity as evaluative cognition presupposes rationality. To show that a belief is objective is to provide reasons. It shows why it is rational to endorse the belief.

"Rationality" comes from "ratio," which, originally, pointed to some order or discernable proportion in what exists. Rationality helps to make sense of things. The world makes sense if reason can discern in it some ratio, some pattern, some cause, or some measurable feature. This "reason in things" makes them knowable and controllable. My friend's curious, furtive behaviour at a party makes sense when I realize that he is trying to avoid speaking to his former wife. How someone makes music on a guitar makes sense when I understand the ratio of notes and harmonics expressed by different strings. Otherwise things are irrational or beyond reason. Something may be so complex or unusual that we cannot understand it. Terrorism strikes some people as frightening *and* irrational because it seems to lack meaning and justification – it lacks clear causes and justifiable reasons. What "has reason" is contrasted with what is absurd, random, or lacking any discernable reason for being. Sometimes, as existentialists are fond of saying, life seems absurd or beyond reason. We and the universe have no reason to be here.[28]

Less metaphysically, rationality can refer to the mundane capacity to give reasons for ordinary beliefs and decisions. We exhibit our rationality when we explain some phenomenon by citing a general principle, or structure

28 Albert Camus says the "one truly serious philosophical problem" is that of suicide. Should we go on living in a world that seems neither made for us nor responsive to our desires? Camus, *The Myth of Sisyphus*, 11.

our reasons into chains of reasoning, inductive, deductive, or otherwise.[29] We show that our beliefs and actions are not arbitrary but rational and reasonable to others. They are "agreeable" to reason. What one counts as rational has much to do with what one accepts as a valid type of reason and cause. Many people today would reject, outright, an explanation of mental illness as caused by demons inside people, because demons are not on their list of causes of things.

Rationalism and Empiricism

In philosophy, the terms rationality, reason, and rationalism are used in technical ways. They are concepts in theories of mind, logic, and epistemology. Of particular importance to this book is the philosophical debate between rationalists and empiricists. Histories of philosophy and science describe the debate in dualistic terms as a confrontation between two camps who share few common beliefs: the rationalists, mainly on the Continent, represented by Descartes, Leibniz, Gassendi, Arnauld, Pascal, and Spinoza; and the empiricists, mainly in England, represented by experimental scientists and philosophers such as Bacon, Hooke, Boyle, Locke, and later Berkeley and Hume.[30]

Rationalism, as a philosophical school, is not the common view that humans should offer reasons for what they believe. On this score, most people are rationalists. Rationalism in philosophy is something stronger and more specific. It is a belief in the knowledge-making power of a special human faculty called Reason (encouraging some believers to spell reason with a capital "R"). The rigorous use of Reason, through strict reflection within the mind, can deliver clear and necessary knowledge about ourselves and the world. Reason provides fundamental principles of knowledge, compared with the shifting, relative, non-fundamental beliefs of ordinary experience and perception. Knowledge of reality through Reason has been called the philosopher's "dream of reason."[31] This view can be called "strong rationalism," as opposed to the mild rationalism that sees value in giving reasons. Strong rationalism contrasts with strong empiricism, with its strong belief in the power of another faculty: the faculty of perception.

29 Aquinas distinguished between ratiocination, knowing God and his plan (i.e., "intelligible truth") through inference from other things known, and God's capacity to know such truths directly. To need inference to know things is the mark of a second-rate (human) mind. Honderich, *Oxford Guide to Philosophy*, 782.

30 For an example of an introduction to philosophy that leans on the contrast between rationalism and empiricism, see Stokes, *Philosophy: 100 Essential Thinkers.*

31 Gottlieb, *The Dream of Reason.*

How does Reason work? Partly through the presumed power of Reason to intuit conceptual or logical truths of great importance and with great certainty. My Reason, for example, suddenly grasps the truth of a principle, causal explanation, or proof. Also, Reason works through the logical sifting of ideas and the use of formal reasoning. Reason analyzes ideas through definitions, clarifications, intellectual intuitions, and theoretical insights.[32] Many rationalists believe in the power of logic and mathematics, and in deductions from abstract principle. Descartes thought the rules for the "proper direction of the mind" were rules for the logical use of Reason, not rules for the use of perception. Descartes's method consisted of the analysis and synthesis of ideas in the mind. Through analysis, the mind breaks down complex ideas into clear and simple ideas. It intuits simple ideas – for example, that something exists, that three lines only bound a triangle, that nothing which is "A" can be "not A." Synthesis works in the opposite direction. The mind takes simple ideas and deduces more complex ideas. The method of analysis and synthesis "springs from the light of reason alone" and is the only way to "sure and indubitable knowledge."[33] Hobbes expressed this rationalism when he argued that it is by Reason alone that we know that if a figure is a circle, then a straight line through the centre will divide it into two equal parts.[34]

Many rationalists like Descartes believed that Reason's power to discern the most important truths about the world could only be explained if the mind came equipped, or innately endowed, with certain ideas about God, geometry, and so on. These truths are known a priori and with a certainty that rules out their origin in experience. Our minds are not, at birth, a tabula rasa, or blank slate, upon which the world "writes" through the operation of our senses.

Rationalists are skeptical of the senses. Where sensory beliefs are not false, illusory, or contradictory, they amount to second-rate, relative beliefs that should be grounded in a higher knowledge of certain propositions and placed within a system of thought provided by Reason.[35] Rationalists

32 Arnauld (1612–1694), a leading figure in the Catholic Jansenist movement in France, said in *The Art of Thinking* that clear, precise thinking by Reason was crucial to separating truth from falsity. The four main operations of the rational mind are conceiving, judging of concepts (using language), reasoning (used when concepts are not clear enough for judgment), and the ordering of ideas into inferences.

33 Descartes, *Rules for the Direction of the Mind,* 1:7, 1:3.

34 Hobbes, *Leviathan,* 147.

35 Descartes's dismissive attitude to the senses and the imagination is evident where he discusses the two methods of knowing, by intuition and by deduction. Intuition by reason is the clear, certain, and evident conception of an "unclouded and attentive mind." This intuition is not the "fluctuating testimony of the senses, nor the misleading judgment

tend to think knowledge must be organized deductively, as in mathematical deduction, with our less certain beliefs resting on the firm foundational principles established by Reason. Induction gives us only what is true here and there, and "for the most part." Attempts to use reason to organize knowledge into deductive form is evident in Euclidean geometry, in Aristotle's deductive syllogisms, in Aquinas's *Summa Theologica,* in Descartes's metaphysics, in Hobbes's *Leviathan,* in Kant's *Critique of Practical Judgment,* and in Spinoza's *Ethics.*[36] The influence of a mathematical-deductive tradition is evident in the methods of Galileo, and in Newton's *Principia.*

Empiricists, to the contrary, believe that knowledge originates in observations, in induction upon observations, and in observed facts established by experiment. Data received from the senses is worked up into ideas through various combinations and associations. Experience is nature's way of teaching humans. Scientific knowledge is the product of careful experimentation and observation of empirical objects to reach new facts. Empiricists are skeptical about the alleged power of Reason to know a priori truths and to provide a correct method for science. They resist the positing of innate ideas. All we know comes from the senses, originally. If this places limits on what people can claim to know, as in Hume's skepticism about God and causality, so much the worse for those beliefs.

A classic of empiricism is Locke's *An Essay Concerning Human Understanding,* a study of how the mind constructs complex ideas from simple ideas originating in sensation, not in reason. Locke posits innate psychological mechanisms, such as the mind's capacity to receive and associate ideas; but he does not posit certain ideas as pre-existing in the mind. For Locke, the mind begins its life empty of ideas – a piece paper upon which nothing is written. Then, external objects cause sensations to enter into the mind. The mind reflects on these sensations and produces the ideas of colour, heat, shape, and pain in the mind. It combines these ideas into judgments, such as judgments of cause and effect. The mind can also reason, moving by inference (by analogy or induction) from ideas to other ideas. Locke concludes: "Knowledge then seems to me to be nothing but the perception

---

that proceeds from the blundering constructions of imagination." Deduction is also praised as "necessary inference from other facts that are known with certainty." *Rules for the Direction of the Mind,* 9–10.

36 Kant, in his *Critique of Practical Reason,* 17–42, begins his analysis of the elements of the idea of pure practical reason – truths known a priori by reason – by organizing his material in classic deductive style, beginning with "definition," "remarks" and "theorems." In his *Ethics,* Spinoza uses the "geometrical method" of definitions, axioms, and propositions so the reader could see the evidence for every statement as they read along. For an explanation of why Spinoza adopted the less accessible deductive style, see Lord, *Spinoza's Ethics,* 10–11.

of the connection and agreement, or disagreement and repugnancy of any of our ideas."[37]

Reason, with or without a capital "R," has had many historical meanings. In the Enlightenment, "reason" played a central social role in arguing for reforms. Reason referred to the ability and right of humans to think for themselves, to search for reasons rather than accept the dictates of authority. The French *philosophes* sang the praises of reason in defiance of absolute monarchy and entrenched church hierarchy, and they appealed to "innate" or self-evident truths. Interestingly, unlike the later logical positivists, they did not regard beliefs as meaningless unless reducible to truths of logic or knowledge of fact. Scientific knowledge was thought to rely on more than facts and logic – the scientist's creativity, skill, and experienced judgment.

Situated and Unsituated Rationality

Rationality requires the capacity to critique one's beliefs and current circumstances. Philosophers have differed over the degree to which rationality is capable of transcending its worldly situation. Can the person who does the thinking transcend her era, class, and society?

One view, which I favour, is situated rationality. It is the view that all rationality is significantly limited by its context. It is a form of constructionism. It asserts that one can never completely transcend, conceptually, one's situation. The aim of knowledge is modest: to arrive at justified but ultimately situated beliefs and theories about the world. Knowledge is situated knowledge. An opposing view is unsituated rationality, which is popular among strong rationalists and absolute realists. Given correct methods and conditions, reason can slip the bonds of its earthly situation and come to know things as they exist objectively.

Situated rationality is popular among people with an empirical, pragmatic cast of mind. However, there have been empiricists who believed that at least some transcendence was possible. Locke endorsed the idea of transcending one's situation, by stepping back from beliefs provided by society and critiquing their validity. Hume recommended that individuals look at art and history from an impartial view.

What is objectivity for unsituated rationality, in its clearest and strongest form? *It is the disengaged reason of a thinking subject pursuing non-relative, general, theoretical truths (or principles) about the world, often in deductive form, which provides secure foundations for the rest of what we believe. It is objective, necessary knowledge of reality through unsituated reason.*

37 Locke, *An Essay Concerning Human Understanding*, 2:167.

On this view, objectivity is both a goal (absolute, objective truths) and a regulatory method for inquiry (rigorous, necessary reasoning). Objective knowledge is accurate, unchanging cognitions of a similarly unchanging rational order in the world, usually found below the flux of life and its changing appearances.

What is objectivity for situated rationalism, in its clearest and strongest form?

It is an engaged agent pursuing well-justified (but not certain) truths from within a situation, for a variety of practical and theoretical purposes. Objectivity uses a plurality of faculties, norms, and ways of reasoning to obtain the best possible beliefs for practice. It is non-necessary knowledge of reality through situated reason.

Objectivity is a situated testing of beliefs and norms of action, using the best available standards and methods of rational inquiry in a given situation. Both the results of inquiry and the norms of evaluation belong to situated traditions of thought and practice. The inquirer aims at an impartial "stepping back" from current beliefs but such transcendence is always partial – a critique from within some context and using some established norms.

As we will see in chapter 4, the difference between viewing the knower as a subject or as an agent is very important.

Objectivity and Facts

Views of objective knowledge disagree on the correct conception of fact.

The most general notion of a fact is some actual and independent state of the world, whose existence does not depend on whether anyone knows it exists. Something is either a fact or not a fact. Wittgenstein famously opened up his *Tractatus* by declaring that "the world is everything that is the case. The world is the totality of facts, not of things … For the totality of facts determines both what is the case, and what is not the case … The world divides into facts. A fact is any true statement about the world, about what is the case."[38]

Objectivity, it appears, is closely related to the idea of fact, especially empirical fact. According to some people, knowledge of empirical fact is the closest that humans ever get to objective knowledge of reality. An objective belief is a belief about fact. Subjective belief fails to record a fact, for whatever reason. When people affirm the great importance of facts, some form of realism is usually in the background, since knowing a fact is correspondence of idea to object. Also in the background is a common-sense

38 Wittgenstein, *Tractatus Logico-Philosophicus,* 29. Alston, in *A Realist Conception of Truth,* uses this notion of fact to explain his realism.

empiricism. Most people, when they think of facts, think of familiar experiences and observations: the car is blue, Mary is a student in my class, I have a headache, and metal expands when heated.

But the idea of a fact is *deceptively* clear. It hides the fact that there are many candidates for the label of "fact." There is not only disagreement on whether something is a fact, but on what constitutes a fact. There are mundane, "particular" facts or truths – for example, the grass on my lawn is green, this fireplace warms my body, Moscow is the capital of Russia, and the moon is 384,400 kilometers from the earth. Yet, people also count as facts propositions of great generality which describe things that are abstract and remote from the senses. For example, the abstract laws of physics are said to be general facts. We also think gravity is a fact. Yet what do we know of gravity beyond its effect on our bodies? Moreover, theories are said to be facts. Natural selection – a long and largely unobserved process – is held to be a fact.

Bernard Williams has observed that there are two "parties" when it comes to facts and truth. There is the "common-sense party" which points to simple statements, such as grass is green and Moscow is in Russia, to argue that it is obvious that there are such things as facts and truths. There is also the party of "deniers" of fact and truth. A notable example is Nietzsche's statement, which contradicted his other statements in support of fact and truth: "Facts are precisely what there are not, only interpretations."[39] Williams thinks both sides are wrong. The common-sense party is right that there are everyday truth and facts, but the common-sense party is not helpful in dealing with much more complex cognitions. It is impossible when constructing a scientific theory or a historical interpretation of some large event, such as World War II, to stick to these everyday facts and no more. As for the deniers, Williams thinks it is wrong to deny facts. Not only are there the common-sense facts alluded to, but facts can be contrasted with such things as historical and psychological interpretations.

OBSERVABLE FACTS

It would be convenient if we could limit facts to the "basic" facts of observation – states of affairs and objects directly observable – and then justify all our other beliefs on the basis of such observations. This would be an objective form of constructionism, a constructionism consistent with realism. Many philosophers have attempted it. But be forewarned: this epistemic project, a favourite of empiricists and positivists, has proven difficult to

39 Nietzsche, *The Will to Power*, 481.

carry out. One problem is the vagueness of "observable." Another problem is disagreement about the epistemic status of observation statements.

For a philosopher, "observable" may refer to something more technical and abstract than the layperson's idea of what is observable. Common sense may think that observable refers to the wide world of physical objects and human activities. But philosophers have used "observable" to refer to sense data such as "hot," "blue," and "hard," which are elements of common sense's complex experiences. For the scientist, "observable" may refer to any quantitative magnitude that can be measured in a relatively simple, direct way, such as the temperature of 80 degrees centigrade or the weight of 94 pounds.[40] Both temperature and weight are regarded as observable because they involve relatively simple procedures of measurement. But is simplicity and directness of method enough to define observability? Do we actually observe the intensity of an electric current, or simply have a means to measure it? Does a physicist "observe" an electron when she sees the path of a particle through a bubble chamber through an electron microscope? Are such perceptions "direct observations of fact" if theory and sophisticated instruments are needed to interpret what one sees? What is observable is not a dualism of (direct) observation and (indirect) interpretation but rather a continuum that starts with direct sensory observations and proceeds to "enormously complex, indirect methods of observation."[41] The line that an ordinary person or a philosopher draws between the observable and non-observable can be arbitrary or based on current purposes.[42] Apart from what is an observed fact, we can also disagree on the status of such observations. Is the fact the subjective experience of seeing an object or property, or the external object or property itself? Are observation reports incorrigible, or fallible?

What is a fact is treated differently by schools of philosophy. What was a fact for rationalists? They were facts of reason, not facts of the senses. Reason shows us the truth of facts of geometry, mathematics, and logic – and many other areas of non-empirical knowledge. We know that axioms of Euclidean geometry and the logical principles of the excluded middle or non-contradiction are true when our Reason contemplates the concepts

40 For the meanings of "observable" in science, see Carnap, *An Introduction to the Philosophy of Science*, 225–8.

41 Ibid., 226.

42 Unable to give a principled definition of observable and non-observable, Carnap turns the distinction into a matter of common practice. In actual practice, physicists agree that some things are observable or are empirical laws based on observations (e.g., laws on the pressure and volume of gases). And, in practice, we decide that some things are theoretical laws about non-observables, such as laws about molecules. Ibid., 228.

involved, apart from perceptual experience. But the rationalists did not stop at logic or geometry. They claimed that the principles upon which they founded their systems of thought were facts about the self or the world. Descartes considered his famous statement, "I think, therefore I am," to be a certain proposition known through Reason. It describes a fact about myself. It is not a fact of the senses.

Kant claimed that we could know, through reason, synthetic a priori judgments about our minds, mathematics, and the world. It was a fact of reason, for example, that space and time were innate categories of the mind, used to order our sensible intuitions. In his *Critique of Practical Reason*, Kant maintained that our knowledge of ourselves as free was not based in experience, since experience is the domain of "appearances" governed by causal laws. We know we are free because reason gives it to us as a fact, as a necessary fact about ourselves.[43]

Facts for the empiricists will be defined in the next chapter. For now, we can say that the empiricist's fact is some state of the world available to observation and empirical verification. Empiricists take our common-sense idea of observable fact and made it more precise and narrow to suit their epistemological and scientific aims.

OBJECTIVITY AS PHILOSOPHICAL RATIONALITY

Let us turn to the first step that Western culture took towards rational and objective knowledge of the world.

The Rational Turn

Objectivity's story begins in Greek antiquity with the momentous transition from mythical explanations of the world to rational, proto-scientific explanations in the form of philosophy, mathematics, and science. Thinkers began to use the many faces of rationality – reason, observation, argument, and mathematical thinking and measurement – as a primary instrument for inquiry into the world. The idea of rational inquiry, as an organized investigation, was born. Rational inquiry is found in an impressive array of different kinds of Greek thinkers: natural philosophers, physicians, historians, mathematicians, philosophers, and sophists. Their use of rationality tended to be philosophical, addressing large questions that resulted in theories and speculations about the basic elements of nature, the nature of mathematics, and abstract problems such as whether reality was "one" or "many."

43 Kant, *Critique of Practical Reason*, 29–31.

Philosophical rationality as a method of explanation contrasted with non-rational methods of explanation, such as appeal to sacred texts, myths, religion, priests and oracles, revelations, and the weight of tradition. Thinkers used their natural capacities to identify first causes in nature, to explain nature and society, and to posit a rational order beneath the flux of experience.[44]

The emergence of philosophical rationality was gradual. Much of Greek mathematics and philosophy was infused with mythical and metaphysical elements. Pythagoras was both a mystic and a mathematician. Many of the period's writings are in poetic or aphoristic form. The difference between the emerging rational thought and the older "non-rational" narratives was not the difference between being rational and irrational. After all, Homer's tales and the Greek myths were not irrational or absurd. They made sense, if one accepted the existence of the gods, and other anthropomorphic devices. The difference was in the sources of authoritative knowledge and the kinds of causes that came to be accepted in explanations.

The change in explanation is evident early on with the natural philosophers, such as Thales, Heraclitus, Anaximander, and Empedocles. From the seventh to the fifth centuries BC, these naturalists thought the first causes of nature were material elements like water, air, and fire.[45] Anaximander posited an invisible element he called the "indeterminate" – a raw material that took the shapes of objects. Democritus proposed an unseen world of atoms moving in a void.

Natural philosophers offered logical explanations, not myth; they appealed to natural causes to explain events, not gods. The belief in atoms, although speculative, was a rational conjecture. The philosopher put forward an idea to be tested by logic and experience. He did not tell a traditional myth or story that gave events meaning, but was closed to rational critique. The poet Pindar explained the flooding of the Nile as the result of a god moving his feet, whereas Herodotus considered natural causes,

44 McMullin, *The Concept of Matter in Greek and Medieval Philosophy*, 1–54.

45 Knowledge of the natural philosophers is difficult because we have only fragments of their writings. Many of them lived on islands in the Aegean Sea and along the coast of Asia Minor. Some created schools, some wrote books, some wore splendid clothes and drew large audiences to their talks. Stimulated by contact with Egypt, Persia, and Babylon, these philosophers were freethinkers who had no emperor to placate or sacred book to defend. See Boardman, Griffin, and Murray, *The Oxford History of Greece and the Hellenistic World*, 126–41.

including the melting of snow on distant mountains.[46] If the explanatory factors were not physical elements, they were mathematical formulae, as in mathematics and geometry from Pythagoras to Euclid. The Pythagoreans, for instance, believed in an order of numbers and ratios that explained geometric figures, the order of the heavens, and musical harmony. Nature had a mathematical basis.

The natural philosophers were followed by the philosophical systems of Plato and Aristotle, firmly establishing rational philosophy as the leading source of explanation.

The use of reason to construct conjectures about nature or mathematical explanations co-existed with an empirical impulse and curiosity. The Greek medical tradition associated with Hippocrates of Cos is an early source of empiricism. The human body was approached as a lawful, physical system. Diseases were treated by physical means, not by rituals of purification. Historians followed the rational turn in thinking. If nature was governed by natural principles, historical events could be explained by facts about humans and their circumstances. To explain the Greek victory over the Persians, Herodotus traveled to Egypt, Persia, and Greek cities to gather evidence.

Philosopher Edmund Husserl provided an interesting insight into the Greek revolution. He said the most dramatic moment in the ancient Greeks' turn to reason was the creation of a "theoretical attitude."[47] What was new was not so much the specific beliefs of the philosophers, but their attitude toward the objects of the world. The theoretical attitude, which became the very idea of science, was the task of finding non-relative, universal truths about the world, apart from the practical applications of such ideas. Discovering reality behind the appearances was the task of reason. Egyptian geometry was pursued practically as a method to mark the fields, after the inundation of the Nile. Babylonian astronomy was pursued practically to predict the future. But Greek geometry and astronomy became intellectual pursuits for their own sake. In contrast, the non-theoretical or "natural" attitude to life is directed toward "this or that" as an end or means, as relevant or irrelevant, as interesting or indifferent: "toward what is daily required or obtrusively new."[48] This pre-theoretical or practical life is *not* naïve, totally devoid of theory or critical reflection. But its criticism is typically practical, and relative to our goals in a specific situation.

46 Aristotle divided the early Greek writers into two groups: "theology," who explained the world by appeal to the gods, and "physici," who explained the world by natural principles. Frankfort, *Before Philosophy*, and Graves, *The Greek Myths*.

47 Husserl, *The Crisis of European Sciences*, 281, and *Ideas*, Vol. 1, 40.

48 Ibid.

Situated and Unsituated Rationality: Greek Origins

GREEK UNSITUATED RATIONALITY

The debate between reason and religion, between absolute realism and constructionism, and between situated and unsituated rationality, began during the Greek transition.

Thinkers, from Parmenides and Pythagoras to Plato, sought to inquire about the world using an unsituated form of reasoning, a strong rationalism that emphasized the power of the faculty of reason. They claimed to arrive at abstract truths, proofs, and ideal models concerning the nature of reality, society, and human nature. The truths were universal and known with certainty. They developed a form for expressing this higher knowledge – the deductive argument, as in geometry, where theorems are deduced, with necessity, from self-evident principles. The claim to certain knowledge was not new. Outside philosophy, other sources of alleged certain knowledge were (and continue today to be) cited, such as mystical experience, oracles, special intuition, and religious revelation.

Parmenides, in the fifth century BC, followed "the way of truth," the way of unsituated reason in its purest form. Parmenides writes that, while on a search for knowledge, a goddess taught him the difference between absolute truth and the beliefs of ordinary people. Truth lies far "from the beaten track of men." The opinions of mortals are false yet they have the "semblance of being."[49] The way of seeming is what happens to be the case, while the way of truth is knowledge held fast by "necessity" such that "no judgement of mortals may outstrip you." Parmenides uses reason to deduce truths that are paradoxical to common sense. He starts with a single premise – "it is" – and deduces that reality is one: complete, unchanging, and eternal. These puzzling "proofs" of Parmenides, and the paradoxes of his student, Zeno, were meant to undermine faith in the senses, in favour of reason.

With Plato, knowledge is the progress from the relative beliefs of perception and common sense to an intellectual grasp of principles that are true independently of context. The ultimate form of knowledge is the rational apprehension of the pure forms of being, a transcendent reality. Knowledge is a rigorous, austere path from the beliefs of experience to mathematical ideas and finally to philosophical truths. For what sort of knowledge does Plato search? Listen to this passage from his *Phaedrus*, where the immortal soul and the minds of gods are "nourished" in heaven by "pure knowledge" of justice, self-control, and other things, as they really exist. They see what is real: "Knowledge – not the knowledge that is close

49 Kirk, Raven and Schofield, *The Presocratic Philosophers*, 267.

to change; that becomes different as it knows the different things which we consider real down here. No, it is the knowledge of what really is what it is."[50] This is strong rationalism's view of (ontologically) objective knowledge, an absolute realism.

The search for unsituated knowledge brought to the foreground the need for impartiality, which meant the capacity to "detach" from, for the purposes of critical review, one's current beliefs and partialities. Hannah Arendt has claimed that objectivity, as impartiality, can be traced back to Homer's *Iliad* where he praised the defeated Hector as well as Achilles, the hero of Homer's kinfolk.[51] Pythagoras compared intellectual impartiality with the detachment of a spectator at the Olympic Games. In Rome, centuries later, Cicero argued that the cultured mind was best trained by philosophers because they were spectators without self-interest. The knower as spectator would become a central metaphor in Western epistemology.

GREEK SITUATED RATIONALITY

Greek situated rationality is evident in the practices of an assortment of sophists, magistrates, political leaders, and, later, the pragmatic Hellenistic philosophers of life – the Epicureans, the Stoics, and the skeptics.

The sophists were itinerant teachers, the "street philosophers" of the ways of practice. A series of sophists, from Protagoras to Thrasymachus, converged on Athens during the second half of the fifth century, attracting large crowds to their orations. For a fee, the sophists provided a higher education in grammar, music, law, and human affairs. Protagoras tells Socrates that he teaches the management of personal affairs so that a student can become "a real power in the city, both as speaker and as man of action." This attention to practical skills was stimulated by the development of city-states with public spheres. As Lloyd said, "testing arguments, weighing evidence and adjudicating between opposing points of view were … a common part of the experience of a considerable number of Athenian citizens."[52]

Sophistic practice was justified by what we now call philosophical relativism. The sophists doubted universal truths, especially in matters of ethics, politics, and society. They pointed to the plurality of opinion. This relativism fit the fifth-century Greek "enlightenment," where regular contact with other cultures had made obvious the plurality of belief systems.[53] Xenophanes said the Thracian gods resemble the Thracians, and if cows and horses could draw, they would depict their gods as cows and horses.

50 Plato, *Phaedrus*, 525.
51 Arendt, *Between Past and Future*, 263.
52 Lloyd, *Magic, Reason and Experience*, 252. Buxton, *Persuasion in Greek Tragedy*, 5.
53 Guthrie, *The Fifth Century Enlightenment.*

He wrote: "No one has ever known or ever will know for sure, for even if what he says is exactly right, he does not know it – it is all a matter of opinion." The dualism of either being certain or having only opinion – a dualism to play an enormous part in Western history – is evident in such remarks. Protagoras's famous statement that "man is the measure of all things" meant that truth was how the world appeared to each individual. Nature was ruled by necessary laws, but human societies were ordered according to customs and conventions. Beliefs and rules in society are constructed through agreement, custom and contract. "The laws of men are fixed by agreement, not by nature," wrote the sophist Antiphon. Knowledge of nature could be unsituated and universal; knowledge of humans and society could not. The sophists are the first "constructivists" about knowledge and objectivity.

The sophists are worldly "imperfectionists" who embody a rationality appropriate to their purposes. They are satisfied with well-spoken, reasonable opinion that persuades others. In retrospect, we can see sophistic practice as pointing toward notions that are very modern – the social nature of thinking, the importance of concrete experience and cultural diversity, and the idea of situated rationality. However, it is not always recognized that sophistic practice was more than just a subjective use of rhetoric. It also required a form of impartiality. The sophist must be able to adopt the perspectives of others, or switch sides in an argument. The sophist stands back, to some degree, from his own place and time. He views his own norms as one set among many. The ideas of partiality and impartiality were well known to the Greeks. They did not need Plato to remind them about the problem of wise judgment and reliable evidence, the persistence of partiality, or the biasing influence of political allegiances and ambitions. Biased testimony in the courts could execute an innocent man, like Socrates. The debates in the agora demonstrated how facts could be interpreted in different ways.

The sophists came into conflict with philosophers who insisted on unsituated reason and universal truths. Plato, in his dialogues, the *Georgias, Protagoras, Euthydemus,* and *Sophist,* criticized the sophist for seeking victory, not truth, in argument; and for teaching relative opinion, not knowledge.

Aristotle's Facts

Prior to the seventeeth century, objective knowledge was not centred on the idea of specific, observable facts or their associated experiences. For Aristotle and many Greek rationalists, particular facts were neither the main content of knowledge nor the fundamental test of belief.[54] Systematic

54 Daston and Park, *Wonders and the Order of Nature,* 236.

knowledge – systems of thought based on general principles and their necessary, deductive implications – was superior to contingent factual observation of what generally occurred, or might have been otherwise. The role of observation of particular experiential facts (or even generalization from these facts) was not to ground science. Its role was to serve as an example of a general principle, or fill in a gap by extending the theory. Knowledge was "deep" and achieved by reason. Objectivity was following the rules of deductive logic.

Aristotle was fully aware of the role of observation and sense experience in cognition. As a biologist and naturalist, he took delight in observing and categorizing natural phenomenon, from autumn rains to the mating behaviour of pigeons.[55] But Aristotle did not define knowledge or science as empirical fact. For Aristotle, scientific inquiry begins with observational knowledge that certain kinds of events occur or certain properties *generally* coexist – for example, that bloodless animals are smaller than blooded animals. But science does not end there. Science is ultimately about the causes of things, where the knowledge of causes takes the form of an explanation in syllogistic form. Aristotelian science is most interested in general, necessary knowledge of experience – not empirical observations or the description of observable facts. Aristotle, for instance, distinguishes his natural histories of animals, based on observations, from scientific inquiry into the causes of various features of species, which was an inquiry of scientific reason. Science, through necessary causes, explains the Herculean flux of experience.

Daston and Park describe Aristotle's empiricism as "smooth," placing particular facts under general concepts and universal statements; while the empiricism of the seventeeth century was "grainy with facts," "full of experiential particulars detached from explanatory or theoretical moorings."[56] Also, the modern fact could be strange or surprising; Aristotelean facts were often commonplace. The scholastic notion of "experience," so heavily influenced by Aristotle, was gradually modified in the seventeeth century from general statements about how things usually occur to descriptions of particular things known through experiment.

Though it was gradual, the change was momentous. As long as knowledge aimed at the apprehension of universals, essences, and deductions from principle, empirical inquiry was a second-class occupation. Alone, it produced only unorganized, specific observations or unreliable (and unexplained) generalizations. Philosophers from Aristotle to Aquinas recognized observation as a source of information, and medieval science was not

55 Aristotle applied the same approach in writing about politics. He collected many constitutions of Greek city states as background for his work on politics.

56 Daston and Park, *Wonders and the Order of Nature*, 237.

lacking an empirical spirit.[57] But most philosophers did not regard facts as the basis of science, and relatively few conducted experiments to force nature to reveal new facts. The new empiricists of the seventeeth century did. Experimental fact would replace the bishop or Bible as an authority on nature.

Yet an Aristotelian view of knowledge was not quickly overthrown. Hobbes, despite being a modern mechanist and materialist, followed Aristotle in his 1651 classification of the branches of knowledge. Like Aristotle, Hobbes separates natural and civil history from necessary knowledge of causes and first principles. The former is "The Register of Knowledge of Fact," while the latter is the "Registers of Science" which are "Demonstrations of Consequences" – demonstrations of what must be the case in general. Science is far from a contingent and uncertain description of fact or what did occur here or there.[58] Perception, memory, and the evidence of witnesses, in law or in life generally, were regarded as "notoriously unreliable sources of truth."[59]

Variations and Mixtures

For ease of comprehension, I have explained the two forms of Greek rationality in rather stark terms, with clear differences. I want the reader to get a sense of the differences without getting lost in the complexities. Now that these ideas are on the table, it is important to note that Greek intellectual history displays a variety of forms of rationality.

Not all unsituated thinkers were as dismissive of experience as Parmenides. Scholars have argued that Plato would not dismiss experience as worthless.[60] For Plato, this realm of relative belief is a second-rate reality that philosophy must explain. Also, facts about society and human nature are grist for the philosopher's theorizing mill, a step on the way to higher knowledge.

The contrast between situated and unsituated rationality would receive an explicit and influential formulation in the works of Plato's greatest student, Aristotle. Rather than create a dilemma where we must choose between situated or unsituated rationality, Aristotle showed that both forms of rationality have a valid place in inquiry and life. He developed theories of theoretical and practical reason. For science, we exercise a theoretical reason that discovers the "first principles" of natural phenomena. For ethics and politics, we exercise a calculating, deliberative, practical reason that

57 Crombie, *Science in the Middle Ages*, Vol. 1.
58 Hobbes, *Leviathan*, part 1, chapter 9, 147–9.
59 Daston and Park, *Wonders and the Order of Nature*, 237.
60 Losee, *A Historical Introduction to the Philosophy of Science*, 18.

generates action-guiding judgments. The distinction divides knowledge into the theoretical sciences (philosophy, mathematics, and natural science) and the practical and productive sciences (ethics, politics, and the arts). Aristotle thought the right response to imperfect knowing is not to dismiss it but to make it a separate and potentially valid form of reasoning. We should adopt distinct methods for imperfect inquiry, as in ethics or politics, and not impose the methods of deductive science on non-scientific activities. This is a modest objectivity in practice, with a human face. Aristotle does not force on us the false dilemma of philosophical absolutism *or* illusory opinion. A deep Platonic skepticism about the world of becoming is absent in Aristotle.

We get a hint of how rationalism and empiricism would combine in future scientific thinking in the work of Ptolemy (100–178 AD). In *The Almagest*, he produced a synthesis of Greek astronomy, updated with new observations of planetary motion. But he lacked a satisfactory explanation for these "appearances." He introduced the concept of objects having a circular motion with uniform angular velocity. He also introduced the idea of an equant point, a point at some distance from the centre of the circle. By using equants, in addition to epicycles and deferments, Ptolemy could predict with fair accuracy the motions of the planets against the zodiac.[61] The particulars of planet motion, what we would call observational facts, became meaningful as facts within a larger causal and explanatory scheme.

Moreover, Greek rationality bridged the theory-practice gap in the teaching of the three Hellenistic philosophies that followed Aristotle – the Epicureans, Stoics, and skeptics. These were not schools for the abstract contemplation of propositions. They were schools that *used* theoretical and philosophical truths to figure out how to live well. They wrote manuals that promised a happy life, or tranquility. The Epicureans taught a balanced life of pleasure and pain, without troubling beliefs. The Stoics valued a virtuous life of reason that accepted the dictates of Fate. The skeptics sought mental tranquility reached through the suspension of judgment about the truth of philosophical dogma.

The Stoics put realism – an ontologically objective knowledge of the world – at the heart of the good life.[62] The Stoic believed in a rational order or *logos* in the cosmos behind the appearances. God is the soul of the world, an eternal, subtle fire (*pneuma*) that acts on, orders, and permeates matter, including our bodies. Human reason is made of the same fiery substance,

61 Ibid., 17.

62 Stoic ideas were elaborated over 500 years from the third century BC to the second century AD. The Stoic writers of antiquity ranged from Zeno and Chrysippus in Athens to Seneca, Cicero, Epictetus, and Marcus Aurelius in Rome.

and animates our material bodies. Men are a universal brotherhood because they share the spark of divine reason. Stoic virtue is a matter of "living according to nature" or God. But to live according to nature one must have objective truths about nature.

Skepticism was a therapeutic practice. The skeptic sought tranquility through detachment, but it was detachment from false or disturbing dogma about how the world really is. Skepticism is sometimes wrongly regarded as an inconsistent, debunking philosophy that undermines all claims to truth and objectivity.[63] The skeptics practised a detachment called *epoche*, a suspension of judgment about philosophical theories. They trained their guns on the "conceit of the Dogmatists." The dogmatists were the spinners of theory, such as the Platonists, the natural philosophers, and the atomists. The skeptics attacked anyone who claimed to know the nature of reality, behind the appearances. The ancient skeptic was an imperfectionist who thought that Plato's ideal of absolute philosophical knowledge was beyond human reach.

Lurking Dualisms

Given these variations, our treatment of Greek thought should be nuanced. Yet no amount of nuance can escape the fact that there were dualisms lurking in the writings of major thinkers and their theories. The dualisms were elaborated by future thinkers, for centuries.

Consider Plato. Although Plato's thought is complex, thinkers yesterday and today read his work as supporting antagonistic dualisms. This dualistic reading of Plato is not without basis. Plato's writings contain historically important dualisms: the universal and the particular, reality and appearance, soul and body, reason and desire, theory and practice, certain knowledge and uncertain opinion.[64] At many places in his dialogues, Plato depicts reason as being at war against non-reason or desire. He describes the soul (or rational psyche) as "imprisoned" by the body. Plato uses a tripartite theory of the soul – reason, emotion, and desire – and he thinks justice in the soul is the *right ordering* of these three elements. The right ordering is

63 Skepticism begins with Pyrrho of Elis in the third century BC and becomes the official philosophy of Plato's Academy under Arcesilaus (315–240 BC). Bertrand Russell called skepticism a "lazy man's" philosophy. Russell, *A History of Western Philosophy*, 6.

64 In Plato's *Republic*, Socrates says: "Nothing imperfect is a measure of anything, though sometimes people think that it is enough." Plato's praise of "pure" theory over practice can be found in such dialogues as the *Statesman*, *Philebus*, and *Republic*. In the *Philebus*, Socrates praises the "purity" of education over the impure technical arts.

reason controlling and repressing unruly desires. Reason persuades the emotions to side with it to control desires.

In the *Phaedrus,* Plato compares the soul to a chariot driver who is pulled by two winged horses, a dark horse representing desire and a white horse depicting emotion.[65] The dark horse is described as a deformed animal who is obstinate and selfish. The white horse is noble and clean, a lover of honour and modesty. The goal of the chariot driver is to reach heaven and view the immortal forms or essences of things, but he cannot get there and achieve such knowledge unless he can rein in the two conflicting steeds. In Plato's *Republic,* only the philosopher whose reason is not distracted by appetites and interests can judge what is truly valuable and real. Only reason has the independence and insight to evaluate our conflicting desires. The philosopher reaches a "standpoint of perfection" necessary for knowledge and a rationally ordered soul.[66]

Realism and Empiricism in Journalism

How do these concepts from philosophy and science apply to journalism? What sort of metaphysics and epistemology lurks in claims by journalists to report objective truth?

Historically, journalists, in attitude and to a great degree in practice, have been realists and empiricists, not constructivists or rationalists. Journalists follow an epistemology that is a realism about truth and an empiricism of method. Journalists are realists. They believe in a real, external world that they report on truthfully. They believe that empirical observation and the facts of experience justify reports and underwrite their claims to knowledge. A journalist's main path to truth is through the senses. Empiricism is a natural method for journalists since they chronicle the world about us. In the main, journalistic realism is a *specific* form of realism, a common-sense realism. It adopts common sense's belief in an external world as experienced in everyday affairs. Seeing is believing, as the slogan goes; and facts make it so.

To say that journalists use common sense in epistemology means that they favour beliefs based on observation and experience, and they adopt epistemic beliefs generally held to be plausible and expressed plainly, avoiding complexities. As I noted in chapter 1, such beliefs are based, implicitly, on philosophical assumptions and scientific beliefs, but those presumptions and beliefs do not normally enter into discussion about

65 Plato, *Phaedrus,* 530–2.
66 Nussbaum, *The Fragility of Goodness,* 160.

practice or editorial decisions. For most of its history, Western journalism has explained itself to others (and to journalism students) by using a narrative that helps itself to a minimum of theory and philosophical complexity. Sometimes, practical, procedural maxims such as "Report just the facts, comments can come later," or "If a story is too good to be true, it *is* too good to be true – verify!" are the extent of its "principles."

CONCLUSION

This chapter has prepared us for the discussion ahead, by defining objectivity as a natural cognitive capacity, and by examining notions of rationality and objectivity. These concepts will be used later in the book to shape journalistic notions of rationality and objectivity. In the next chapter, I focus on one type of objectivity. I explain the idea of objectivity of fact, which arose in the early modern period as a standard for the new empiricism, the new experimental science, and Europe's fledgling culture of fact. Objectivity of fact would become, with some alterations, the form of objectivity adopted by journalists.

3

Objectivity of Fact

But facts, Hastings, facts are the cobbles that make up the road on which we travel.

Inspector Hercule Poirot in Agatha Christie, *Murder in Mesopotamia*

The conception of objectivity that influenced the formulation of journalistic objectivity was an objectivity of observable or empirical fact, ascertained by a neutral inquirer. For brevity, I call this an objectivity of fact.

Appeal to fact is our "default" position when challenged on a belief. It is a *fact*, we insist, perhaps tapping our toe impatiently. What else could an objective belief be but a true belief about fact? What else could objectivity be but an unbiased description of experience or observation? As this chapter will show, appeal to empirical fact in the early modern era became the defining component of theories of objectivity, knowledge, and science. Yet, as the history also shows, the appeal to fact was, and is, far from innocent or clear. There is a gap between having a belief true to the world and reducing it to a neutral recording of observation. Moreover, as noted in chapter 2, much depends on what we take a fact to be and how we know the fact. In the early modern period, granting facts priority in guiding inquiry and in deciding truth and falsity was a sea-change in epistemology. Journalism objectivity, with its slogan of "just the facts," was a late application of this objectivity of fact for a practice that was growing in power, size, and social significance, and which had ambitions to be professional.

In this chapter, I divide the history of objectivity of fact into two steps. First came the early modern veneration of fact, especially in the new experimental science, in the new rationalist philosophies, in social institutions such as law, in adventures to discover "new" lands, and in an emerging "culture of fact." By the end of the 1600s, the ancient notion of objective rational explanation (described in chapter 2) had become a scientific rationality of fact. Then came the development of objectivity of fact into a more demanding objectivity of pure fact. We find this stricter conception in positivism, in the use of instruments and numbers, and in the epistemologies of the new special sciences as they distanced themselves from natural philosophy. By the late 1900s, objectivity was a neutral knowing of pure fact, a "given" in experience, stripped of all taint by hasty inference, subjective interpretation, and personal bias. Objectivity is, in large part, a nineteenth-century creation of science and scientific philosophy.[1]

The chapter has two sections. The first section outlines the early history of objectivity of fact and explains how this led, in the Enlightenment, to similar notions of "disengaged" inquiry for both theoretical rationality (as in science) and practical rationality (as in ethics). I also point out how the empiricism that developed this objectivity bequeathed to future generations three difficult problems: normativity, representation, and construction.

The second section describes how the idea of hard, pure facts arose as science became more specialized and "depersonal."

EARLY OBJECTIVITY OF FACT

Fact as a Weapon

Prior to the seventeeth century, objective knowledge was not centred on the idea of specific, observable facts or their associated experiences. As noted, for Aristotle and his medieval "followers" in philosophy, including the scholastics, particular facts were neither the main content of knowledge, nor a fundamental test of belief. Systematic knowledge – systems of thought based on general principles and their necessary deductions, often on theological or metaphysical topics – was superior to observation of the ordinary world.

The slow pace of new empirical knowledge had a social explanation. The church, the state, and other actors both preserved and limited inquiry. They preserved "higher learning" by studying ancient texts and by supporting scholarship and universities. But, they also stood in the way of change and new learning.[2] Critical thinking and new learning by independent thinkers could undermine the authority of religious and

1 "Subjective" and "objective" enter German, French, and English dictionaries as a pair of terms in the 1820s and 1830s. By the mid-nineteenth century, the term "objectivity" was popular in the academy and in the public sphere. It became popular at about the same time that the term "scientist" entered common usage.

2 I do not intend to paint the pre-modern era as a totally bleak period for learning. That would insult scholasticism and the great theological and philosophical works of the medieval period. What I am pointing to is the slow pace and lack of interest in the sort of empirical inquiries that culminated in the scientific revolution. There were periods of increased learning and "revivals" in the medieval ages. For example, as Strayer notes, the revival of Europe around the twelfth century saw a "rapid growth" in the number of educated men, which

traditional doctrine. Yet change was in the air. In Europe, the horrific religious factionalism of the sixteenth century undermined a consensus interpretation of Christianity. A "crisis of knowledge" ensued. What authority provided truth?[3]

Amid turmoil, the debate over "sources of knowledge" – that dry phrase of philosophy textbooks – was not a cool discourse among detached philosophers. The debates were seeped in the religious and social conflict of this fractious era, and never divorced from issues of power. Who determined what was knowledge and what was heresy? Spinoza's books were burned. Locke's proto-liberal idea of government by consent angered conservative monarchs. Exile for philosophers who were out of favour, from Hobbes to Locke, was a necessary strategy. For progressive thinkers, the task was to *resuscitate, improve,* and *advance* independent and scientific inquiry. This is why Bacon worked on a new method of inquiry. His letter to King James I explains why he wrote *The New Organon*, published in 1620: "The work … is no more than a new logic, teaching to invent and judge by induction … thereby to make philosophy and sciences both more true and more active. This, tending to enlarge the bounds of Reason and endow man's estate with new value."[4] The idea of empirical fact as the basis for knowledge was a philosophical "weapon" to use against traditionalists. The success of science turned the tide. The discoveries of Copernicus and Galileo on the Continent provided impressive examples of the new method.[5] In England, Harvey, Hooke, and Boyle showed how experiments and calculations led to discoveries and laws. By the end of the seventeenth century, science was the most successful model of inquiry, able to boast about Galileo's laws of motion, Harvey's discovery of the circulation of blood, and Newton's dynamics.

A Culture of Fact

In the seventeeth century, society at large became fascinated by new, strange, and experimentally produced facts, stimulated by coverage in the fledgling news press. Shapiro called England in the sixteenth and seventeeth centuries

indicates an increased desire for learning. Flocks of young men attended schools of law and ecclesiastical institutions, as the emerging institutions of the modern state needed officials with legal and other skills. See Strayer, *On the Medieval Origins of the Modern State*, 24.

3 On the crisis, see Beiser, *The Sovereignty of Reason.*

4 Cited in the introduction to *The New Organon*, viii–ix.

5 The phrase "natural philosophy" gave way to "sciences of nature" only in the eighteenth century. The first scholar to write of "scientific method" appears to have been the skeptic and philosopher Francisco Sanchez (1552–1623), in *Why Nothing Can Be Known* (1581). He argued that humans can make only limited claims about appearances – a cautious approach he called "scientific method."

a "culture of fact" that stressed perception, particulars, factual inquiry, and non-necessary knowledge.[6] Gutenberg's printing press created an "objective" print culture of repeatable and recordable fact.[7] Scientific and social "discourses of fact" emerged. Shapiro argues that impartial fact-determination first took root not in science but in English common law.[8] Law courts were among the first institutions to discuss the idea of impartiality and to produce tests for reliable, objective testimony. A judge who puts facts "on trial" resembles the scientist who tests ideas before nature. The new objectivity of fact, then, was first an objectivity of practice. Other disciplines adopted the same norms of factuality. Eventually, the legal "fact" became the editor's "newes" of the Thirty Years War, the explorer's "chronicle," the experimenter's "matter of fact," and the merchant's "facts of finance." Historians claimed that their writings were factual chronicles. Travel writing reported on exotic journeys. Editors claimed journalism was a discourse of fact.

Bacon's Facts

Francis Bacon, lawyer, chancellor, and author, was the father of the modern fact. London's Royal Society, inspired by Bacon, called him the "father of modern science." Daston called Bacon "the patron saint of objectivity."[9]

Bacon said that inquirers must "freely and faithfully" report with "impartial veracity" and follow "the rule of writing nothing but Matter of Fact." But obtaining scientific fact was not a matter of everyday perception or common sense. It was hard work, using the inductive method to exclude subjective factors in inquiry. Particular facts, downplayed by Hobbes and "smoothed over" by Aristotle, would play an unprecedented scientific role. Yet Bacon was keenly aware that the senses could be misleading and that the mind misinterprets facts. The mind "adds" its own biasing gloss on things. The greatest hindrance to good understanding is the "dullness, incompetency, and deception of the senses."[10] Bacon classified forms of mental bias the "idols" of the mind. There were the idols of the tribe (errors due to the limits of perception), of the cave (individual bias), of the theatre (the influence of systems of philosophy) and of the marketplace

6 Shapiro, *A Culture of Fact.*

7 See Eisenstein, *The Printing Press as an Agent of Change.*

8 Poovey, however, argues that the "modern fact" began in the double-entry bookkeeping of sixteenth-century merchants. Poovey, *A History of the Modern Fact*, 29–91.

9 Daston, "Baconian Facts," 37.

10 Bacon, *The Essays*, 277.

(the use of vague terms).[11] Human understanding is prone to illusion, like a "false mirror," which distorts the objective rays it receives from external things "by mingling its own nature with it."

Therefore, our knowledge of facts is not whatever strikes one's senses. We begin with beliefs that are prima facie plausible. These beliefs must remain valid *after* we have subjected them to scrutiny, and have eliminated the influence of the idols. Much analysis and ordering of facts is necessary before the mind can discover new principles, as well as new facts. Bacon wanted facts "scrubbed clean" of conjecture, bias, hasty generalization, inference, and precocious theorizing. Scrubbing presumes a capacity to *encapsulate* facts – an independent capacity to observe facts, separate from other cognitive capacities. The goal of encapsulation led to the long and tortured attempt by empiricists to identify a "given" in perceptual experience, a pure, direct contact with reality as foundation for knowledge.[12] What distinguished the new empiricism was "the sharp distinction between a datum of experience, experiential or observational, and any inference drawn from it."[13] Also, Baconian facts were not known with certainty. In the nineteenth century, the fact of observation would become incorrigible.

Fact and Faculty

A Baconian fact is a special element in cognition *produced* by a stringent method of inquiry. Bacon is not a monist about how such elements are produced. Epistemic monism is the view that knowledge is achieved primarily (or only) through the use of one dominant faculty, for example, through observation. Bacon is an epistemic holist who calls for a synthesis of observation, imagination, categorization, and inference, all utilized in the right manner and in the right order. In Book 1 of *The New Organon*, Bacon writes: "Those who have handled sciences have been either men of experiment or men of dogmas. The men of experiment are like the ant, they only collect and use; the reasoners resemble spiders, who make cobwebs out of their own substance. But the bee takes a middle course: it gathers its material from the flowers of the garden and of the field, but transforms and digests it by a power of its own."[14] The bee combines observing and thinking about what one observes. Bacon did not want to eliminate the interpretation of facts or theories. What he wanted was a

11 The idols are catalogued in Bacon, *The New Organon.*

12 In 1929, C.I. Lewis would declare that the "given" as a pure stream of unmediated sensations, was a "myth." Lewis, "The Given in Experience."

13 Daston and Park, *Wonders*, 237.

14 Bacon, *The New Organon*, 79.

reliable supply of facts for interpreting nature. He sought a "lawful marriage" between reason and observation. Other experimentalists agreed. Hooke described the experimentalist's method as a circular process involving the senses, memory, understanding, and reason. Empirical natural philosophy, in the hands of Galileo and Newton, displayed the power of a synthesis of facts, hypotheses, logic, and mathematics. The logical positivist Rudolf Carnap, writing three centuries after Bacon, argued correctly that the tension between rationalism and empiricism is not a dualistic choice between reason or experience.[15] Early empiricists, Carnap said, did not realize the importance of logic, while rationalists mistakenly thought reason alone could produce empirical knowledge.

Guided by Nature

In chapter 2, I stated that realists believe that knowledge is a truthful description of what is real, as it exists in itself. The same realism motivated the creators of the modern fact. A favourite phrase was that their inquiries were guided by nature, not by their biases. Bacon claimed that, unlike the Aristotelian logic, which teaches how to grapple with abstract classes, his method trains the understanding "to dissect nature truly and to discover the powers and actions of bodies and their laws limned in matter. Hence this science takes its origin not only from the nature of the mind but from the nature of things."[16]

How do we know what belongs to nature and what is added by our minds? One way is to avoid the idols of the mind. Another way is to pay attention to the "primary" properties of things. Rationalists and empiricists made a distinction between primary and secondary qualities (or properties). In science, Galileo distinguished between objective, primary properties – an object's shape, size, mass, and motion – and subjective, secondary properties – an object's colour, taste, sound, and smell. "Tastes, odours, colours, and so on, are no more than mere names so far as the object in which we place them is concerned, and … they reside only in consciousness."[17] This was not a new strategy. In ancient Greece Democritus said that his theory of atoms and their properties was true to nature while properties of ordinary objects, such as the bitterness of some foods, were subjective properties of human convention. He wrote: "By convention colored, by convention sweet,

15 Carnap, *The Logical Structure of the World*, preface to the 2nd edition, vi. Carnap thought logical positivism had achieved the correct synthesis by combining empiricism and logic.

16 Bacon, *The New Organon*, 219–20.

17 Clavelin, *The Natural Philosophy of Galileo*, 435.

by convention bitter; in reality, only atoms and the void."[18] Descartes argued that physical reality was only matter in motion, with the primary properties of extension, shape, mass, and motion. Locke distinguished between secondary qualities – ideas in our minds which do not resemble anything in the external objects that are what actually cause those ideas – and primary qualities, which refer to "real" or objective properties, such as solidity, extension, figure, motion or rest, and number.[19] Into the second-class category of secondary properties, moral properties would soon be thrown. However, there were dissenters, such as Berkeley and Bayle, the latter of whom noted that the same arguments used to reduce sensory properties to a "secondary" status could be used against primary properties such as extension.[20] Today, the distinction remains popular. Many people, for example, accept the claim of brain science that colours are not properties of external objects, but are subjective projections of our nervous system onto objects.

How did scientists construct their list of primary properties? In large part, they were the properties popular in physical science and mathematics. The properties answered this question: What ontology is needed – what objects must we assume to exist – in order to make science understandable and true? Scientific method favoured properties that were observable and measurable, as nature came to be conceived of as mathematically lawful and materialistic.[21] Extension, size, shape, and motion were better suited to the prevailing methods of science than colour and tastes.

Objectivity as Disengagement

Early objectivity of fact, however, was not just a set of methods for discerning outward facts. It was also an inward attitude of disengaging from and transcending the prejudices of one's place and era. In chapter 2, we noted that most notions of objectivity require inquirers to disengage, fully or partially, from their current beliefs and situation to investigate and critique. The difference between situated and unsituated rationality is the degree to which disengagement is thought possible and desirable.

In the early modern period and into the Enlightenment, norms of disengagement and transcendence were developed in two areas: (1) disengagement in the use of theoretical rationality for philosophy and science, and (2) disengagement in the use of practical reason for ethics, politics, and aesthetics.

18 Democritus, in Kirk and Raven, *The Pre-Socratic Philosophers*, 422.

19 Locke, *Essay Concerning Human Understanding*, Book 2, 166–74.

20 Bayle, *The Dictionary Historical and Critical*, Book 4, 612.

21 Burtt, *The Metaphysical Foundations of Modern Science*, 105–24.

Objectivity for Theoretical Rationality

Recall that Bacon required inquirers to review facts impartially. Recall also that Descartes attempted to follow, in the strictest manner possible, the path of transcendent thinking. Echoing Plato's disappointment with common opinion, Descartes complains that he travelled the world and found either conflicting beliefs or consent to "extravagant and ridiculous" opinions. He resolves to "believe nothing too certainly of which I had only been convinced by example and custom," which "rendered us less capable of listening to Reason."[22] In *Meditations on First Philosophy*, Descartes adopts the liberating attitude of disengagement as he sits by a fire and thinks. Radical doubt allows him to step back from his beliefs. Doubt, systematically practised, lead him to clear, indubitable ideas, such as that he exists as a thinking or experiencing subject. Correct method and disengagement aim ultimately at an "absolute conception" of the world: to know things independently of historically and socially conditioned perspectives.[23] Locke, for his part, rejects any "Authority" in deciding philosophical questions. "The floating of other men's opinions in our brains, makes us not one jot the more knowing, though they happen to be true."[24] Truth is his only aim.

For Bacon, Descartes, and Locke, disengagement is the first step in a reconstruction of beliefs. Disengagement contains a fundamental presumption: that reason is a faculty autonomous from context and situation. Through it, we enjoy intellectual freedom. If reason was not autonomous, it could not adopt an objective attitude, it could not discover its own truths, it could not transcend its entanglement in tradition. In Augustine, God's grace illuminates confused minds. In Descartes, the "natural light of reason" provides the illumination.

Objectivity and Intervention

However, there were differences in disengagement in philosophy and the new science. The search for philosophical fundamentals encouraged philosophers from Plato to Descartes to prescribe a form of disengagement suitable for an *inactive* "thinking subject." However, the search for new empirical truths in science redefined disengagement as one of the mental virtues of an *active* investigator who tests ideas through intervention in nature. In 1699, the *Histoire* of the Royal Academy of Sciences in Paris said that scientists wrenched "matters of fact" from nature by a "kind of violence"

22 Descartes, *Discourse on Method*, in *The Philosophical Works of Descartes*, Vol. 1, 87.

23 Williams, *Descartes*, 65.

24 Locke, *An Essay Concerning Human Understanding*, Book 2, 115.

through experiment.[25] This engaged empiricism used instruments to probe nature, far beyond the powers of the unaided human eye. Instruments were generators of objective facts. The air pump, telescope, camera obscura, and microscope were showpieces of the new scientific method, appearing in numerous paintings.[26] The verification of experimental results was an active, social affair. Verification meant demonstrating one's experiments *before others.* Sprat said that meetings of the Royal Society made "the whole process (the experiment) pass under its own eyes," correcting idiosyncrasies of observation and judgment. "It is not I who says this," Sprat said, referring to experiments sanctioned by the Royal Society, "it is all of us." The social aspect of verification was crucial.[27]

The test of scientific objectivity was twofold: the test of nature (through hypothesis and experiment) and the test of public scrutiny (through demonstration before other scientists). The experimentalists were not isolated intellectuals, writing in a garret. They were part of a very public and international "Republic of Letters," whose members believed that their work transcended factions and countries.[28] Scientists developed a modest, impartial style for communicating the results of their inquiries. Objectivity, as the impartial pursuit of truth and fact, occurred *within* an active, engaged form of inquiry, with its own goals and interests.

Objectivity for Practical Rationality

The spread of science in the seventeeth and eighteenth centuries did not crush work on ethics. Some of the best minds of the age, like Hume, wrote treatises on morality. However, given the emerging mechanical worldview, there was a decline in theology-based moral philosophy that explained man's place in nature while ascribing purpose and goodness to the latter. Instead, there arose a naturalistic wave of ethics that rooted goodness and rightness in more parochial facts about human nature and society – such things as human sentiment, utility, and social contracts. Hobbes defined good and bad as objects that psychologically attract or repel us. Locke identified good and bad with pleasure and pain. Hume argued that desire,

25 Daston, "Fear and Loathing of the Imagination in Science," 75.

26 Shapin and Schaffer, *Leviathan and the Air-Pump.*

27 In modern times, Popper argued that scientific objectivity was a method with an intrinsic social aspect. Scientific objectivity is "not a product of the individual scientist's impartiality, but a product of the social or public character of scientific method." Popper, *The Open Society and Its Enemies,* 2:217–20.

28 On the Republic of Letters, see Burke, *A Social History of Knowledge.* On experimentalism, see Butterfield, *The Origins of Modern Science,* 77–95.

not reason, sets the ends of action. Bentham's utilitarianism reduced moral (and other) decisions to the calculation of pleasures and pains, the greatest good for the greatest number.

This was the factual side of naturalized morality. It was founded not in God's will but in facts about what individuals generally desire and what rules should limit self-interest so that individuals could reap the benefits of society. Yet moral reasoning needed more than facts about humans. It required virtuous attitudes, of which the most important was an impartiality when reasoning about what to do. Situated agents must be willing to transcend calculations of self-interest and prudence. They need to reason impartially about what is best for all parties affected by some action or policy.

Theories of moral impartiality took many forms. For Hobbes, society was only possible if partial individuals surrendered their rights to the more impartial judgment of a Leviathan with the power to penalize non-compliance with the social contract.[29] Impartiality in utilitarianism was considering each person to be equal when we calculate the overall utility of any decision. Impartiality in Kant was "universalizing" one's moral maxims to see if what I judge to be right for me would be right for other people in similar situations. One reduces partiality in moral judgment by seeing if a proposed rule of conduct would be sanctioned by the common, or universal, view. For Kant, an action is an objective duty if reason regards it as a duty for all rational beings. Universalizability, impartiality, rational consistency – these are the signs of agreement with impartial practical reason. Most importantly, for Kant, the agent respects the objective, moral law. Kant makes the "voice" of morality not sentiment but the stern voice of self-legislating reason. Acting objectively is an expression of autonomous human nature and dignity – the same autonomy that underlies theoretical reason in Descartes and Locke.

Other theorists of morality emphasized the sentiments of benevolence and sympathy as a counter-balance to naked self-interest. Such naturally felt sentiments, not reason alone, were what encouraged us to adopt the common view. Condorcet believed that nature endowed all people with "benevolence … and generous sensibility." Hume said that, to judge another person as vicious, one must appeal to common feelings of sympathy and antipathy towards certain actions, arguing from a "common point of view." For, he added, "the humanity of one man is the humanity of every one." Hume extended this common view to other areas. He advised the art critic to take the position of a "man in general, [and] forget, if possible, my individual being, and my peculiar circumstances." He believed that historians

29 See Ward, "Thomas Hobbes: The Ethics of Social Control."

must "have no particular interest or concern to pervert their judgment." In politics, Hume encouraged impartiality and public zeal, not the "ends of ... faction."[30]

Adam Smith, in *The Theory of Moral Sentiments,* argued there must be controls on self-love. Individuals must be able to put themselves imaginatively in the place of others and to feel sympathy for them.[31] But sympathy is not sufficient. In ethics, it is not enough to feel sorrow or joy. One must judge whether someone's actions display propriety, given their situation. We look on the actions from the perspective of an external, impartial judge.[32]

In summary, many writers treated the search for objective ethical judgment as an *analogue* to the search for objective empirical judgment. Scientific and moral objectivity are treated as different expressions of our natural capacity for objective evaluation of belief. Scientific and moral quests for objectivity share the desire for correct cognition or judgment through logic, facts, and norms of rationality and consistency. Impartiality, transcendence of partiality, and social verification are common themes.

THREE PROBLEMS: NORMATIVITY, REPRESENTATION, CONSTRUCTION

The rise of the modern fact created three problems for subsequent thinking in epistemology, philosophy of science, and ethics: the problem of normativity in terms of an "is-ought" dualism, the problem of objective representation, and the problem of construction.

Problem 1: Is versus Ought

The "is-ought" distinction was stated explicitly as a dualism by Hume.[33] By the time Hume published his *Treatise* in 1739, the scientific and human images of the world had already begun to diverge.[34] The world known by science began to look quite different from the world known by ordinary experience. For the former, it is a world of matter in mechanical, law-like motion consisting of primary properties and devoid of purpose, value, or freedom. The world of ordinary experience is a world of secondary

30 Hume, *Essays: Moral, Political and Literary,* 562, 278–9.

31 Smith, *The Theory of Moral Sentiments,* 3.

32 Ibid., 22.

33 Hume's is-ought distinction and his main discussion of morality as sentiment occur in Book 3, Part 1, of *A Treatise of Human Nature,* 455–76.

34 Sellars, in "Philosophy and the Scientific Image of Man," called these the "scientific" and "manifest" images of men.

properties and values – colours, tastes, sounds, mental life, purposes, and actions that presume freedom. Weber called this the "disenchantment" of nature – the elimination of "enchanting" values from a scientific description of the world.

The "is-ought" distinction is both an explanation and product of this worldview. The explanation is: Science deals with objective fact, and ethics deals with subjective values. The former involves the observation of fact; the latter is the expression of emotion or values.

Hume's version of this distinction occurs within a discussion of morals. His chief aim is not to support a dualistic, mechanical worldview, but to support his naturalistic ethics – to show that ethics originates in natural sentiments and the need for social coordination. Hume says that "the operations of human understanding" (or cognition) are of two kinds: the relations of ideas, i.e., logically combining or separating ideas, and matters of fact, i.e., cognizing facts of observation and using reason to make inferences from such observations.[35] So the question for ethics is: to which category of cognition do moral judgments belong? They are not relations of ideas, and they do not appear to be matters of fact. Not if by "fact" you mean a sense impression of an external moral property or moral fact. We do not literally "see" or "bump into" goodness or justice through the senses. Nor are they inferences from facts. As Hume famously says, you can't deduce what ought to be from what is.[36] So moral judgments are not creatures of reason or logic. Therefore, Hume concludes, moral judgment is not a form of cognition; it is not some representation or description of an external fact.

Yet many people talk about what is right or wrong as a matter of fact. Is it not a fact that torturing a baby for pleasure is wrong? So, what *are* ethical judgments? Hume's reply is that ethical judgments are emotive or sentiment-based approvals (or disapprovals) of actions. They express our feelings toward some fact, but they do not describe the fact. Recognizing an action as an instance of torture is a factual judgment but the ethical condemnation of this fact is an emotional response. The mind "adds" an ethical appraisal to the fact that an action occurred. We call it right or wrong, good or bad. Ethical judgment is a non-cognitive form of evaluation.

The implications of Hume's is-ought dualism are far-reaching. If ethics is a non-cognitive response to the world, then it seems that ethics is highly subjective and outside of rational evaluation. As we will see, the logical positivists, influenced by Hume's is-ought dualism, regarded ethical statements as cognitively meaningless. Many ordinary people have adopted the

35 Hume, *Treatise*, 463.
36 Ibid., 469.

distinction as obvious. But the dualism is far from obvious. It relies on crucial premises that need to be argued for, not presupposed. For example, Hume's argument goes through *only* if we grant him a crucial assertion: That facts are reducible to sense impressions. But is this too narrow a psychology of facts and of cognition? Regardless of its validity, the "is-ought" distinction created a problem for anyone who wanted to defend ethics as rational, let alone an objective field of study. Hume did not think his distinction threw ethics into the category of hopelessly subjective topics. Instead, he thought it opened the door to better, sentiment-based ethics. But for many people who came after Hume, the lesson was not that ethics had to be reformulated as sentiment, but rather that ethics was whatever anyone thought was right.

Problem 2: Objective Representation?

The second problem was the problem of objective representation of the world. Locke said that knowledge was an analysis and combination of ideas. Where did these ideas come from?

According to the seventeeth century's psychology, ideas were either innate to the mind, or they reached the mind through the senses. Either way, ideas represent objects, facts, and truths. Representation was viewed in Locke and Hume as a sort of "picture" or image that resembled the object. But how do I know that the pictures in my mind, encased in my body, accurately represent an objective thing "out there" in the world? How do we even know there *is* an external world? How do we know that some ideas represent primary qualities? Perhaps idealists like Berkeley were right when they claimed that we only know our mental ideas, which exist in a mind or the mind of God. In Berkeley's famous phrase, to be is to be perceived.[37] Berkeley asked the skeptical question that would haunt future empiricists: "For how can it be known that the things which are perceived are conformable to those which are not perceived or exist without the mind?"[38] These problems arose directly from defining knowledge as the outcome of a thinking self that (as Hume said) considers ideas in the "theatre" of its mind.[39]

To make matters more complicated, Kant developed a critical philosophy that viewed representation as much more than the association of ideas

37 Berkeley, *Principles of Human Knowledge*, para. 88, 292.

38 Ibid., para. 86, 291.

39 Hume says, in discussing personal identity: "The mind is a kind of theatre, where several perceptions successively make their appearance; pass, repass, glide away, and mingle in an infinite variety of postures and situations." *Treatise*, Book 1, Sect. 6, 253.

derived from the senses. Kant reversed the approach to knowledge hitherto favoured by most philosophers and metaphysicians. The latter went from outer to inner. Philosophers start with a metaphysical view of the world and then study the place of humans and the human mind within that scheme. We start with objects in the world and then study how our minds conform to the object. Kant proposed that we proceed from the inner to the outer. We start with the mind and show how its capacities construct objects. Nelson Goodman summarized this trend by saying that modern philosophy began when Kant "exchanged the structure of the world for the structure of the mind."[40] What was needed was a "transcendental" philosophy that investigates how the mind's structure makes possible our experience. Kant compared his approach to Copernicus's revolutionary decision to try a new standpoint in astronomy – to hypothesize that the "entire celestial host" did not revolve around the earth-bound observer, but rather that the observer revolved and "left the stars at rest."[41] Kant writes of his own revolution:

> Up to now it has been assumed that all our cognition must conform to the objects; but all attempts to find out something about them *a priori* through concepts that would extend our cognition have, on this presupposition, come to nothing. Hence let us once try whether we do not get farther with the problems of metaphysics by assuming that the objects must conform to our cognition.[42]

For Kant, we represent the world though a complex conceptual scheme innate to the mind. Humans use the faculties of understanding and reason to make sense of sensory intuitions – the data from external objects. All sense experience is *rationally interpreted experience.* The mind comes equipped with basic concepts (or "categories") without which no experience would be possible. These categories, such as space, time, and causality, determine the structure of all perceptual experience. Kant called these categories "a priori" because they do not derive from particular, empirical experiences. They belong, innately, to all rational minds. We have knowledge of external objects only as they appear to us, through the mediation of the categories. Reason cannot know "things-in-themselves" – how things are, apart from how they appear. Nor can reason know "supersensible" objects, such as

40 Goodman, *Ways of Worldmaking,* x.

41 A similar "revolution" occurred in modern physics of motion when natural philosophers such as Newton began to regard motion as natural and believed that objects would move and continue to move eternally unless some force like inertia inhibited their movement. This standpoint was almost the complete opposite of the long-lasting Aristotelian view that rest (or non-motion) was natural and motion had to be explained.

42 Kant, *Critique of Pure Reason,* 110, Bxvi.

God, that go beyond the appearances. Science knows nature as a lawful system of appearances, filtered through a priori categories.

So, in this view, mental representation is a complex interaction of sensory intuitions and conceptual structures. It is a view that combined notions from rationalism and empiricism. But, we may ask: Have we not "conceptualized" and softened the idea of the independent empirical fact? The external world and the world of fact seem to lose their robustness. In Kant, the world becomes an "idea" of reason – something we must presume to exist but of which we know nothing. Empirical facts become beliefs about mentally constructed appearances.

Work on the problems of objective representation would live on. A long line of philosophers – rationalists, empiricists, and philosophers of common sense – would try to bridge the gap between mental idea and external object. For example, the Scottish philosopher Thomas Reid said people were justified in believing the common-sense principles that philosophers doubt or feel require special proof, like belief in an external world. Reid said that the mind had an irresistible tendency to believe in an external world because our ideas "suggest" the presence of external bodies. Reid's "Principle 5" holds: "That those things do really exist which we distinctly perceive by our senses, and are what we perceive them to be."[43] This principle's denial, Reid argued, is more improbable than its affirmation. John Stuart Mill would not follow Reid's common-sense approach. Instead he would construct external objects from sensations. He said that the mind constructed the perceived object as an association of actual and expected sensations. Matter was the "permanent possibility of sensation."[44]

Problem 3: Beyond Sense

The third problem originated in the empiricists' thesis that all knowledge *originates* in the ideas of sense. This thesis places the burden on the empiricist to show how all forms of knowledge are derived from sense experience; that is, from a meagre input of shifting perceptual data. The empiricist is asked to rationally justify our most important and probable beliefs and theories by showing how they are constructed from empirical experience. Objective belief is either the direct recording of experience, or belief correctly constructed from an experiential base. As we will see, this construction proved to be fraught with difficulties. For example, it does not appear that the principles of logic or mathematics are generalizations from perceptions.

43 Reid, *Essays on the Intellectual Powers of Man*, 452, 476.
44 Mill, *An Examination of Sir William Hamilton's Philosophy*, IX, 183.

Are universal scientific laws so derivable? What about statements about the distant past or future? If our knowledge "starts" logically from perceptual experiences, are the latter incorrigible? How can subjective experiences ground public, objective science?

OBJECTIVITY OF PURE FACT

Inoculating Science

Objectivity of fact became objectivity of pure fact in the nineteenth century. There was, in many quarters, an almost religious veneration for the fact. "Sit down before a fact as a little child," wrote Thomas Huxley. "Be prepared to give up every pre-conceived notion, follow humbly wherever and to whatever abyss nature leads, or you shall learn nothing."[45]

The time period does not coincide exactly with the nineteenth century. The period in view extends from the publication of Mill's *System of Logic* in 1833 to the rise of logical positivism, as the Vienna Circle, in the late 1920s. Objectivity of pure fact was the invention of an empiricism and a plurality of new sciences that ardently wanted to be accepted as scientific. Epistemology would be developed by scientists themselves, from Comte and Mach to Duhem.

Over this hundred or so years, empiricism became a positivism of sensory experience, avoiding metaphysics by reducing worldly knowledge to regularities in a Kantian world of appearances. Empiricism became stricter, more strident, and ideological, and, with logical positivism at the turn of the twentieth century, more intolerant of thinking that did not closely conform to natural science. Empirical philosophy had always been associated with empirical and natural science, but, in the nineteenth century, it became science's ideological servant, at times defined as only a "logic" of science. As a logic, its mandate was to clarify and justify the basic concepts, methods, and principles of science. But this clarification had an ulterior goal: to explain how science was distinct and superior to other pursuits of knowledge; to "protect" science from non-science, especially metaphysics. Philosophy, as epistemology, sought to explain how *scientific* knowledge was constructed from experience, and how other forms of belief could not be so constructed.

The attempt to inoculate science from both bias and non-science launched the quest for pure objectivity. Carving out a space for science encouraged the belief that the distinctness of science was in its factual

45 Quoted in Stevens, *A History of News*, 221.

rigour, defined in terms of a pure notion of fact and a demanding, depersonalized notion of the impartial investigator. If science was to defend its claim to be the exemplar of true and rational knowledge, it seemed that philosophers and scientists would have to show how science, in method, is a superior and stricter pursuit of objectivity. This required that epistemologists do two things. First, philosophers had to identify a point of clear and immediate contact with reality – typically understood as perceptual awareness of the world – that would serve as an incorrigible foundation for scientific knowledge and the testing of theory. Philosophers needed to articulate rigorously this "given" in experience, this "anchor" of theory to the world. Second, philosophers and scientists should welcome new methods by which the role of human judgment and interpretation could be reduced, perhaps even eliminated. Judgment and creativity would be replaced with the impersonal objectivity of scientific instruments and numerical analysis. Science needed an "objectivity without a person." Objectivity should be an objectivity of depersonalized "purified reason."[46]

Positivism, Mechanics, and the Sciences

Positivism is the view that empirical knowledge is knowledge of what appears to us through the senses – the empirical facts.[47] Positivists took to heart an idea of German idealism: Kant's maxim that science can know only appearances, not things in themselves. The goal was not to explain what we experience by unobservable entities or metaphysical processes but to show how our appearances follow empirical laws and generalizations, such as those concerning how the pressure of gas is related to volume and temperature. Fourier's mathematical laws of the diffusion of heat, for example, formulated regularities among phenomena without assumptions about the nature of heat. Since "appearances" was understood, following Hume, as matters of fact that appear to our senses, knowledge was a matter of careful observation and collection of facts, and induction upon such facts. Science did not "explain" by citing hidden or theoretical causes "behind" experience. Rather, science limited itself to a description of the lawful order of experience.

The opposite of positivist thinking was called "metaphysical" thinking. Positivists defined metaphysics as highly general, philosophical theories

46 Newell, *Objectivity, Empiricism, and Truth*, 29.

47 The term "positivism" first appeared in 1831 in a document published by followers of the French utopian socialist Saint-Simon. In England, nineteenth-century positivism is virtually identified with J.S. Mill, ignoring the writings of Pearson and Clifford. For instance, Pearson said that a scientific law is only a brief description of the order of our perceptions.

about the world that appealed to entities (and causal factors) beyond empirical experience. Positivists thought that science had shown metaphysics to be outdated and discredited. Mill said positivism was "the general property of the age." He defined positivism: "We have no knowledge of anything but phenomena, and our knowledge of phenomena is relative, not absolute. We know not the essence, nor the real mode of production, of any fact, but only its relations to other facts in the way of succession or of similitude."[48]

Why was positivism so popular? It was not only because, in philosophy, it was heir to the empiricism of Bacon, Locke, and Hume; it was also popular because it expressed the spirit of an age of fledgling sciences, technology, and social industrialism, with its stress on the factual and experiential. As the new scientific thinking jostled for recognition in universities and in society, it adopted an aggressive, skeptical perspective on other disciplines. Positivism was, as empiricism was earlier, a viewpoint "on the offensive" against tradition.

When casting aspersions on metaphysics, positivists had specific writers in mind. The list included the post-Kantian idealists.[49] Hegel postulated a world spirit; in England, Bradley postulated an "absolute" reality behind the contradictory appearances of sense.[50] Metaphysics in this form is an expression of strong, unsituated rationalism, of an absolute realism seeking to see the world as a whole, as it exists in itself. Clearly, this form of philosophy is not hospitable to the positivist's reduction of knowledge to sensory appearance.[51] Idealism tended to downgrade the reality of "particular things" – individuals and sense experiences.[52] Sometimes, positivists simply

48 Mill's positivism was not influenced by Hume and his is-ought distinction. Mill knew next to nothing about Hume.

49 Idealism here is not Berkeley's view that to be is to be perceived by a mind. It is the view that to be real is to be a member of a rational, world system that is ideal or spiritual. For Platonic idealism, a thing is real insofar as it participates in the ideal essences. For Absolute Idealism, something is real if it is a manifestation of Spirit or a member of a community of spirits.

50 See Bradley, *Appearance and Reality*. Bradley's metaphysics was a chief target of attack by G.E. Moore in "The Refutation of Idealism" – an article that became a manifesto for Moore and Russell.

51 For example, British idealist Thomas H. Green attacked the empirical view that to be real or to be a fact is to be a "phenomenon" given to us in experience as an isolated sensation. The real consists of objects in relations. Relations exist only for a thinking consciousness, and therefore, the world is constituted by mind. We know an objective world through our mind and as participant in the eternal consciousness.

52 This downgrading of the individual thing and the individuality of experience was the basis for Søren Kierkegaard's anti-Hegelian "existentialism" in the mid-1800s. From the standpoint of world history, he writes, "the individual subject is indeed unimportant,

cited, with derision, examples of unverifiable metaphysical statements such as "the Absolute is Plural" and its rival, "the Absolute is One." What facts could show that one assertion was true and the other false? Yet metaphysics, as idealism, would continue to enjoy periods of renewed interest in England and the United States after Hegel died in 1831.

Positivism was associated with phenomenalism as a theory about perception of the external world. Phenomenalism claimed that the solid, external objects of perception are really the mental "phenomena" of an experiencing subject. Mill, as seen, reduced the belief in external objects to the experience of groups of sensations. Experience, at its most elemental and direct, is a stream of raw or undigested sensations and feelings, and our belief in external objects is an inference from patterns in these sensations. Mill was following the constructivism of earlier empiricists. He had absorbed the empiricism of "experience" and association of ideas from David Hartley in his *Observations on Man* and from his father, James Mill. The human mind and knowledge could be explained by the operations of a few psychological laws upon the materials of sensation. Mill preferred this phenomenal empiricism because it supported his reformist leanings. It swept away religious talk of the soul and replaced it with more precise psychological analysis, and it suggested that, because humans start with the same psychological faculties, humans could be perfected. Like the Baconian fact, the ideas of psychological association and direct experience were political weapons for social reform, opposing the Establishment with its "necessary" laws and "sacred truths" known by Reason. Mill calls himself an experimentalist and not an empiricist since, in Baconian fashion, he regards the latter as unsystematic common sense, which is not rigorous inquiry and is often uninterested in new ideas.

Meanwhile, French positivism took over Hume's reduction of cognition to matters of fact or relations of ideas. Auguste Comte said: "Any [empirical] proposition which does not admit of being ultimately reduced to a single enunciation of fact, special or general, can have no real or intelligible sense." For Comte, science was the culmination of the march of human thought from theology to metaphysics to positivistic science, and now sociology. The accumulation of facts would lead to predictive laws of society to guide reform. At first, Mill approved of Comte's *Course in Positivist Philosophy*, but later was aghast at Comte's *System of Positivist Polity* which outlined a totalitarian order with a secular religion where humanity is

but, ethically, the individual is infinitely important. The task is in "becoming subjective." See Kierkegaard, "Becoming Subjective," 132.

treated as a deity.[53] Mill called Comte's book the "completest system of spiritual despotism which has yet to emanate from the human brain."

Scientists as Positivists

In the second half of the nineteenth century, leading scientists wrote philosophical treaties to promote their methods, eliminating any reasoning that might upset a positivist conscience. Mechanics, the science of bodily motion in nature, received a positivistic interpretation. G.R. Kirchhoff's *Principles of Mechanics* in 1874 asserted that scientists should explain physical motion and the interaction of bodies in the simplest and most complete manner. They seek regularities among phenomena. They do not try to explain, metaphysically, why such regularities exist. The most important philosopher-scientist was Ernst Mach, whose *The Science of Mechanics* contained ideas close to Kirchoff's principles.[54] In an article for *Popular Scientific Lectures* in 1896, Mach said Kant's first critique of pure reason "banished into the realm of shadows the sham idea of the old metaphysics." Science deals economically with experience. What is this experience? In *The Analysis of Sensations*, Mach, after starting with science's "anti-metaphysical" form of thought, says "the world consists only of our sensations ... In which case we have knowledge *only* of sensations."[55] The table, the tree, and so forth are "my sensations," and are eventually constructed into beliefs about physical objects. Science brings a diversity of such experiences under singular and widely applicable laws, reducing the risk of finding ourselves confronting a wholly unfamiliar situation in the future. Science takes away the magic of experience by showing how what was strange and unfamiliar is a specific example of a familiar connection among experiences.

But what about the entities of theory – atoms and the absolute space of physics? Mach adopts an instrumentalism. They are merely useful "posits" for predicting phenomena. For example, there is no absolute space and time. Such talk is meaningless. There is only spatial location relative to another body, and temporal position relative to some instrument for measuring time. Mach attacked the Platonic-Cartesian idea of science as strict demonstration. He believed that principles do not need to be deduced from first principles. Science can get along with the testing of hypotheses about empirical regularities.

53 See Nussbaum's account of Comte's positivist-directed secular society in chapter 3 of *Political Emotions*.

54 Mach, *The Science of Mechanics*, first published in 1883, in English by 1893.

55 Mach, *The Analysis of Sensations*, 12.

Realists and Complexity

As scientific empiricism traversed the nineteenth century, it was challenged by a new generation of realists, logicians, and pragmatists who questioned positivism (and phenomenalism) as an account of experience and scientific knowledge. Is it really true that we only know our own sensations? This inner world of sensation does not resemble the robust world of everyday external objects. It seems to reduce the world to what is in my mind.

Further challenges came from science itself. Scientific theories became more and more complex and theoretical, putting pressure on the idea that these theoretical concepts could be defined by sensations, immediate experience, or any other phenomenal base. To rectify this problem, physicists, positivists, and others introduced epistemologies of science that tried to hang on to the positivist view of science by devising increasingly complex explanations of the relationship of theory and experience. Scientific thinking was now said to include conventional, pragmatic, and holistic elements. Such amendments made this more sophisticated empiricism look increasingly *unlike* positivism.

The mathematical physicist Henri Poincaré was a noted critic of positivism. He introduced "conventionalism" as an explanation of scientific laws. Laws are conventions. They are free creations of the human spirit, not mechanical generalizations over facts. Positivism wrongly portrays the scientist as no more than a sensitive recording device. Laws are definitions in disguise – we create a language to talk about the movements of particles. This claim was criticized for questioning the objectivity of science. Poincaré replied that experience guides the selection of conventions. Objectivity occurs when a convention (or law) is proposed and scientists agree on its superiority in describing or predicting some phenomenon. But this didn't sound like the old emphasis on strict objectivity of fact.

Physicist Pierre Duhem disagreed with Poincaré, but he too introduced doubts into the positivist theory of science. Duhem was an empiricist but not a positivist. He did want beliefs to "answer" to facts, but he did not think, contra Mill and others, that scientific theory, especially in physics, was simply the description of regularities in our perceptions. He advanced a multi-levelled view of the nature of physical theory that anticipated the holistic epistemologies of the next century. Duhem agreed with Poincaré that something *other* than recording the particular facts of experience guides science. Theories are retained long after counter-evidence exists. But, he said, calling this process a matter of convention was misleading. What the philosophy of science needed was an account of how theories are subjected to the test of experience while acknowledging that the testing is indirect and complex. Duhem thought that the theories of physics are symbolic structures containing (1) abstract theoretical laws, (2) empirical laws about regularities in phenomena, and (3) empirical hypotheses or conjectures. The hypotheses cannot be conclusively verified. Moreover, their meaning is at least partly determined by the theory in which it is embedded. To believe that a column of liquid in a laboratory is copper because of its green colour is to apply, implicitly, a scientific theory. Moreover, when a conjecture fails in terms of observations, we may conclude that we need to revise our empirical, not our theoretical, beliefs.

Duhem ends up with a Mach-like view of physics as a system of mathematical propositions which attempt to represent, as simply and completely as possible, a group of experimental laws. But he draws a sharp distinction between experimental laws and theory, and abandons the idea that a conflict between theories can be decided by a "crucial experiment" or a set of observations. Even if we have observations, there may be indeterminacy as to which theory is best and what corrections are necessary. The verification of science is a complex process involving not only observations but experimental and theoretical laws. For Duhem the links between beliefs are holistic and cannot be reduced to a positivism of experience, where individual statements are verified by individual observations.

Duhem, who died in 1916, was signalling that centuries-old epistemic assumptions about the dominance of empirical fact were insufficient to deal with the new theoretical complexities in science, especially physics. The latter would require a questioning of objectivity of fact as a positivist reduction to sensory fact. A new form of empiricism would have to be constructed to deal with knowledge of special relativity, the space-time continuum, Heisenberg's theory of uncertainty, quantum mechanics, and such strange phenomenon as black holes and dark matter.

Meanwhile, a realist and non-positivist view of cognition was being revived in psychology and philosophy by Brentano, Husserl, and others in Europe. The primary question was not the genetic question of origins – how did this judgment come to be? – but the realist question: Is this true or false? They challenged the view of positivists and phenomenalists that humans have direct knowledge only of subjective ideas in the mind, making knowledge of external objects a matter of inference. They argued that the mental states were "intentional," and always about some object that was not reducible to sensations. Some argued that we have direct perceptual access to external objects.

Franz Brentano, for example, developed a "descriptive" psychology. Just as a natural scientist has only indirect or inferential knowledge of her theoretical objects, so a psychologist has direct, immediate, and certain apprehension of her subject matter: mental acts. Each mental act is perceived itself, directly. Knowledge of the mental is peculiarly direct and objective.

Brentano said the essential feature of the psychological is to "point towards an object" beyond the act itself. Physical things lack this act of pointing. Brentano called this feature "intentionality," although he later abandoned the term because people confused it with intending to do something.

Husserl followed Brentano in stating that consciousness is always consciousness *of* something, some object that exists independently of the act of knowing it. Examining the acts and structures of consciousness as it comprehends objects is the task of Husserl's "phenomenology."[56] If philosophers adopt strict methods of describing the objects of consciousness, for example, by bracketing biasing "natural" attitudes about what one is experiencing, they obtain a knowledge that is objective and certain, fulfilling the Cartesian quest for foundations for human knowledge.[57]

By the early 1900s, realism appeared to be replacing phenomenalism as a dominant view of perception and experience. Both Mach and William James denied that what is immediately perceived is mental, or a state of mind. James, in his "radical empiricism" phase, talked about a realm of pure experience where conscious act and object were fused. Only later do we distinguish the mental and the physical, the act and the object. Moore and Russell rejected idealism and its view that to be is to be perceived. Following James and others, Russell posited sense data that were neither mental nor physical. The originator of pragmatism, Charles Peirce, would proclaim in 1896: "We have *direct experience of things in themselves.*"[58]

Objectivity without a Person

In the second half of the nineteenth century, many practitioners of science, rather than entertaining doubts about positivism, advocated an even more strenuous objectivity of fact. Scientists embraced a conception of objectivity that replaced "subjective" human capacities, such as judgment and interpretation, with the "objective" capacities of machines, tools, and numbers. Objectivity acquired a negative meaning. "Objectivity" was *not* being subjective, *not* interpreting.

The invention of pure objectivity was largely the development of science as a powerful institution, linked to the economy, the education system, the military, and the race to develop new technology. By 1900, scientific inquiry was a professional, salaried occupation established at universities and industrial laboratories. Scientists also worked at schools that taught the applied sciences. Social acceptance of science depended on impressive discoveries

56 See Husserl, *The Idea of Phenomenology.*

57 See Husserl, *Cartesian Meditations.*

58 Passmore, *A Hundred Years of Philosophy*, 260. Italics by author.

in physics, physiology, medicine, and chemistry, along with new technologies, from the locomotive to electricity. As the institution of science expanded, it fragmented into specialized disciplines. Science became "the sciences," natural, historical, and social. The modern sciences of biology, psychology, economics, sociology, and statistics emerged, and new disciplines abounded: hematology, toxicology, climatology, ethnology, epidemiology, topology, and criminology. Specialization made scientists impatient with system-builders. Progress in a scientific career required the learning of specific methods and a more narrow focus of inquiry. It became scientific to be cautious about speculating on the wider, philosophical implications of one's experimental results. The sciences distinguished themselves from the "subjective" non-sciences and arts by objective methods, a suspicion of theorizing without empirical control, and a devotion to facts. Scientists gave birth to three species of epistemic objectivity: mechanical, aperspectival, and numerical.

Mechanical and Aperspectival Objectivity

Mechanical objectivity was objectivity through machines. Machines, it was thought, record facts automatically, uncontaminated by interpretation. Among the instruments used were the camera obscura, lithographs, photoengraving, photographs, and X-rays. Atlases, which proliferated from 1830 to 1920, were other tools of inquiry, and symbols of objectivity. Scientists employed machines to create images of the body, biological and botanical species, and eventually elementary particles, stars, and embryos. In an industrial age, scientific machines seemed tireless, ideal observers, ignorant of theory and devoid of personal ambition.

The mechanical production of images was influential. Edgar Allan Poe wrote how the daguerreotype, compared with a work of art, discloses "a more absolute truth, more perfect identity of aspect with the thing represented." Photography was a tool of realism, providing a "mirror" of nature, a correspondence of image and object. In 1885, William Anderson said that medicine no longer needed artists to construct atlases of the body because cheaper photographic methods "reproduce the drawings of the original object without error of interpretation." In 1875, the ophthalmoscope helped two authors, Hermann Pagenstecher and Carl Centus, to create an atlas of the eye. About their atlas they said: "[We] have kept it purely objective ... to preserve to the reader the advantages of unprejudiced view and unbiased judgment." In 1878, French physiologist E.J. Marey said that machine-made pictures are "patient and exact observers, blessed with senses more ... perfect than our own ... they accumulate documents of an unimpeachable fidelity." Charles Babbage praised machinery because it avoided "the inattention, the idleness, or the dishonesty of human agents."[59] In 1874, Gaston Tissandier, the French popularizer of science, said: "That which man cannot do, the machine can accomplish."

Aperspectival objectivity meant the transcendence of partial viewpoints; not the mechanical copying of facts, but the reduction of distortion caused by local perspective. Scientists needed to "escape from perspective" to apprehend nature as it really is.[60] They needed to become unsituated. One way to do so was through peer review by scientific societies and journals. Science's internationalization encouraged the search for objective standards and terminology so that scientists could communicate across national borders. Scientific congresses established objective standards of measurement, from the ohm to standard time. Another way was to study phenomena in teams of scientists. Aperspectival objectivity increased when many "subjectivities" reasoned together – when many scientists worked on the same problem. In the United States, Peirce said that truth was what emerges in the long run from communal inquiry. Claude Bernard declared: "L'art c'est moi, la science, c'est nous." Ernest Renan observed that scientists were "transported to the viewpoint of humanity," while philosophers provided "the subjective fact of the solitary thinker."

Meanwhile, the social sciences contributed their own norm of objectivity – the idea of neutral, or "value-free" social science. Robert Proctor has shown how a campaign for neutral social science grew in Germany (and elsewhere) in the late nineteenth and early twentieth centuries. Max Weber, among others, tried to rescue German social science from the control of socialists, politicians, and industrial leaders. Neutrality and objectivity were to act as shields against those who would politicize social theory. Weber argued that social science had practical application, yet it should study social phenomena from a neutral perspective. Scientists might determine the consequences of different programs, but they should not judge the value of the rival programs.[61] Citizens, not scientists, would resolve major questions of value. Weber said that a sociologist studying the conditions of factory workers should not see this as an opportunity for political pronouncements but should observe them "simply as a phenomenon … whose progress it is his business objectively to explain." The ideal of neutrality assumed the objectivity of facts and the subjectivity of conceptions of the good. "Whenever the man of science comes forth with his own values, full understanding of the facts ceases," Weber wrote.[62]

59 Daston and Galison, "The Image of Objectivity," 81–127.
60 Daston, "Objectivity and the Escape from Perspective," 597–618.
61 Weber, "Objectivity in Social Science and Public Policy," 50–5.
62 Quoted in Proctor, *Value-Free Science?* 139, 150–1.

Numerical Objectivity

Since Protagoras, some of the strongest realists have not been empiricists or positivists who look to concrete, observable facts. They have been people who look to more abstract forms of knowledge, that is, logical and mathematical formulae, and calculations. Numbers and logic appeal to reason. They appear to express what we can know objectively about some object. Bertrand Russell, for instance, thought that when we become aware of a logical implication or understand a mathematical proof, we are understanding something objective, independent of how I or anyone think. Russell, Frege, and Husserl all opposed a "psychologism" in the philosophy of logic and mathematics that explains logic as how humans happen to think – human psychology. Russell distinguished logic from empirical psychology. Logic studies implications that hold objectively and realistically between propositions whether we grasp the relationship or not. In inferring, a person is simply "receptive" and "registers" the fact that an implication is present. Numbers, like logical relations, are objective because they are abstract, impersonal entities, governed by formal rules of calculation that hold for all rational beings.

From the early modern period on, the search for objective knowledge spurred on the development of a method for empirical inquiry. Philosophers, logicians, and mathematicians developed notions of probability, statistical inference, and induction. The notion of evidence, originally equated with verbal testimony at a trial or an occult "sign" of things to come, received a scientific sense: empirical support for belief, a support that came in degrees. Sciences of fact worked out "standards for well-founded, reasonable, highly probable, but non-certain belief."[63]

This "trust in numbers"[64] created new social facts and revealed patterns in welters of data. Objectivity was a professional ideal for the expanding ranks of experts, officials, and sociologists. An "objective society" based on facts, not on patronage, seemed possible. Governments, politicians, and interest groups appealed to the numerical facts to justify decisions or to deflect complaints. In the nineteenth century, numerical objectivity extended into studies on public health and social conditions. Writers turned to numbers for objective support for their conclusions about empirical matters. The numerical analysis took many forms: surveys, equations, graphs, measurements, statistical inferences, cost-benefit analyses and the

63 Shapiro, *Probability and Certainty in Seventeenth-Century England*, 4–5.

64 For the rise of probability theory and statistics, see Porter, *Trust in Numbers*. See also Stigler, *The History of Statistics*; Gigerenzer, et al., *The Empire of Chance*; and Hacking, *The Taming of Chance*.

application of probability theory to decisions. For example, the US Army Corps of Engineers early in the twentieth century explained its plans for major public works projects by developing detailed cost-benefit analyses. It helped to create a consensus among engineers and to persuade politicians that the corps could do the job.

Numbers were used to support analyses of social trends, or problems, from overcrowded cities to mortality rates for insurers. For example, early nineteenth-century surveys of the crowded cities of Britain were interpretive accounts of how overcrowding had occurred with tables of numbers and statistics. The tables purportedly described the same fact – a crowded city – without analytic commentary. Mary Poovey, in *The History of the Modern Fact*, studied the use of these tables of facts. What role did the numbers serve and why were they attractive to officials? She found that these writings assumed a dualism between uninterpreted numbers and an interpretive commentary that uses the numbers. Poovey judges this assumption to be questionable. The two types of texts are intertwined. Even the collection of numbers is interpretive because it embodies theoretical assumptions about what should be counted, how one should understand material reality, and how quantification contributes to systematic knowledge of the world. Poovey argues that this dualism is part of a larger dualism between the description and interpretation of facts (or theoretical analysis). It is the story of how one kind of representation – numbers – came to seem immune from theory or interpretation. In our terms, this dualism has roots in the idea of isolatable facts in the early modern era.

CONCLUSION

By the late 1900s, objectivity of fact was the dominant notion of objectivity in the academy, in science, in philosophy, and in culture, despite disputes about phenomenalism and worries about the subjectivity of experience. Moreover, large areas of science and culture were seeking an objectivity of pure fact.

Yet this history is incomplete until we add the movement toward "objectivity of correct construction" which arose at the turn of the twentieth century.

To this form of objectivity we now turn.

4

Objectivity as Correct Construction

Objectivity of fact has been discussed mainly as an objectivity of one level of experience: our perception of objects in the world and how they give rise to beliefs about fact. Yet our exposition, here and there, has pointed to other levels of knowledge: scientific theories, universal laws, mathematical regularities in nature, our knowledge of logic (what follows from what), and theoretical entities such an unseen subatomic particles and forces. As indicated in chapter 3, any complete theory of objectivity, and any complete epistemology, has to do more than explain our knowledge of perceptual fact. It should also tell us how to determine if our beliefs at these other levels of knowledge are objective, or not. I called this the problem of going "beyond sense" (our sense experience). The problem is this: Let us grant that carefully observed observations correspond to objective fact. But what else of what we believe is objective, and why? What is the relationship of perceptual fact to the rest of what we deem to know?

Many positivists and other empiricists in the nineteenth century and early twentieth century tried to explain that relationship by "reducing" theoretical beliefs to certain types of perceptual experience, aided by logic. A belief in other people's minds or in subatomic particles is said to be objective if we can show how it is correctly constructed, or derived from, more basic perceptual beliefs. For example, perhaps my belief that other people have a mind is an inference from experience, by analogy: other people act like me so perhaps such conduct is caused by a mind, as in my case. Empiricists also sought to "reduce" theoretical concepts to concepts of experience, and theoretical statements to statements of observation. Or, to look at it from the other direction: they sought to show how we can construct higher-order concepts and statements from lower-order concepts and statements of experience.

The empiricist's goal was to construct an epistemology for our many types of belief, and to separate the valid from the valid, the necessary from the superfluous. This could be done if we could show how higher-order beliefs could be correctly constructed from experience. Construction in epistemology uses definition, conceptual analysis, and methods of verification and justification to connect valid observational beliefs to valid non-observational beliefs. The objectivity of many beliefs relies on the possibility of a correct construction from objective, perceptual fact. Across the nineteenth century, and into the next century, empiricists sought to show how this construction was possible. But how beliefs were linked was not always clear.

Objectivity of correct construction was part of scientific empiricism. It retained the thesis that objectivity was based, *ultimately*, on the empirical encounter of the mind with the world. But, stimulated by developments in logic and mathematics, epistemology became interested in the construction of "logical systems" – of showing how our corpus of beliefs, and the theories within it, are logically derived from elemental, empirical facts. Objectivity was both an objectivity of fact and an objectivity of correct, logical construction from fact.

THE TURN TO LOGIC

In chapter 3, I noted that attempts at epistemic construction in classical empiricism, roughly from 1600 to 1860, from Locke to Mill, had limited success and failed to garner general acceptance. There were several reasons. The construction was an awkward mix of psychological questions (how do we come to believe *x*?) and normative questions (*should* we believe *x*?). For example, Locke gave a psychological explanation of how we experience external objects. The objects act causally on our senses and produce ideas. But does that explanation *justify* our beliefs about external objects, or just explain their genesis? Moreover, in constructing knowledge are we describing, psychologically, what actually happens over time, as we grow up; or, are we more interested in philosophically reconstructing our beliefs into a well-ordered set of propositions, with side glances at psychology? Also, there was, as seen, the general problem of explaining objective mental representation. If empiricists struggle to show the link between idea and observable object, then they fail to take the very *first* step in the construction of our multifarious, multi-levelled beliefs. The ambitious program of constructing knowledge cannot even get started. It resembles the unfinished Tower of Babel.

To make matters worse, proposed constructions by leading empiricists were controversial – among empiricists. Hume's reductions of the "self" to impressions, and causal beliefs to regularity in impressions; or Mill's definition of physical objects as permanent possibilities of sensation – all were contested. Finally, empiricists struggled to construct the formal part of our knowledge. If all knowledge was based on experience, were mathematical and logical principles empirical generalizations? Mill thought so,[1] but many – including Russell, Frege, Moore, Wittgenstein, and Husserl – rejected the view.

Logical Construction

So, by the mid-to-late 1800s, what was the way forward for an empirically minded philosophy? First, empiricists needed a better conception of logical and mathematical knowledge. Second, empiricists needed a better model of epistemic construction.

To help the reader, let me state what the main answers would be, before explaining them in more detail. The answer to the first problem would come from thinkers such as Wittgenstein, who treated statements of logic and mathematics as conceptual tautologies that dealt with the meaning of terms and made no empirical claim about the world. The answer to the second problem would come from advances in the philosophies of mathematics and logic.

The knowledge to be constructed consisted of two types: (1) symbolic systems in mathematics and logic, where the construction used axioms, deductions, logical definition, and theorems; and (2) empirical systems containing scientific statements and theories about the world, grounded in some way in experience. The idea grew that the methods of construction in logic and mathematics could be applied to the logical ordering of empirical knowledge. We can affirm the objectivity of our higher-order scientific concepts about the world because they are the product of rigorous, logical construction from some given in experience.[2]

Originally, this application of formal ideas and methods to epistemology was called "philosophical analysis" or logical empiricism. It differed substantially from existential and phenomenological philosophy, which regarded the use of definition and logical analysis to be an abstract and narrow approach to philosophy.[3] Philosophy, in the early 1900s, would begin to divide into an "analytic" camp and an existential camp.[4]

1 See Mill, *An Examination of Sir William Hamilton's Philosophy.*

2 For a summary of the emergence of mathematical formalism and formal logic, see Putnam, "Peirce the Logician."

3 By the early 1900s, at Cambridge, Russell represented a love of logic-based analysis directed in large part at the concepts of science. At Oxford, John Austin came to lead a movement called "ordinary language philosophy" which looked at the details of how we use words in everyday situations. At Cambridge, philosophers John Wisdom and Susan Stebbing were part of the Cambridge "common sense" school of language philosophy.

4 When I was a philosophy graduate student in the mid-1900s, this division was still vibrant. Cohorts who admired existentialism and the "continental" philosophy of Husserl and Heidegger could not understand the attraction of analytic philosophy. It seemed trivial, an

Bertrand Russell and, later, Rudolf Carnap,[5] were leaders of this epistemology of logical construction. Philosophy was to be scientific, systematic, and rigorous. Statements would need careful analysis and verification, and concepts would be clearly defined. For Russell, analysis went hand in hand with his deep interest in what the world is like if science is true. Ontologically, what sorts of theoretical entities must be presumed to exist and how are they constructed from empirical concepts and experiences? What entities can be reduced to other entities – for example, can physical objects be constructed from sense data?

The logical construction of our belief system required a clear view of the relations among its epistemological, logical, and psychological aspects. In *An Inquiry into Meaning and Truth*, Russell says epistemology explains why I should believe any particular belief. In a "perfected epistemology" the propositions must be arranged in a certain logical order, from best known to known on the basis of the best known.[6] The best known or "basic propositions" are "perceptual premises" or matters of fact that "appear to us credible independently of any argument" in their favour.[7] Epistemology has a logical element, mapping the inferential relations between basic propositions and those things we believe on their basis. It also has a psychological element. It studies how propositions are generated from experiences, and it examines our feelings of doubt or certainty about various beliefs.

Russell chose carefully the name of his constructivist philosophy: logical atomism. The "atoms" were basic, logically simple propositions discerned by analyzing more complex propositions. The philosopher would then combine these logical elements to form "molecular" propositions. Logical construction could not be accomplished by using the vague, unscientific terms of ordinary language. It would require a reconstruction of the language of philosophy. For Russell and Carnap, that meant an ideal language with clearly defined terms that refer to clearly defined aspects of reality. The aim is the most economical, rigorously constructed system of beliefs consistent with our best science. The idea of scientific philosophy was not new. It had been advocated by Bacon, Comte, and others. But this new approach would employ powerful methods of logical and linguistic analysis.

---

abandonment of philosophy's task to make sense of the world. Within departments of philosophy, ideological sides were taken. Some students followed the leading philosophers on both sides like they were religious leaders, their doctrines unquestioned. The divisions were bitter, despite deep (often unseen) commonalities.

5 For the role of logic in philosophy, see Schlick, "The Turning Point in Philosophy."

6 Russell, *An Inquiry into Meaning and Truth*, 14.

7 Ibid., 15.

One can wonder why philosophers thought the formal sciences could help empiricism. They seem so far apart, in nature and in method. Do formal sciences not *abstract* from experience? To the contrary, logical constructivists thought formality, clarity, and independence from particular experiences was just what epistemology needed. Logic would provide new and clear ways to define concepts and analyze statements in terms of experience. Logic would show how the epistemic relations among beliefs – in terms of evidence and justification, for example – could be reconstructed as logical relations of derivation, implication, and deduction. These logical relations would be firmer and more certain than relations provided by psychology or more informal methods of philosophizing. As Carnap said, the use of logic would make epistemology independent of "the contingencies of the real world."[8] In Carnap and Russell, empiricism is shaped by a rationalist love of certainty, formal propositions, and clarity.

Why this optimism about constructing worldly knowledge from logic? Philosophers were impressed by the success of construction in mathematics and logic, as in the work of Peano[9] and in Frege's work on arithmetic.[10] These analyses resolved contradictions in the foundations of mathematics, while showing how formal knowledge in mathematics and logic could be deduced from a small, clear set of concepts. The ancient view of mathematics as stating deep truths about the world was giving way to a view of mathematics as the construction of symbolic systems where the emphasis was on formal proof, completeness, and consistency. In logic, Boole, Frege, Jevons, Peirce, Schröder, Boltzmann, and others developed systems that represented inferences as the formal manipulation of symbols, replacing Aristotle's logic of syllogisms. Here, it seemed, three centuries after Bacon, was the emergence of a new, logic-based, "organon." Russell himself was responsible for enthusiasm about analysis and logical construction. In the early 1900s, he

8 Carnap, *The Logical Structure of the World*, preface to the 2nd edition, vi. Russell's attraction to formal thinking was a Cartesian quest. He came to philosophy, like Descartes, through a desire to find knowledge, not questionable current belief. He sought "indubitable truth" in mathematics, and was "profoundly dissatisfied" with Mill's *Logic* and it view of mathematics as based on generalizations from experience. See Russell, *Logical Atomism*, 31. Putnam called this yearning the "craving for objectivity." Putnam, "The Craving for Objectivity," 120.

9 In 1908, Peano and his Italian colleagues showed how the concepts of arithmetic and algebra could be constructed, via definition and analysis, from a few elementary logical ideas such as classes, class inclusion, and material implication, three primitive ideas (zero, number, and the idea of the next number), and six elementary propositions.

10 Frege, among his many accomplishments, argued in *The Foundations of Arithmetic* (1884) and *Fundamental Laws of Arithmetic* (1893–1903) that he could make the truths of arithmetic "secure" by deriving them from the laws of logic.

and Whitehead published *Principia Mathematica*, which constructed mathematical notions from basic notions of logic.[11]

Tools for Construction

What were the logical "tools" for empirical construction? They were techniques for defining, translating, or reducing one set of terms and statements to another set of terms and statements that were regarded as clearer and linked to empirical experience. In a 1928 article, Russell looked back on his writing.[12] He introduced the term "logical construction" to describe how he analyzes terms and statements.[13] The constructed terms were a logical construction of the terms and techniques used to analyze it. Russell pointed to examples of his logical constructions. Examples ranged from his use of contextual definition,[14] his analysis of physical objects (and matter) into sense data,[15] and, in the formal sciences, his reductions of arithmetic, numbers, points, and classes to notions of logic. Logical constructions were not the "inferences" used by previous empiricists, such as simply "positing" physical objects as a necessary inference from our experiences. Logical constructions provided details on the object constructed and the objects into which it was constructed. Russell said that the "supreme maxim in scientific philosophizing" was, "whenever possible, substitute constructions out of known entities for inferences to unknown entities."[16] Russell declared that philosophy in a scientific world was "essentially that of logical analysis, followed by logical syntheses." Yet he never gave up a larger role for philosophy to be "comprehensive, and should be bold in suggesting hypotheses as to the universe which science is not yet in a position to confirm or confute."

11 *Principia Mathematica* was published in three volumes in 1910, 1912, and 1913. Based on logicism (mathematics is reducible to logic), the book developed and popularized symbolic logic and stimulated research in the foundations of mathematics.

12 Russell, *Logical Atomism*. For an analysis of logical construction, see John Wisdom, "Logical Constructions," in *Mind*, 1931–33.

13 There is disagreement on the precise meaning of "logical construction" in Russell and its validity as a method. To get a sense of the complexities and disagreements, read Bernard Linsky's account of Russell's logical constructions in *The Stanford Encyclopedia of Philosophy*, https://plato.stanford.edu/entries/logical-construction/.

14 Unlike an explicit definition, which translates a term into another term, a "contextual definition" translates statements containing the term into statements that do not contain the term. The statement is the term's context.

15 See Russell, *The Problems of Philosophy*, 4. In the preface, Russell agrees with G.E. Moore that we are immediately acquainted with sense-data such as colours, smells, sounds, tastes, hardness, roughness. Physical objects are not immediately known.

16 Russell, *Logical Atomism*, 34.

To understand why Russell did not think logical construction was a game with words and logic, consider a famous example – Russell's theory of definite descriptions, which Ramsey called a "paradigm of philosophy" in the analytical mode.[17] Russell analyzed definite descriptions, such as the present king of France, as they occur in sentences like "the present king of France is bald." The "surface" grammar of such sentences suggests that the definite description acts as a denoting term, that is, "the present king of France" is the subject of the predicate "is bald." But since there is no present king of France, how can this sentence have meaning? Is it true or false? Russell used logical analysis to show that the sentence does not have a subject-predicate form. It is an existential sentence. It claims that something exists which is the king of France and that object is bald. Since there is no king of France the sentence is false, and we do not have to posit a non-existing entity as the denotation of "the king of France." Unfortunately, the example of a bald king of France tempted some to think that this was a trivial discussion. But Russell and his analytical colleagues thought differently. It was an illustration of a logical method with application to many issues in philosophy. For one thing, it showed that Brentano and Meinong were wrong to assume that all terms in a language have meaning by referring to an existing object. It demonstrated the "profound and almost unrecognized" influence of language on philosophy.[18]

In the end, Russell remained an empiricist who saw knowledge anchored in "acquaintance" or experience of the world.[19] But it is not sufficient. We need to add principles of mathematics and other forms of knowing – although we must do it with trepidation. In *The Analysis of Matter*, Russell said that a "strict empiricism" that confined knowledge to immediate experience would be a "solipsism of the moment," denying the reality of anything but our present sense-data. Hence the issue is what other principles and postulates must be added.

Meanwhile, Carnap argued for the view that philosophy's task was not to explain the world. That was the job of science. Nor was the task to construct metaphysical systems about a reality deeper than that known by science. Philosophy's task was conceptual analysis and epistemological construction (via logic) of knowledge, and of science in particular. Philosophy was a "logic of science."[20] A student of Frege, Carnap set out to show, in concrete form, what a logical construction from the given in experience might actually look like. The result was his early major work,

17 Russell, "On Denoting"; Ramsey, "Philosophy."
18 Russell, *Logical Atomism*, 38.
19 Russell, *The Problems of Philosophy*, 32.
20 Carnap, *The Unity of Science*, 24–7.

The Logical Structure of the World, in 1928. The aim was a "rational reconstruction of the concepts of all fields of knowledge on the basis of concepts that refer to the immediately given."[21] By immediately given, Carnap meant concepts of "elementary" and unanalyzable sensory qualities and relations present in the "raw material of experience," such as hot, red, loud, and firm, and similarities among instances of these properties. From this base, Carnap set out to construct, though chains of definitions, the concepts of many other things such as the visual field, the temporal order of experience, physical objects, and other people.

Carnap's book does not complete the construction, and many of his discussions are of mainly technical interest. Nevertheless, Carnap is an example of a philosopher caught up in the excitement about the new logic. Over his career, he uses many terms to describe his constructions – reductions, translations, transformations, derivations, definitions, and partial explications. "Rational reconstruction" is "the searching out of new definitions for old concepts." He calls logical construction a "reduction of cognitions."[22] To reduce *a* to *b* and *c*, or to "construct" *a* out of *b* and *c*, means to produce a general rule that shows how, in each case, a statement about *a* can be transformed into a statement about *b* and *c*. This "translation" is a constructional rule of constructional definition.[23]

Logical Positivism

By the late 1920s, the logical turn in philosophy gave birth to one of the most active and controversial schools of philosophy in modern times. Its very name testified to the belief in logic as a method for empiricism – logical positivism.[24]

After the First World War, around 1928, a group gathered around Moritz Schlick at the University of Vienna to form the Vienna Circle, the incubator of logical positivism.[25] Its program, influenced by Wittgenstein, Russell, Frege, Mach, and others, was published in 1929. Many of the members

21 Carnap, *The Logical Structure of the World*, preface to the 2nd edition, vi–vii.

22 Ibid., preface to the 1st edition, xvi.

23 Ibid., 6–7.

24 The term "logical positivism" came mainly from an article of the same name published by Blumberg and Feigl in the *Journal of Philosophy* in 1931. Schlick called it "consistent empiricism" and Carnap preferred "logical empiricism." It was also called neo-positivism.

25 For a laudatory yet still useful history see Kraft, *The Vienna Circle*. Some of the members were Carnap, Waismann, Feigl, Neurath, and Gödel. It worked with the Society of Empirical Philosophy at Berlin led by Reichenbach, Kraus, and Grelling. Its main publication was the journal *Erkenntnis* (1930) which was renamed *The Journal of Unified Science* (1939–40), edited by Reichenbach and Carnap. A.J. Ayer was the most notable English

were scientists and mathematicians who knew little about classical philosophy and were devoutly anti-metaphysical. For about thirty years (1930–60), the movement virtually defined analytical philosophy. A journal was started; international conferences on the unity of science were held. The movement spread from Austria and Germany to England, Scandinavia, and the United States. The movement dissipated before the Second World War as its leading figures died, took up positions at other universities, or decamped to England and the United States to escape the Nazis' suspicions of the movement.

Like its nineteenth-century predecessor, logical positivism caught the spirit of its times. In the 1920s, both the political left and right in Austria and Germany were calling for a radical reconstruction of society after a disastrous world war. For positivists, a modern society would be built on uncompromising new modes of thought that were practical, scientific, and technological. Logical positivism, with its austere methods, resembled the austerity of Bauhaus architecture. Carnap issued a call for "clarity, for a science that is free from metaphysics," for an attitude that "will win the future."[26]

Logical positivism as a whole is difficult to summarize because members of the movement disagreed on key concepts, such as verification; and key figures, such as Carnap and Ayer, abandoned or revised their positions. However, it can be said that logical positivism inherited the "problem space" of nineteenth-century positivism: the need to verify statements, define the foundational "given" in experience, show how knowledge was constructed from experience, and avoid metaphysics.

But logical positivism was *not* a cautious extension of empiricism. Logical positivists wanted stricter, clearer distinctions between verifiable and non-verifiable, empirical and non-empirical, meaningful and meaningless, science and non-science. It was prepared to cast all of metaphysics and most of traditional philosophy, including ethics, into the category of cognitively meaningless expressions of emotions or unverifiable speculation. To be non-scientific was the philosophical equivalent of the Bible's original sin. It was to fall outside of meaningful, cognitive discourse. Logical positivism wanted such a firm division between philosophy and science that some members were suspicious of attempts by like-minded philosophers, such as Russell, to construct large views about the world.

---

logical positivist. Other leading thinkers, such as Popper, and earlier pragmatists such as Peirce and James, were not affiliated with the movement but were part of a larger international conversation on scientific empiricism.

26 Carnap, *The Logical Structure of the World and Pseudoproblems in Philosophy*, xviii. See also Richardson, *Carnap's Construction of the World.*

Logical positivism, also like its nineteenth-century forerunner, could be radical and belligerent, and at times functioned as an ideology for the superiority of science, especially natural sciences such as physics.[27] Especially in its early phase, logical positivists issued strongly worded *dicta* whose strength attracted support from those who sought rigour in philosophy. But its intolerance – and sometimes disdain – for forms of thinking outside of natural science and logic (and mathematics), made enemies in the humanities, social sciences, arts, traditional philosophy, and religious studies. Carnap, in *The Unity of Science*, portrayed many philosophical topics as "pseudo-problems." Later, A.J. Ayer's overconfident *Language, Truth and Logic* in 1936, a popular work of philosophy, became the manifesto of the positivist's war on metaphysics. In the book, Ayer claims to have "explained the nature of truth." Within a few pages, he dismisses all of ethics as the subjective, non-cognitive expression of emotion. Ayer later admitted that his arguments could have been more persuasive if not presented in "so harsh a form," and that the questions with which *Language, Truth and Logic* dealt are not as simple as he once thought.[28]

FAILURE OF CONSTRUCTION

Construction remained a priority for logical positivism. As we saw, Carnap, a leading member, devoted a book to constructing the world as we know it, and he continued to search for better methods of correct construction throughout his career. In taking over empiricism's problem space, the logical positivists were occupied with defining the starting point for construction – the "given" in experience – and explaining how this given grounded scientific theory. Moreover, construction was important due to the logical positivist's goal of "the unity of science." The goal presumed that it was possible to show that all sciences share a common language, and are all verified, directly or indirectly, by experience. Some logical positivists asserted the in-principle possibility of conceptually reducing all sciences to physics.

27 To get a taste of the aggressiveness of early logical positivism, read Carnap's small book *The Unity of Science*, where many traditional concerns of philosophy are dismissed. Kraft countered the charge of belligerence by saying that the most controversial theses were not the views of all Circle members but the views of a subset of "radical" members such as Neurath. Kraft, *The Vienna Circle*, xx.

28 Ayer, *Language, Truth and Logic*, 5.

Dualisms for Construction

Logical positivism never realized its ambitious goals and its varied attempts at construction failed. Some of the reasons have been noted. Science itself was growing increasingly abstract and theoretical, especially in physics – the model science for positivists. At first, logical positivists hoped to provide explicit definitions of scientific concepts in terms of observation. But it soon became evident that explicit definitions could not even be given for relatively "empirical" dispositional properties such as solubility. Any reductions or constructions would have to be indirect and partial. Construction was more difficult than imagined. Also, as examined in chapter 3, Duhem, followed by others, concluded that only a sophisticated empiricism could explain the complex ways in which scientific theories are verified. There seemed to be no hope for verifying empirical theories or laws by testing them with a finite, conclusive set of observations.

Another reason was internal bickering. Logical positivists disagreed, often vociferously, on basic tenets such as the principle of verifiability and what should be the starting point for rationally constructing science: statements about subjective experiences, or statements about physical objects? Phenomenalism, or realism? Were such empirical reports incorrigible or fallible? Moreover, no one seemed capable of actually *producing* a general construction of empirical knowledge. Carnap's uncompleted sketch was the best example available.

There was also another reason, which I believe was logical positivism's fatal mistake. They chose to develop principles of scientific epistemology that not only would prove to be questionable, but were untenable because they were implausible cognitive dualisms. Logical positivism embraced four dualisms: (1) meaningful statements versus meaningless statements (or verifiable versus non-verifiable statements); (2) analytic versus synthetic judgments; (3) matters of fact versus theory (or interpretation); and (4) fact versus value. As discussed earlier, these dualisms took ordinary, everyday distinctions and turned them into firm divisions. Dualistic thinking would protect scientific objectivity by drawing hard lines between forms of thinking.[29] But the dualisms would also prevent logical positivism from building the right sorts of construction. In short, they were working with the wrong set of basic concepts and distinctions.

Let's consider, briefly, each dualism and how it defeated, or made impossible, the construction of a plausible empirical epistemology.

29 Because these dualisms of logical positivism are much discussed in the philosophical literature, I provide summaries that focus on what is essential for this chapter and book.

Meaningful and Meaningless: Verification

Is it possible to draw a hard line between statements that have meaning and those that are, literally, meaningless?[30] The logical positivists thought so, if one defined meaning as actual or possible verification by experience. What was new in logical positivism was not the interest in verification. All empiricists face the question of how experience verifies our beliefs. What was new and more radical was twofold. First, there was the strength of the positivist's belief in the *necessity* of drawing a hard line, lest science and clear thinking end in a muddle, or be corroded, retarded, or co-opted by sloppy metaphysics or emotionality. Little progress could be made in scientific inquiry unless one had a bold empiricist criterion of meaning. Second, there was the logical positivist's decision to make *meaning* and not just truth (or justification) a matter of verification. Meaning and verification are usually kept apart. Common sense suggests that first we determine the meaning of a sentence and *then* we verify it, as a second and separate step. The Vienna Circle view of verification, which was inspired by Wittgenstein,[31] collapsed the two steps. The meaning of a sentence was the empirical facts that would verify it. No verification, no meaning.[32]

The verification criterion of cognitive meaning was formulated in several ways, and debate about those formulations led to reformulations.[33] Schlick wrote: "To understand a proposition, we must be able exactly to indicate those particular circumstances that would make it true and those other particular circumstances that would make it false."[34] Ayer wrote: "To test whether a sentence expresses a genuine empirical hypothesis ... I require ... not indeed that it should be conclusively verified, but that some possible sense-experience should be relevant to the determination of its truth or falsehood. If a putative proposition fails to satisfy this principle and is not

30 Here we are speaking of cognitive meaning, which was defined in chapter 1 as a representation or statement about some object or state of the world.

31 Carnap, among others, attributes the idea of meaning as verification to Wittgenstein, through his writings and conversations with the logical positivists. Wittgenstein later rejected the idea that he was advancing a verificational theory of meaning. Verification was only one way to get clear about the meaning of a sentence. See Passmore, *A Hundred Years of Philosophy*, 368.

32 The stress on "doing things" to verify a sentence and ascertain its meaning runs through the pragmatism of the early twentieth century as well. As James asks: What difference in experience would it make if *x* was true or false?

33 The criterion was first explicitly stated by Waismann in 1930 in *Erkennis*. For a review of the changes to the verification criterion, see Hempel, "The Empiricist Criterion of Meaning."

34 See Schlick, "A New Philosophy of Experience."

a tautology, then I hold that it is metaphysical, and it is neither true nor false but literally senseless."[35]

I forbear to trace the winding path of reformulation and weakening of original *dicta* that occupied logical positivists as they tried to defend this strong criterion of meaning. I will only remind readers of some of the sticky questions it raised: Is the verification principle itself verifiable? What is it that verifies – what type of statement? Are statements about the distant past or future that are not strictly verifiable meaningless? Are general statements, such as universal general laws, beyond firm verification and therefore meaningless? How are we to verify statements about theoretical entities? Is it possible to erect a dualism between isolatable facts of experience and other kinds of cognition and judgment, such as theoretical and interpretive cognitions, and evaluative cognitions? Are there any statements, or at least any *significant* statements, that do not mix observation and interpretation? These questions, alone, indicate how the principle of verification, in such a strong and dualistic form, was not just implausible but a conceptual obstacle to a more accurate description of science and how we test our higher-order beliefs.

Analytic and Synthetic

The verification principle worked in tandem with the analytic-synthetic distinction to answer the question that had long troubled empiricists: How could knowledge be reducible to experience if the formal sciences elude reduction to experience? The answer, as noted above, was that knowledge about mathematics, logic, and other formal topics was not *about* the world. They were "analytic" and completely different from synthetic or worldly statements. Such statements describe the language or conceptual system that we use to describe the world. As Wittgenstein said in his *Tractatus*, formal statements were tautologies that made no claim about the world, and were known to be true independently of experience. One reflected, instead, on the meaning of the terms involved and the rules of language.

If this is true, then formal knowledge did not constitute a counterexample to the empiricist's thesis that all knowledge was based on experience. Rather, the thesis was modified to read: All *empirical* knowledge was based on verifiable experience; non-empirical (analytic) knowledge was based on the meaning and relationship of symbols in some language. This idea of analytical knowledge suggested that formal knowledge, at least to some extent, was a matter of linguistic convention, or pragmatic agreement on what

35 Aye, *Language, Truth and Logic*, 31.

languages to construct and use. This presumed that one could firmly distinguish the conventional and the empirical in knowledge. All knowledge was synthetic or analytic.

But the analytic-synthetic dualism could not be philosophically defended over the long term. In 1951, Quine wrote a devastating critique of the "two dogmas" of empiricism – the analytic-synthetic distinction and the verifying of empirical sentences one by one.[36] He argued that one cannot clearly separate what is conventional and what is empirical in our web of belief. These two elements are fused like different strains of thread in a rope. Also, the pragmatic choice of language is not something separate and external to doing science. Rather, in many cases, what is pragmatic in the way of ideas is the best evidence we have for their truth. Finally, Quine picked up on Duhem's theme that scientific theories were not verified one sentence at a time. They were verified holistically as a "corporate body" which as whole is tested by experience. The logical positivists' principle of verifiability was wrong. Once again, dualistic ideas blocked the construction of a better view of evidence for science.

Fact and Value

The attempt to distinguish analytic and synthetic judgments and to promote a strict empiricist criterion of meaning was not a philosopher's idle pastime. These ideas would be used not only to explain empiricism and the foundations of logic but to declare entire types of judgment – evaluative, metaphysical – as meaningless. Such statements were not analytical. Nor, as the positivists would claim, were they synthetic (or verifiable). Hence, these judgments were meaningless.

The most controversial exclusion from the arena of meaningful statement was the category of ethical judgments. This exclusion followed Hume in denying that ethical judgments are a matter of cognition. We don't perceive ethical objects or facts in the world. But logical positivists went further than Hume in their anti-realism toward ethical statements. It was one thing to dispute whether ethical statements were synthetic or how they could be verified. But it was entirely a different and bolder claim to say they were *meaningless*. Logical positivists thought ethical judgments were meaningless because they express emotive or other non-cognitive responses to matters of fact, such as acts of murder or kindness to strangers. They do not represent or describe the act or object in question. They respond to the object as preferred, valued, loved, hated, disliked, or admired, and

36 Quine, "Two Dogmas of Empiricism."

therefore as something to be promoted or condemned. Ayer put forward a classic example of this "emotivist" view of ethical judgments.[37] This was the beginning of modern non-cognitivism as a meta-ethical theory.[38] Later, Hare analyzed ethics as imperatives to do certain things.[39] Stevenson divided ethical judgments into two parts – a factual part that identifies the action as of a certain kind (e.g., cruel) and an "ethical" part that expresses an emotion toward the action. The first part is factual and objective, the other part psychological and subjective.[40]

For logical positivists, facts were of service to science only if they were scrubbed clean of ethics and values. Carnap, in *The Unity of Science*, writes: "All statements belonging to Metaphysics, regulative Ethics, and (metaphysical) Epistemology have this defect, are in fact unverifiable and, therefore, unscientific. In the Viennese Circle, we are accustomed to describe such statements as nonsense (after Wittgenstein)."[41] Carnap says people can associate images, emotions, and other concepts to such "logically invalid statements" but that has nothing to do with logic. For Carnap, a dualistic chasm separated scientific and ethical judgments. He wanted not only to question ethical statements in science, he wanted to eliminate them.

The fact-value dualism was the final component needed to secure the reduction of knowledge and science to meaningful, verifiable, empirical facts. If valid, the dualism would be a coup de gras for metaphysical and evaluative judgments as claimants to meaning, knowledge, or scientific status. We end up with a demandingly narrow sense of empirical meaning: narrow because it reduced what was verifiable and meaningful to either an observation or a fact of experience, or the capacity to *reduce* (or translate) any statement to observation or experience.

In the years to come, a legion of philosophers and other writers would criticize the fact-value dualism. They would argue that logical positivism itself is based on values: for instance, the value of the unity of science. They

37 For an early statement of this view of ethics, see Reichenbach's "The Nature of Ethics" and Ayer's "emotive" theory of ethics in *Language, Truth and Logic*, chapter 6, 102–13.

38 On non-cognitivism, see my *Ethics and the Media*, chapter 1. Non-cognitivism is not identical with logical positivism's emotivism. After logical positivism, neo-cognitivists developed theories of greater subtlety and plausibility, as found in the works of philosophers such as Blackburn, and contractualists such as John Rawls. See Blackburn, *Ruling Passions*.

39 Hare, *The Language of Morals*. Calling an ethical judgment an imperative does not automatically categorize it as non-rational or purely subjective. Kant, for example, believed that ethical judgments were imperatives and so not descriptive, but he disagreed with Hume in saying that such judgments could not be justified by reason.

40 See Stevenson, *Ethics and Language*.

41 Carnap, *The Unity of Science*, 26.

would argue, as Putnam did, that cognition in general, and science itself, is based on epistemic norms and values of good inquiry, such as verification.[42] If all value judgments are meaningless, then positivism, science, and any other inquiry is based on meaningless or subjective norms. The dualism proves too much. It is self-refuting and blocks new thinking.

Like Hume, the logical positivists distinguished statements of fact and value, but then erected a dualism that made ethical judgments meaningless and ethical philosophy a seeming waste of time for philosophers or scientists – a claim Hume would never make.

As Putnam says, it was a "vastly inflated version" of Hume's distinctions. Hume never thought that a fact-value dualism would rule out ethics as a serious area for study and philosophical analysis. His naturalism leads him to write entire treatises on the origins of morals and justice. But, for Carnap, the dualism did rule out the worth of philosophers writing texts on ethics.

In retrospect, logical positivism got both forms of objectivity wrong. It got objectivity of fact wrong: there are no certain or pure facts (or "given"); and, as I will argue, no such thing is needed to talk about the factual objectivity of beliefs. It got objectivity of correct construction wrong: it used implausible dualisms of cognition to both defend science and to show how science is constructed from experience.

Death of Empirical Objectivity?

With the collapse of logical positivism in the middle of the twentieth century, it appeared that the project of rigorously constructing empirical knowledge had run its course, and failed. When the dualisms of logical positivism crumbled under prolonged attacks and attempted revisions, so did the credibility of objectivity and the modern project of empiricism.

Since at least the mid-1900s, announcements of the death of empiricism, especially the death of logical positivism, have been stated, sometimes with undisguised glee. Dewey found empiricism's notion of experience too narrow, its foundationalism unnecessary, and its dualisms a form of thinking to be overcome. Passmore said that, by the 1960s, logical positivism was as dead as any philosophy could be. In 1984, Putnam wrote a chapter called "After Empiricism" aimed at the views of Ayer. In 2002, he published a book on the "collapse" of the positivists' fact-value dichotomy and the way forward, philosophically. In the meantime, a long train of "continental" philosophers, from Habermas to Foucault, steered clear of classical empiricism in the mode of Hume and Mill. Historians of science and social

42 Putnam, *The Collapse of the Fact/Value Dichotomy*.

constructionists rejected positivism's ahistorical view of scientific objectivity and stressed the human and conventional elements in inquiry. The critics did not say that all empirical principles are false. None of the important critics would deny the existence of facts, the role of the senses in knowing, or the need to test scientific beliefs by empirical standards. Most of us are empiricists in that general sense. Rather, what was questioned was logical positivism's intellectual arrogance and its contentious, narrow dualisms of fact, value, and cognitive meaning.

Yet despite the obituaries, we still have not uprooted the conceptual errors from our culture. Knowledge of positivism's failure was limited, in large measure, to philosophers and epistemologically minded theorists in the history of science and in the social sciences. The positivist's dualistic approach would continue to define ideas of objectivity in the professions, such as journalism, as well as in public discourse and everyday life. Many people today are positivists when they think about facts and ethics. In philosophy, the fact-value dualism lives on but is supported on other grounds. One popular argument is the ontological (and anti-realist) argument that ethical properties, such as "is good" or "is right", are strange posits that cannot exist, or violate the naturalistic ontology of science.[43] Here are the main ideas that never died: (1) the idea that facts can be scrubbed clean and become pure encapsulated facts; (2) the belief in a strict, neutral attitude that, through numbers and machines, can eliminate the bias of the human inquirer; (3) a strict division between observation and all else that we know and cognize; (4) a fact-value dualism that serves as the default position of people when they discuss morals.

For instance, Vivian Walsh has written that, by the end of the 1950s, the "necessary theses" to maintain the positivists' fact-value dichotomy and notion of cognitive significance had fallen. Yet economists whose "philosophical heritage" is logical empiricism still write as if the old fact-value dichotomy was beyond challenge.[44] In discussing objectivity, Newell welcomed the "exorcism" of positivism from philosophy although he acknowledged that there is still "much plausibility" in the general features of Humian empiricism, for example that we need rational controls on argument through fact and logic.[45] This encourages thinkers to see some form of Humean empiricism as the difference between intellectual order and anarchy.

43 Putnam, *Realism with a Human Face*, 165.

44 Walsh, "Philosophy and Economics."

45 Newell, *Objectivity, Empiricism and Truth*, 1–2.

CONCLUSION

The persistence of these ideas underlines the need for a new and more plausible conception of objectivity that avoids two extremes: a subjectivism that dismisses objectivity, and a dualistic, positivistic, objectivity. Most important, it is time to stop working from within the positivist's problem space.

In the next chapter, I seek to learn from the criticisms of objectivity of fact. I propose a different notion of objectivity that does not start from the problematic of traditional empiricism and its dependence on purified fact. My view does not share logical positivism's tendency to erect dualisms, or objectivity of fact's suspicion of human judgment and interpretation. I do not search for absolute foundations in some fictional "given" of experience. Instead, I propose a situated objectivity with a human face which uses an imperfect human practice of testing beliefs through a holistic set of standards.

PART TWO

Reconstructing

5

Objectivity with a Human Face, Part 1: *Objectivity* in Situ

If our "objectivity" is objectivity humanly speaking, it is still objectivity enough.
Hilary Putnam, *Reason, Truth and History*, 168

We have deconstructed notions of objectivity in journalism, in philosophy, and the history of ideas. It is time to learn from these exercises, and to construct. It is time to philosophize in a positive manner by reinterpreting objectivity.

The purpose of the rest of this book is to provide a pragmatic view of objectivity that is useful for ethics and journalism ethics. It is an alternative to both rationalistic and empirical notions of objectivity. That is, it is an alternative to conceiving of objectivity as a theoretical grasp on rational truth and as a methodological faithfulness to empirical fact, respectively. I call my view "objectivity with a human face" because important versions of rationalism and empiricism favour a de-personalized idea of objectivity.[1]

My conception is part of a trend in philosophy and the social sciences toward an objectivity for practice and engagement, a situated rationality that does not lapse into relativism or absolutism. Objectivity with a human face avoids cognitive dualisms and the problem space that empiricism inherited from seventeenth-century materialistic science. As Newell said, we need an epistemology that grounds objectivity in human actions without "sacrificing" rational control on judgment or scuttling the idea of truth.[2] Objectivity with a human face recovers the notion of objectivity from centuries of captivity in the castles of absolute philosophy. It understands

1 "Objectivity with a Human Face" echoes the title of a book by Hilary Putnam, *Realism with a Human Face.*

2 Newell, *Objectivity, Truth and Empiricism*, 5.

objectivity as objectivity *in situ*[3] – the evaluative practices of fallible humans in society.

Some would regard the notion of an objectivity between relativism and absolutism as a contradiction in terms, or an impossibility. This view reflects the dominance of absolutism and relativism in our culture. It forgets an obvious fact. We regularly and inescapably engage in objective evaluation in everyday life without thought of philosophy or absolutism. This engagement may not be perfect, but that is to be expected. Objectivity just *is* the objectivity we practise daily even if our theories say it is impossible, given our relativist moments; or even if our theories argue that objectivity must be transcendent of situations, given our absolutist moments. Our culture has not provided deep, philosophical understandings of this daily practice.

Objectivity with a human face is empirical, but it is not an objectivity of fact. It is a scheme-dependent, holistic application of standards by agents with pragmatic purposes in which facts play a limited, albeit important, role. There is no searching for pure facts. It acknowledges that objective evaluation is affected by such human factors as attitude, worldview, perspective, and passion. It is not a de-personal objectivity restricted to the "hard" sciences, as discussed earlier. It is a multi-dimensional approach to testing interpretations wherever they arise, in science, philosophy, the arts, and the professions, including journalism.

If someone despairs that objectivity relativized to humans is not objectivity at all, or it is not "enough," I can only say that it *better* be enough, since it is all the objectivity we will ever have. Either we can define objectivity as evaluation within our normal practices, or objectivity is truly a myth. At best, objectivity would be of interest only to philosophers at the most arcane reaches of thought.

The explication of objectivity extends across two chapters. In this chapter, I outline the philosophical basis of objectivity with a human face, applicable to inquiry wherever it occurs. In the next chapter, I use this philosophy to define a specific conception of objectivity, pragmatic objectivity and how it is used in forms of social engagement. But, first, let us examine the phrase "objectivity with a human face" more closely.

OBJECTIVITY WITH A HUMAN FACE

Objectivity, like the Roman god Janus, looks out to the world with two, quite different, faces. The faces represent, metaphorically, two approaches to objectivity – personalized or depersonalized objectivity.

3 By "*in situ*" I mean both the idea of someone being in a situation and something in its natural and original place.

Objectivity with a human face is an objectivity that most human inquirers can hope to achieve to a significant degree. It does not require extraordinary capacities, purity of character, heroic effort, or an austere transcendence of all things human. Objectivity with a human face is a form of valuation that is embedded in, and useful to, practices in the real world. It is situated evaluation within the practice of some discipline, project, or science.

What is "human" in this form of objectivity is its use in everyday human affairs. It also refers to the all-too-human factors of inquiry: the human penchant to interpret, to judge, to value and evaluate, to follow traditions and practices, to seek goals and interests, and to allow oneself to be moved by such "non-logical" faculties as passion, imagination, creativity, emotion, and aesthetic sensibility. Moreover, the "human" refers to human agency and inquiry, a domain of the probable, the fallible, and the uncertain. Objectivity with a human face is hospitable to such factors, and it shows how to incorporate them into the process of evaluation.

Far from being a myth or an ideal beyond our capacities, objectivity is an evaluative practice that many people carry out every day, as professionals, judges, teachers, or baseball umpires; although their attempts are imperfect, the practice of objectivity is crucial to society, with its need for impartial practices and institutions. Our natural evaluative capacity has produced a plurality of methods for testing objectivity, from the sciences to the practice of law. That the practice of objectivity exists is beyond doubt. What is up for questioning is the nature of that practice and its limits.

Michael Polanyi, in explaining "personal knowledge," expressed the basic idea behind objectivity with a human face.[4]

> As human beings, we must inevitably see the universe from a center lying within ourselves and speak about it in terms of a human language shaped by the exigencies of human intercourse. Any attempt rigorously to eliminate our human perspective from our picture of the world must lead to absurdity.

Polanyi contends that "personal knowledge" seems to be a contradiction if we think of knowledge as impersonal, universal, and objective. The seeming contradiction is removed by "modifying the conception of knowing" so that we think of it as an "active comprehension of the things known, an action that requires skill." The personal participation of the knower in all acts of knowing does not make our understanding "subjective" or arbitrary. Comprehension is neither arbitrary nor passive but a responsible act

4 Polanyi, *Personal Knowledge*, 3.

claiming universal validity, a willingness to commit oneself to a hypothesis as objective because the hypothesis is successfully applied in life and correctly predicts future experience. For Polanyi, "into every act of knowing there enters a passionate contribution of the person knowing what is being known ... this coefficient is no mere imperfection but a vital component of his knowledge."[5]

"Objectivity without a human face" refers to a group of conceptions of objectivity that have dominated Western thought to the point of being identified with objectivity per se. Objectivity without a human face may require extraordinary capacities, purity of character, heroic effort, or transcendence of all things human. In some cases, such as as in Plato's theory of intellectual ascent to knowledge of reality, the path is so difficult that objectivity is the achievement of the few. Objectivity becomes an ideal that only an absolute philosopher could love – an abstract ideal, largely unachievable for a great mass of humanity. This approach to objectivity opens the door to skeptical suspicions that objectivity is a myth or is useless for actual inquiry. It forgets objectivity's more humble origins in daily life.

Objectivity without a human face favours methods and principles that are impersonal, universal, and transcend human perspectives. One form of this objectivity prefers methods that can be followed in an algorithmic manner, without personal judgment – a method without a person. In other cases, the objectivity of science is said to depend on the existence of absolute principles and ahistorical standards of evaluation. Objectivity without a human face can be ostentatious, coolly demanding that our "ordinary" human beliefs appear before the austere "bar of Reason," an autonomous (and supreme) court of evaluation that does its work far from the fray of human disputes, questionable doctrines, and perspectives. Human factors in inquiry are viewed with wariness, as sources of subjectivity. These biasing factors are not to be incorporated into a conception of objectivity. To the contrary, they are to be minimized and, if possible, eliminated from inquiry.

What are some examples of objectivity in either group? For objectivity without a human face, we have already discussed several: the mechanical and aperspectival objectivity of nineteenth-century science; the absolutist views of knowledge from Parmenides onward; the veneration of pure facts. A classic statement of objectivity without a human face is Popper's theory of objective knowledge. I agree with his exposition on rationality in *Open Society*, where he describes his rationalism as a "modest and self-critical rationalism," which recognizes the limitations of human nature. The attitude

5 Ibid., vii–viii.

of critical rationality involves being ready to listen to critical arguments and to learn from experience. The rationalist attitude, Popper says, is characterized by a desire for objectivity and impartiality.[6] But I disagree with his description of objective knowledge, in another work, as objectivity (and epistemology) without a knowing subject.[7] This is the Platonic ideal of an abstract realm of knowledge that exists independently of "anybody's claim to know … knowledge without a knower." In my view, knowledge is intrinsically related to real humans and their perspectives. Knowledge arises only when someone's beliefs, in a given situation, are in tune with the way the world is. It is against such de-personalized philosophies of objectivity that this book rebels.

What is wrong with this approach is not its admirable alertness to biases in cognition. What is wrong is its proposed solution to the possibility of bias: (1) the erroneous idea that we need to go to great lengths to minimize or eliminate the experiences that may cause bias; (2) the erroneous idea that the pursuit of objective truth is a pathway that leaves behind our all-too-human faculties; (3) the erroneous idea that good inquiry is the impersonal operation of a logical intellect; and (4) the erroneous idea that inquiry requires the construction of implausible dualisms to wall off personal elements from the citadels of knowledge and science.

Naming examples of objectivity *with* a human face is more complex. This is due to the dominance of objectivity without a human face. The prime example of objectivity is thought to be an absolute ontological objectivity, such as realism's ideal of knowledge of what truly exists, apart from human interpretation. One result is that the debate between objectivity and subjectivity is misconceived as reducible to the debate between relativism and absolutism. In recent decades, however, pragmatic philosophers, such as Putnam and Lynch, have developed notions of truth, rationality, and objectivity along the lines of objectivity with a human face.[8] They develop actual alternate conceptions, and do not settle for just another relativistic attack on absolutism and realism.[9] The goal is a philosophy of objectivity that is constructivist and situated but which still has a place for truth. It can propose non-arbitrary criteria for deciding what is rational to believe.

6 Popper, *The Open Society and Its Enemies*, 2:224–40. Popper calls his view "pragmatic rationalism." The world is not rational but we still try to subject it to reason as far as possible.

7 Popper, "Epistemology without a Knowing Subject."

8 Pragmatists see value in seeking impersonal methods so long as they do not aspire to eliminate the personal or presume complete transcendence of situation. As an example of the latter, see Rescher's *Objectivity: The Obligations of Impersonal Reason.*

9 See Putnam, *The Collapse of the Fact/Value Dichotomy*, and Lynch, *Truth in Context.*

Although objectivity with a human face is a fledgling approach, there have been many anticipations of its ideas. The relativists and sophists of ancient Greece were not advancing a theory about objectivity with a human face. But they did discuss situated rationality and human factors in judgment. Aristotle's division of theoretical and practical reason recognizes, in the latter, a thinking that is imperfect and dependent on human factors, yet important.

The revival of Stoic skepticism in the sixteenth century, such as the common sense of Michel de Montaigne with his famous question, "Que sais-je?," pointed to the ineliminable trace of the human in all thought. Montaigne famously declared: "I am myself the matter of my book." He pointed to the human and social factors in belief, and, as he faced death, accepted imperfection: "Our being is cemented with sickly qualities," he wrote. "Whoever should remove the seeds of these qualities would destroy the fundamental conditions of our life."[10] Another anticipation, discussed in chapter 2, was the engaged experimental scientist intervening in nature. In the past century, objectivity with a human face can draw on a rich body of work, from literature to art to science, even where the focus of the writer is not objectivity per se, such as Wittgenstein's work on human practices in *On Certainty*. Contemporary theorists of rationality, emotion, social cognition, and the history of science provide seminal ideas for a new theory of objectivity. Aside from these "indirect" influences, there are writings that are directly relevant to constructing a human-friendly objectivity. Of central importance is the work of philosophical pragmatists such as James and Dewey, neo-pragmatists such as Quine and Putnam, and historians of science such as Kuhn and Hacking. There is also much to learn from nuanced relativists in moral theory about how to evaluate value judgments within conceptual schemes.[11]

Our culture has the conceptual resources to construct an explicit and detailed theory of situated objectivity with a human face. These seminal works have brought us to the point where we can bring together their ideas, scattered across many texts, into a solid conception of objectivity for a world without absolutes. We should not underestimate the challenge. This construction will require that many types of ideas "line up" – the way we solve a Rubik's Cube by making many elements cohere. A general theory of objectivity answers questions belonging to metaphysics, epistemology,

10 Montaigne, *The Complete Works*, Vol. 3, 726–7. Also cited in Bakewell, *How to Live*, 320.

11 See, for example, David Wong's defence of "pluralistic relativism" in *Natural Moralities*.

psychology, ethics, and other disciplines, with the possibility of error or critical objections at every turn.

One can only do what imperfect humans do: propose a reasonable conception without dogmatically assuming that it will anticipate all questions. One puts a theory forward to join the history of ideas. It may advance our thinking, but thankfully it will never silence doubt.

THE "WHOM" AND "WHAT" OF OBJECTIVITY

To rethink objectivity as human and humane, we start by asking for the context in which questions of objectivity arise. This breaks down into two sets of questions: (1) To *whom* does this evaluative cognition and associated practices belong? Where and why does the evaluation occur? (2) *What* is evaluated – simple perceptions, or rich trains of experience? Judgments of ordinary experience, or sophisticated theories? Literal descriptions of objects, or complex interpretations of phenomena that mix fact, value, and theory? Our theory of objectivity should be based on our answers to the "whom" and "what" of objectivity. We start with the "whom."

Naturalism: The "Whom" of Objectivity

The person who inquires and the person who evaluates inquiry are mind-endowed, purposeful organisms in a natural world. As explained earlier, objectivity is the cognitive capacity for rational evaluation. Objectivity refers to a desire, a need, and a capacity to evaluate cognitions that claim to be apprehensions of some aspect of ourselves or the world.

We naturalize objectivity. Since Quine's celebrated essay on naturalizing epistemology, treating it as a branch of psychology, philosophers have talked about naturalizing various parts of philosophy.[12] In this chapter, naturalism is a philosophical commitment to explaining the world by appealing only to natural capacities and processes. Naturalized epistemology seeks to understand how humans come to have, and evaluate, systems of belief.

Naturalism is my philosophical starting point. Humans are naturally evolved, mind-endowed, purposeful agents embedded and interacting in a natural, evolving society of meanings and practices, and a physical world of animate and inanimate objects. All that humans do, and all of their capacities, are part of their engagement with an environment. Inquiry begins, develops, and ends within this context. An allegedly non-contextual form of inquiry is, in reality, another perspective.

12 Quine, "Epistemology Naturalized," in *Ontological Relativity and Other Essays.*

Our mind is incarnate, entangled with body. Thoughts impregnate our actions and shape our goals, while actions, and the practical consequences of actions, retroactively reshape our beliefs. Our mental operations bear an irreducible reference to our embodied agency in the world.[13] It is not easy to understand incarnate mind. Edmund Husserl and John Searle – philosophers from different perspectives and times – refer to the "enigma of subjectivity": how we can be conscious, meaning-centred creatures in a non-conscious, meaningless world?[14]

Naturalized epistemology approaches the conscious agent as a human-in-the-world. It does not start internally. I, as subject, introspectively review my ideas. I recount what it is like to experience the world through my mind's eye. This phenomenology of experience is important, but it is not a "stand-alone" entity. It should not be studied apart from its incarnation in body and in the natural evolution of minds. Our embedding in this natural world and our construction of societies of intentional, human creatures is a relatively small part of the ongoing evolution of the universe, a local chapter in a global story. It is the context for all our thinking and a fundamental assumption for any inquiry.

Everything in my philosophy follows from this starting point. It defines inquiry and it defines objectivity. My starting point may seem no more than a truism, that is, that we live in nature. But working out the implications of this starting point is anything but obvious. Many thinkers who acknowledge this "truism" – who would deny a world of nature and agency? – go on to betray, ignore, or minimize it. In ancient times, Zeno and Parmenides, while making observations as men in a natural world, used their reason to doubt the reality of a world of many things. Some mystical philosophies say that the natural world and our very individuality are illusions. Berkeley's idealism reduces the apparent material world to a phenomenal, mental world of ideas and minds. Even phenomenologists of experience, like Husserl, seek knowledge by bracketing our natural beliefs so as to discern, through a special, purified introspection, certain beliefs about consciousness.[15]

13 As noted in chapter 2, the importance of body was a theme for Merleau-Ponty. Langan claims that "incarnated intentionality" is his central concept. See Merleau-Ponty, *Phenomenology of Perception*, and Langan, *Merleau-Ponty's Critique of Reason*, 17.

14 Husserl said the "the enigma of subjectivity" created a division in philosophy: "objectivism" or the scientific search for absolute laws of an external world, and "transcendental philosophy" which sees our common world as an achievement of subjectivity – of the human mind. See Husserl, *The Crisis of European Sciences*, 68–9. For Searle's comments on this question, see Searle, *Making the Social World*, ix.

15 See Husserl, *Cartesian Meditations.*

STARTING IN THE MIDDLE

So, the first answer to the "whom" of objectivity is that objectivity is a capacity and a task for a species whose mind is incarnate in body and in society. This means that inquiry takes place in time. All inquiry and evaluation starts in the middle. In the middle of what? In the middle of time. In the middle of lives lived on this blue planet. Inquiry occurs in the context of already existing practices, beliefs, goals, and activities in a culture. Epistemology is reflection on cognition, already under way. This pre-existing world defines our sense of self and the world, guides our choice of issues, and provides resources, methods, and traditions to address problems. Within this context, the distinctive mentality of humans, and their capacity to communicate and cooperate, plays an important part.

There is no First Philosophy in the sense of starting without a world, without a context, without existing beliefs. There is no starting with *nothing*, or only absolute truths, in mind. Aboard our ship of inquiry, we, as bodily agents, get a sense that we are travelling in the right direction, and are prepared to change course, gently or radically, as needed. For the most part, we sail together as communities of inquirers with traditions and practices, not as isolated individuals with idiosyncratic methods.[16] Starting in the middle means starting in a muddle. At least some of our beliefs, or the beliefs of others, will be puzzling and questionable. We think epistemically to reduce error or confusion but, being human, some muddles there will always be.

One part of this "middle" is a social world of shared meanings which Husserl, in his last work, called the *lebenswelt* or lifeworld: "In whatever way we may be conscious of the world as universal horizon, as coherent universe of existing objects, we, each 'I-the-man' and all of us together, belong to the world as living with one another in the world; and the world is our world, valid for our consciousness as existing precisely through this 'living together.'"[17] We do not deduce the lifeworld. It is already there, from our first experiencing.

While empiricists looked to a "given" in sensations or external facts, Husserl's lifeworld is the given of shared experience in the fullest of terms. It is a world of fellow agents, exchanging thoughts and sharing projects.

16 Hacking stresses the creative, social side of that ship-building. We don't reconstruct alone: "It is too big a task for one person, one elite, one generation, one civilization." Hacking, "Natural Kinds," 137.

17 Husserl, *The Crisis of European Sciences,* 108. Husserlian phenomenology now includes the study of consciousness in history. This approach by Husserl caused trouble for Husserlian scholarship. Did Husserl abandon his prior "pure" approach to consciousness? See David Carr's "Translator's Introduction" to *The Crisis of European Sciences.*

The lifeworld is not a static background but an evolving horizon of meaning and purpose. Even Descartes's meditations presumed this world of human agents. Otherwise, to whom is Descartes addressing his thoughts?

Is the lifeworld the world of common sense? Yes and no. Yes, common sense is part of the lived world. But, no, common sense is not coextensive with cognitions of importance. Naturalism is also interested in theoretical beliefs and their relations with common sense. "Common sense" should be used with caution. It does not imply that common-sense beliefs are true, even if widely accepted. Common sense may lag behind the leading edges of science. Nor is common sense limited to ordinary observations. In any era, common sense includes religious, theoretical, and scientific beliefs that have made their way into popular culture. Properly understood, "common sense" refers to beliefs widely held and expressed in a non-theoretical manner. Philosophical and scientific principles may operate as implicit premises.

It goes (almost) without saying, that where we start from may not be where we end up. Naturalistic inquiry may lead us to view ourselves and our world in surprising ways. We follow where inquiry leads.

Humans as Agents

The mind-endowed, pragmatic organism is an agent when it takes action: when one intentionally acts in the world toward some end. Mind and body unite to bring about some new state of affairs. Agency is mindful, intentional action, a form of activity.[18] John opening the door for Fred is an action by an embodied agent with an intention. Searle defines action as the coming together, in various ways, of cognition (belief, memory, and perception) and volition (desire, intention). All actions have two components: an intention-in-action, and, typically, a bodily movement. The intention-in-action is a continuing intention to do something. It must be maintained through the course of action; for example, the intention to spend months writing a book.[19] Not all movement or effort is an action, or a matter of agency. Our bodies may move without intention, as when I accidentally spill my cocktail at a party. Our bodies react to stimuli by reflex. We may be drugged and do things not of our own accord. We can be automata. Much of nature lacks agency. The spontaneous decay of radium lacks both agency and intentionality.

18 On the philosophy of action, see O'Connor and Sandis, eds., *A Companion to the Philosophy of Action*, especially Lowe, "Action Theory and Ontology," 3–4.

19 Searle, *Rationality in Action*, 46.

Where does this leave theoretical activities that do not seem to be forms of agency, such as thinking about an abstract question in philosophy, or mathematically modelling the rotation of a distant planet? One response is to erect a dualism between mental thinking (as non-agency) and physical acting (as agency). The dualism is unhelpful because there is no theory/practice dichotomy. The human can be a practical, acting being, or a theoretical, thinking being, or both at the same time. The theoretical is implicated in action, and the practical is implicated in theory. The dentist knows the theoretical basis for treatment. Theoretical questions arise from practical problems – how to build a tunnel under the river? Science is a theoretical praxis, with its own practices and goals. The physicist tests her mathematics by seeking experimental results, the biologist uses his discoveries about genes to develop gene-repair technology. Even mental activities that withdraw from the world, like quiet meditation on a rug, are usually temporary and have some purpose.

We can avoid a theory-practice dualism by using the concept of a continuum, as discussed in chapter 1. We place kinds of activity along a continuum from the most practical to the most theoretical. The activities differ in the degree that they are immersed in practical actions and the degree to which they withdraw from practice to theorize. Theoretical activity becomes increasingly abstract as we progressively distance ourselves from practical agency and our thoughts from practical application. We can become theoretical temporarily (e.g., to think about a problem), or for long stretches of our lives (e.g., to study theoretical mathematics).

At one pole are forms of abstract thinking that dramatically reduce the need for bodily actions, practical reasoning, and practical goals. At the other pole are practical, bodily activities that are so habitual, or so caught up in the physical manipulation of things, that there is little need for theory. The barber cuts my hair without stopping to theorize his actions. Some reasoning is predominantly interested in arriving at correct ideas – what to believe – and is called theoretical reasoning; some reasoning is predominantly interested in what to do, and is called practical reasoning.

Some people live near one of the ends of the continuum. There are practical people who have little interest in theory; and there are contemplative philosophers who comically fail at practical matters. Socrates, we are told by a Greek satirist, was so caught up with his ideas that he fell into a well. Lives at the poles tend to be relatively thin in diversity and richness of experience. Most people live in the thick, rich, middle area of this continuum where agents mix thought and practice. Our lives have theoretical and practical strands difficult to untangle. Even the otherworldly philosopher must take nourishment, and pay the bills. When thinking abstractly, her body participates. She takes long walks, or paces her study.

The continuum makes agency, or the "I do," the basic category.[20] When I am an agent I unify the many aspects of my person or self. The self that reflects and the self that acts is the same – the same embodied agent. My cognitive, emotional, and reflective activities form a functional unity, as aspects of, and tools for, agency and engagement. Emotions stimulate thinking and acting. Thinking reveals why we have such emotions and values. With practical agency as the focus, "man recovers his body and becomes personal."[21] I can withdraw from agency and become a spectator, limiting my participation in society. But I do not thereby exist as "thought" or as a thinking thing. I cannot "think" my way into being a person. I can only do so by acting. A theory of knowledge is a theory of human agency and action.

One of the most important things we do as agents is to inquire. Inquiry is the natural activity of a highly evolved organism motivated to explore, understand, and control phenomena as it navigates a perilous natural and social environment. The inquirer's mind is not a private theatre where the mind's eye passively views ideas. "Mind" is an umbrella term for a complex of skills, functions, and abilities that aid inquiry into the world. This inquiring organism is pragmatic. He goes into the world to test hypotheses, to solve problems. Ideas are mental tools that organize experience to achieve goals.

Pragmatic inquiry is situated and contingent. It sees contingency, vulnerability, luck, and fallibility at the heart of all things human.[22] Inquiry is the activity of an organism that happened to develop a relatively large brain with remarkable cognitive abilities and self-consciousness. We, as a species, are a contingent product of a contingent evolutionary process. Contingent biological evolution is supplemented by contingent cultural evolution. Rational inquiry is the activity of one fragile species in a tiny part of an expanding universe. Contingency does not surprise nor dishearten pragmatists. The mature acceptance of contingency prevents us from fleeing into the arms of absolutism in knowledge and authoritarianism in politics. Pragmatism is the hard-won but modest wisdom that celebrates constructive activity in a contingent world. Humans give meaning to their lives through purposeful activity. No grand metaphysical plan bestows meaning on our earthly labours. The pragmatist is an imperfectionist, poised between naïve idealism and cynical despair.

20 On the primacy of the practical and the "I do" see Macmurray, *The Self as Agent*, 21–2.

21 Macmurray, *The Self as Agent*, 12.

22 Nussbaum, in *The Fragility of Goodness*, shows how notions of luck and vulnerability influenced ancient Greek ethics and drama.

Inquiry, and its evaluation, is inherently social. We participate in social practices. We also evaluate the practices as groups and communities. I ask other people to evaluate my thinking. As noted, the rise of scientific societies in the seventeenth century made the verification of experimental results a public, intersubjective affair. Through social reflection, we achieve a partial, but never total, transcendence of our situation and partialities. In philosophy, we tend to describe this process in a curiously private way. Philosophers, such as Kant, define ethical objectivity as a process of a person *asking themselves* whether they can "universalize" their maxims of action. But we are not limited to asking ourselves. Other people will gladly tell us what they think of our reasons. Objectivity is not about going "my own way" in terms of belief and evaluation, but asking what other reasonable people would say. One philosopher calls this the "obligations of impersonal reason" – imagining what other reasonable people would believe or do in the same circumstances.[23]

The "What" of Objectivity

If this is the "whom" of objectivity, how to conceive of the "what" of objectivity? What do agents think about, and how do they evaluate their inquiries? It would be convenient if we could restrict these questions to one part of our continuum of activity, for example, how to evaluate perceptual knowledge. Yet, in the last chapter, we saw how no epistemology can restrict itself to this one level. The same need to go "beyond sense" is encountered when we act as agents. Activities all along the continuum produce thoughts, theories, alleged facts, and interpretations of varying plausibility. We need a general description of the cognitions that require evaluation for objectivity. We need to understand how we interpret the world.

I propose we start by regarding all cognitions as different ways of "making sense" – that is, ways of understanding things and experiences. Making sense is predominantly an act of interpretation. Through interpretation I endow meaning on perceptions, texts, behaviour, theory, and countless other objects of cognition. Some people restrict interpretation to the interpretation of texts. This is too constraining. To try to think of interpretations in art criticism, the performing arts, perception, and elsewhere as interpretations of texts stretches the term to the breaking point. It is better to start with the broad notion of making sense, and then pick out sense-makings that require objective evaluation.

23 See Rescher, *Objectivity: The Obligations of Impersonal Reason.*

As Dworkin reminds us, the interpreters and objects of interpretation are many. Historians interpret *events*, psychoanalysts interpret *dreams*, sociologists and anthropologists interpret *societies and cultures*, lawyers interpret *documents*, critics interpret *poems*, *plays*, and *pictures*, priests interpret *sacred texts*, and philosophers interpret "*contested concepts*."[24] The literature on interpretation is immense. It extends from Aristotle's *On Interpretation* and the exegesis of biblical texts to modern hermeneutics in philosophy, art, and the social sciences, as discussed by Davidson, Habermas, Gadamer, Heidegger, Thom, and others.[25]

Interpretation, as I use the term in this book, is conscious, explicit, specific, and symbolic. To interpret is to make sense through description, explanation, theorizing, perceiving, and engaging in artistic expression or performance. I interpret noise on the tracks as an approaching train. I interpret darkness at noon as an eclipse of the sun. A violinist interprets a poignant melody as a composer's crie de coeur. I have a bodily "understanding" of how to ride a bicycle but it is not an interpretation. It is a skill. To have an interpretation of *x* is to have an explicit understanding of the object, or an understanding that can be made explicit through words, symbols, and actions.[26]

Thom provides a general model of interpretation. Interpretation consists of three components: an object of interpretation, a representation of the object, and a "governing concept" that gives the representation meaning. An interpretation aims "to endow a given object with a particular type of significance by subsuming a representation of it under a governing concept."[27] For Thom, objects of interpretation are always somewhat indeterminate. The score of a symphony does not settle all questions on how to perform it. A poem does not tell you how to read it. The object may itself be an interpretation. For example, the musicians who interpret the opera *Eracle* are interpreting a score that interprets another score, Handel's *Hercules*. Thom sees no need to presume that we can specify the object independently of all interpretation.[28] Interpretations are plural. Opera companies interpret an opera differently.

24 Dworkin, *Justice for Hedgehogs*, 123. Italics are mine.

25 See, for example, Davidson's *Inquiries into Truth and Interpretation*, Gadamer's *Truth and Method*, and Thom's *A Theory of Interpretation*.

26 However, interpretation may use unconscious or intuitive materials. See Kahneman, *Thinking Fast and Slow*. Also, we are well acquainted with the idea that the mind processes information below the level of consciousness.

27 Thom, *A Theory of Interpretation*, 71.

28 As Bradley said, why do we insist that for intelligent understanding there must be "datum without interpretation any more than interpretation without datum"? Bradley, *Essays on Truth and Reality*, 204.

Representations transform objects into objects-as-represented, as when a jazz group gives a jazz "standard" a new colouring or rhythm, or alters an original score. Theatrical companies represent a play when they give it an allegorical reading. The interpretation's "governing concept" gives an explicit, stateable meaning that encompasses the object as a whole. For instance, we say a play is about wanting, but lacking the courage, to commit suicide. To take another example, Van Gogh's painting, *The Potato Eaters*, has been the object of differing interpretations. One interpreter sees the painting as expressing the governing concept of family solidarity despite poverty; another interprets the painting as expressing the governing concept of the isolation of family members. The concepts of solidarity and isolation are different views of the picture that structure how we understand parts of the painting. Interpreters who favour the theme of solidarity point to the family sharing a meal with similar coffee cups; interpreters who favour isolation point to a wall between an older woman and man.[29]

Consider, also, a scene from Verdi's opera, *Rigoletto*. Rigoletto believes he has achieved revenge against the Duke for apparently "defiling" his daughter. He drags a sack toward the river which he thinks, mistakenly, contains the Duke's body, killed by an assassin that Rigoletto hired. But Rigoletto's celebratory mood turns to angst when he hears the Duke speaking in the distance and realizes the sack contains his dead daughter. The audience understands the transition in Rigoletto's mood and speech because the musical representation transitions from the governing concept of "revenge" to the governing concept of grief at unintended death.

Representation and Scheme

Thom's model is a valuable schema, but, to be of value to a theory of objectivity, it needs to be filled in with other features of interpretation. The primary addition is that interpretations are based on conceptual schemes and employ a plurality of psychological faculties. The governing concept is "unitary," as Thom states, but the representation is a complex creature – a convergence of psychological processes and a web of concepts.[30]

In its simplest form, an interpretation is an act of categorization. We understand *x* as an instance of F. We perceive *x* as a lion in the dark. We interpret a few black streaks on the sea's horizon as smoke from a ship. But things soon get more complicated. We use a sophisticated knowledge of

29 Thom, *A Theory of Interpretation*, 40.

30 For more extended treatments of interpretation and holism, see my *The Invention of Journalism Ethics*, chapter 8; *Global Journalism Ethics*, chapter 2; and *Radical Media Ethics*, chapter 2.

language and symbols to interpret *x* as a mocking gesture or *y* as a parody. To interpret light as quanta of energy we must draw upon a complex set of concepts. To interpret Johnny's struggles to learn in school as attention deficit disorder requires a psychological theory. More abstractly, we interpret our interpretations. We debate our interpretations of attention deficit disorder. Psychologically, the interpretation, as an explicit judgment of significance, is the tip of the cognitive iceberg.

Thom quotes the chemist Lavoisier on discovering oxygen:

> I have deduced all these explanations from a single principle, that pure air, vital air, is composed of a particular principle belonging to it and forming its base, and that I have named *principe oxygine*, combined with the matter of fire and heat. Once this principle is admitted, the chief difficulties of chemistry seemed to fade and dissipate, and all the phenomena were explained with an astonishing simplicity.[31]

Thom says Lavoisier's description is a "natural interpretation" based on natural laws and the priority of data. True, but it is also a prime example of how a scientist uses a scheme of concepts, data, principles, and explanatory methods to endow a phenomenon with meaning. Included in the process is the convergence of a number of evaluative standards (such as "astonishing simplicity"), the explanation of many phenomena, and the resolution of theoretical difficulties.

Interpretations, then, are internally complex representations that take advantage of the capacity of conceptual schemes to provide a mental grid of intelligibility. Causal, logical, and hierarchical relationships link concepts to each other.[32] A conceptual scheme can fit within other schemes, like figures inside a Russian doll. The conceptual scheme for dogs fits into the conceptual scheme for mammals, which is part of the scheme for animals. Different conceptual systems understand the same objects – there are several systems for categorizing library books. Bruner talked about how conceptual schemes can be "codes" or formulae that order data and allow the mind to go "beyond the information given."[33] Codes can take the form of grammatical rules, memory schemata, cognitive maps, theories, mathematical formulas, modes of inference, or hierarchically arranged categories. We grasp meaning through pattern-recognition,

31 Thom, *A Theory of Interpretation*, 8. The quote is from Thagard, *Conceptual Revolutions*, 46.

32 On conceptual schemes in science, see Thagard, *Conceptual Revolutions*, 30.

33 See Bruner, *Beyond the Information Given.*

whether it is the predictable plot arc of a romance novel or the familiar chord changes we call the "blues."

Conceptual systems can be normative, descriptive, or explanatory. Utilitarianism is a normative scheme, while classical (Newtonian) physics is explanatory. A conceptual system may be loosely organized or precise. Euclidean geometry is a tidy conceptual system. Our understanding of how ordinary objects behave – "folk physics" – is imprecise. A shift in a conceptual scheme can spark a conceptual revolution. In the sixteenth century, Galileo's new way of thinking about the motion of bodies challenged the centuries-old Aristotelian model. Galileo's revolution contained a seemingly simple conceptual change. Think of motion, not rest, as natural. Conceptual schemes may be so encompassing as to be a worldview, a metaphysics.

Holism and Pluralism

The internal complexity of interpretation entails that we make sense of things in a holistic and plural manner. Pluralism is the view that what is to be interpreted is plural in nature. The plurality cannot be reduced to one thing. There are many ways to teach a class, many truths about the world, many concepts of justice, many languages in India, and many interpretations of the Bible. Holism agrees that things are plural, but focuses on part-whole relationships among the many. It adds this idea: We know the part by knowing the whole, and vice versa. Words have meaning within language systems. A concept has meaning within a conceptual system. A holistic theory shows how the parts work together, as when one shows how a healthy ecology is a balanced system of species and natural resources.

Our interpretations, as psychological constructions, are plural and holistic at two levels: (1) they are holistic systems of ideas employing interrelated psychological faculties; and (2) they employ holistic systems of cognitive standards to evaluate interpretations. For instance, Lavoisier's interpretation was an instance of (1) because he brought together a plurality of ideas, principles, observed facts, and experimental results. He employed the faculties of observation, reasoning, deduction, imagination, and speculation. He did not simply appeal to observed facts, or to a brilliant idea that arose in his mind. His reasoning was holistic, moving from fact to theory and back to fact until he reached a sort of "reflective equilibrium" where the main contents of his thought were, like a web, mutually supporting.[34] His interpretation was, at the same time, an instance of (2) because he used

34 "Reflective equilibrium" comes from John Rawls. He used the term to describe the balancing of considerations in constructing a theory of justice. I return to this notion in the next chapter.

a plurality of standards in evaluating the results of his experiments and his theorizing, such as "astonishing simplicity." They too appeared to be in reflective equilibrium. This holism of standards helped to persuade Lavoisier that he had an objective explanation of objective phenomena. The objectivity of theory is how the elements of a conceptual scheme cohere and satisfy cognitive standards.

The place of a concept (or belief) in a conceptual scheme depends on at least six properties: its distance from stimuli, its degree of generality, its interanimation with other concepts, its epistemic status, its relative immunity from revision, and how it participates in holistic verification.[35]

Concepts (and the beliefs of which they are a part) differ in their relative distance from external stimuli or observation. The concept of a quark is farther from observation than that of a rabbit. The statement "It is raining" is closer to observation than "Human aggressiveness is due to inherited genetic factors, a product of evolution." Similarly, "The moon is large and yellow tonight" is closer to observation than "The red shift by the galaxies in our expanding universe shows that galaxies move towards a great attractor." We also distinguish beliefs according to their degree of generality. Our beliefs extend from the particular, such as "I saw Mary drinking in the pub at 7:05 p.m. on 3 December 2017," to the sweeping generalities of physics typified by $E = mc^2$. Logical laws are so general that they apply to all sentences of a certain form, regardless of subject matter.

A third feature is the dynamic relationship (or "interanimation") between the particular and general, and the observational and theoretical – a dynamic for which logical positivism failed to account. To use an example mentioned earlier, a scientist mixes the contents of two tubes, observes a green tint, and says, "There was copper in it." The scientist's assertion derives from something more than the perception of a green tint. It reflects her knowledge of chemistry. The stimulus elicits the observation sentence only in conjunction with other, more theoretical beliefs. There is an interanimation between the observable and theoretical concepts of the scientist's conceptual scheme. Similarly, my decision to drain a subequatorial swamp makes sense relative to my theory of malaria. This dynamic relationship operates on the most prosaic levels of experience. Each morning, I interpret a yellow ball in the sky *as* a rising sun, given my background beliefs about gravitation and a heliocentric universe. The connections between levels of ideas means observation is not passive watching or an encapsulated faculty. It is an active, and often skilled, performance guided by background knowledge. An experienced astronomer easily identifies comets in the sky; a

35 Quine, *Word and Object*, 1–25.

veteran bird watcher "sees more" than the novice; a physician quickly recognizes a mole on the skin as potentially cancerous.

The fourth feature is the epistemic importance of a concept or belief. It depends on whether we treat the concept or belief as basic or non-basic. Basic beliefs logically support less basic beliefs. Darwinian natural selection is basic for evolutionary biology. Strawson defined basic concepts as a set of general, irreducible notions that form a "structure which constitutes the framework of our ordinary thought and talk."[36] Basic concepts come in at least three types: concepts used to understand sensory experience, such as space, time, causality, and external body; concepts to understand the social realm, such as personhood, morality, and responsibility; and methodological and normative concepts about how we should think, such as truth, evidence, fact, logical inference, and objectivity. Quine's model of conceptual schemes recognizes certain beliefs as basic, but they can change. Wittgenstein compared basic beliefs to a river bed that gives shape to its current of water.[37]

We do not change basic beliefs without pressure to do so. Some beliefs of logic, mathematics, or experience are so basic that we can barely imagine what it would be like to alter them. We thereby come upon a fifth feature of conceptual schemes: some of our concepts are more resistant to change than others. Abandon Darwinian natural selection, and one must make many changes in evolutionary biology. A change in the river bed of thought can prompt a conceptual revolution.

Resistance to change reveals a sixth feature: the holistic verification of cognitions, as discussed in chapter 4. We are faced with choices when reflective equilibrium is disturbed. Say I test my scientific hypothesis concerning attention deficit disorder and it results in negative results. I could abandon the hypotheses, or try to "save it" by blaming an idea in my theory, or reinterpret the results, or blame a faulty experimental method. As Duhem and Quine knew, verification is not reducible to the testing of individual statements. When testing a hypothesis, we use a plurality of ideas and faculties, and we employ a holism of standards, from simplicity and logical consistency to prediction of future observations. Testing is more than testing by experience. We abandon the idea of objectivity as reducible to observed fact.

36 Strawson, *Analysis and Metaphysics*, 24.

37 Wittgenstein, *On Certainty*, 15e, para. 97.

WIDE EXPERIENCE

Experience and Cognition

Why is holism so ubiquitous? Because our experience of the world is wide, not narrow; entangled, not encapsulated. We do not construct and revise our beliefs in a tidy, positivist fashion, adding one "atomic" belief of fact onto another. We do not construct belief systems the way we build objects using a Lego kit – adding one uniform piece to another uniform piece in a uniform manner. We experience the world in all its richness and complexity, and we are forced to balance conflicting beliefs and values. It is messy. It is human. To experience the world widely means that our experiential stream is rich with meanings, cognitions, and elements like observations, feelings, and musings. What we call the "present experience" is fat and wide. A wide cognition is a cognition that brings together a plurality of capacities to produce the temporally extended experiences of agents. Human experience is the accumulating experiential "record" of a species with incarnated mind and bodily existence.

One of Dewey's achievements was to show how classic empiricism, with its narrow notion of experience as sensations and inferences drawn from them, was flawed. Empiricism ignored the experiences of bodily intervention and purposeful agency in the world. He thought the ignoring of agency and practice originated in elites, such as the philosophical elites in ancient Greece who looked down their noses at physical "work" carried out by the body. Philosophy originated in elites who had the wealth or social status to enjoy leisure, and had time for intellectual speculation.

Dewey developed a pragmatic notion of wide experience. He states: "Experience becomes an affair primarily of doing. The organism does not stand about, Micawber-like, waiting for something to turn up … The organism acts in accordance with its own structure, simple or complex, upon its surroundings."[38] In acting, the environment responds and the organism experiences the consequences of action. "Experience" is this linkage between doing and what follows from doing.

An agent experiences the world in complex ways over time, strung together by mental and bodily memory. Sequences of actions dovetail to achieve goals. What I call my experience is nothing less than the trace of my agency across an entire lifetime, in conjunction with the lifetimes of others. *Within* this doing and interacting, acting and experiencing, the faculties and capacities of the organism operate and have meaning. These

38 Dewey, *Reconstruction in Philosophy*, 49.

are the faculties of perception, attention, emotion, reasoning, decision-making, and motivation.

Dewey's best description of what he means by experience is found in the early pages of *Experience and Nature*, where he quotes James as saying experience was a "double-barreled word" referring both to *what* men do, suffer and strive for, and believe and endure – as well as *how* men act, suffer, and strive. In short, how people act and are acted upon – a stress on "processes of *experiencing*."[39]

> "Experience" denotes the planted field, the sowed seeds, the reaped harvests, the changes of night and day … It also denotes the one who plants and reaps, who works and rejoices, hopes, fears … [experience contains] no division between act and material, subject and object, but contains them in an unanalyzed totality. "Things" and "thoughts" … refer to products discriminated by reflection out of primary experience … Life denotes a function, a comprehensive activity, in which organism and environment are included.[40]

One task of philosophical reflection is to understand that complexity. The focus of epistemology should not be sense data and how they lead to inferences about physical objects. The focus should be systems of beliefs and practices in the dynamic, experiential matrix of interacting human agents who make meaning.

To get a sense of what wide experience is, imagine this holistic experience. You are playing guitar and writing a song at the seashore on a hot July day. The experience is a simultaneous convergence of multiple faculties. It makes possible a rich experience. There is the linguistic capacity to write lyrics and notes, the imagining of a new melody, the full-body experience of being in front of an apparently infinite sea and hearing its waves come in, relentlessly; the sense of heat and sun on one's skin; the emotions that well up and seek expression; not to mention the musical skills required to sing and play an instrument. The guitarist, as agent, undergoes a wide cognition within a wide experience.

Or, imagine how an accomplished violinist interprets a difficult score in concert. The cognition of the violinist exhibits the same collaboration and convergence of capacities, faculties, and physical skills as the musician at the seashore. There is the feel of the violin strings on her fingers; the "body memory" of her muscles so she can perform difficult passages; her awareness of the sound in the hall and the mood of the crowd; the unpleasant

39 Dewey, *Experience and Nature*, 8.
40 Ibid., 8–9.

heat of the spotlight on her forehead; the nervousness as she approaches the piece's most difficult section; not to mention her interaction with the accompanying orchestra and ever-present conductor. This is wide experience, with rich and wide cognitions. If someone wants a striking example of the narrowness of the positivist's notion of experience, I suggest that they experience the wide forms of cognition and experience that occur at a Quaker meeting. People sit and "communicate" in silence, with occasional comments. In this silence, there is meaning, accumulating over time. To explore *that* form of meaning-making, the aforementioned verification theory of meaning – check off the observational consequences – is hopelessly primitive.

The central question for psychology is how an agent constructs such wide experiences as she interacts with the environment. The central question for epistemology, and objectivity, is what forms of evaluation are appropriate for the interpretations that arise from the experiences. Synthetic theories of the experience of agents engaged in action are needed. Whatever concepts of objectivity and rationality we can construct will arise out of reflection on wide cognition.

Wide Rationality

An agential point of view makes practical rationality paramount. Searle rightly states that we cannot understand rationality unless we first understand intentional minds and human agency. It is through agency that people can create commitments and create reasons.[41]

Rationality is part of our desire to make sense intellectually, and to act in a way that makes sense. The original sense of "rational" – as noted in chapter 1, to find a "ratio" in things – is a way to make sense. Now, if experience is wide and laden with value and purpose, so is rationality wide and value-laden.

Rescher provides a model of practical rationality. He follows Dewey by defining rationality as "the intelligent pursuit of appropriate ends."[42] Practical rationality is normative. It asks for cogent reasons. It asks what I ought to believe, do, or prefer. Rescher divides rationality into three interacting forms of rationality. They are three kinds of *choices*. There is (1) cognitive rationality: the choice of what to maintain about the world. The result is beliefs. (2) Instrumental rationality: the choice of what to do. What are the means? The result is "action recommendations" or injunctions.

41 Searle, *Rationality in Action*, 34.
42 Rescher, *Rationality*, 2.

(3) Evaluative rationality: the choice of what ends to pursue, what to value and prefer. The result is appraisals or evaluations of both means and ends.

Rationality is always "effecting the resolution of choices in the best possible way." As rational beings, we are optimizers.[43] We use the best means at our disposal to achieve the best results, given our resources, information, and limitations. I use intelligence to maximize the probability that my actions will realize my (or our) interests. To live rationally is to live according to the counsels of this world-engaged and situated rationality.[44]

Rationality is holistic in several ways. The agent, in acting rationally, brings together at least four faculties:

1 Cognition: The capacity to accurately cognize the surrounding environment and its potential, including possible means to ends.
2 Imagination: The capacity to imagine alternatives, and consider what might happen.
3 Evaluation: The capacity to evaluate alternatives, both means and ends, given (1) and (2).
4 Selection and will: The capacity to select the best option and the will to implement it.

Moreover, rationality is holistic because each of the three choices of rationality are interdependent. If our acts are based on inappropriate beliefs, they lack rational justification; if our beliefs do not admit of implementation in practice, they suffer a defect; if our ends are inappropriate or wrong, we are led astray. As Rescher says: "Rationality is a matter of establishing harmony within (and between) the spheres of action and belief in the interests of the efficient pursuit of legitimate ends."[45]

Rationality is context-sensitive. It is not just about formulating impersonal principles. It is about how principles apply to situations. Aristotle noted this context-sensitivity of practical rationality when he discussed how the most appropriate diet for an ordinary citizen is not the most appropriate diet for an athlete in training. Rationality would be of little use if it *wasn't* context relative. It would issue only universal, but practically useless, injunctions. Also, rationality is an intrinsic part of the process of inquiry, not an

43 Ibid., 2–4.

44 My notion of situated rationality is consistent with, but broader than, studies of "bounded rationality" in psychology, management science, and computer design. The common idea is that rationality is "a style of behavior that is appropriate to the achievement of given goals, within the limits imposed by given conditions and constraints." Simon, "Theories of Bounded Rationality," 361.

45 Rescher, *Rationality*, 127.

external judge of inquiry after our thinking is completed. Rationality shapes our inquiry from start to end, helping us to identify presumptively valid sets of beliefs, hypotheses, or courses of action, and encouraging us to think rationally *as* we go through inquiry. Rationality, like inquiry, is external and social. Rationality is not just what happens "in our head." We do think things out, but usually with reference to some problem in the external world. Rationality is something best done together. We give reasons to others, and hope they will find them reasonable or plausible. We work within shared standards of what is rational.

Rationality is a virtue of intellect and character. It is the disposition to make my best reasons my motives for acting.

Rationality and Value

Choice makes values an intrinsic part of being rational. Our choices are justified by cognitive and ethical norms. Cognitive norms, or standards, evaluate conceptual systems. Here is a partial list: logical consistency among beliefs (e.g., no contradictions); coherence (e.g., new beliefs should cohere with existing beliefs); economy or simplicity of conceptual scheme; empirical and predictive power; agreement with facts; theoretical elegance; deductive power; self-evidence, or a foundation in intuitively clear ideas; the ability to unify old and new phenomena under laws and concepts; the ability to explain strange phenomena; the reliability of beliefs in the past; usefulness for solving practical problems and producing new technology.

Cognitive norms, such as truth and rational acceptability, form a circle of meaning. We explain one term by another term. We cannot say whether *x* is a fact without some conception of what we rationally ought to believe. Conversely, we ought to believe something as rational if it is supported by facts. Similarly, you can regard a fact as a true statement, or a true statement as a fact. As Putnam asserts: "A being with no values would have no facts either."[46] There is no neutral conception of rationality. Our conception of rationality is defined by a scheme of interdependent cognitive values that belong to one of many possible traditions. These norms of reason evolve over time.

Also in play are ethical notions of what is good. Rationality is about seeking the best means to goals that are often ethical in character, having to do with solving social problems and pursuing human goods. Too often we erroneously presume the sovereignty of reason over goodness. Reason puts the emotions and goodness on trial, or insults them as non-cognitive and

46 Putnam, *Reason, Truth and History*, 201.

"merely" subjective. But, we can ask in reply, what is the good of being rational? The justification for adopting a rational stance, or accepting a rational scheme, such as a scientific method, stands or falls with its contribution to intelligent and valuable action.

Pragmatic values, in terms of ends and consequences, are as important to reason as theoretical values, such as obeying logical laws. Take the debate between objectivity and subjectivity in inquiry. On pragmatic grounds, it is not true in general that we'd be better off in the long run to abandon the idea there are such things as impartiality, consistency, and reasonableness in human thought, even if we only approximate them in our lives and practice. Things go better for us as individuals and as societies if we retain a commitment to objectivity of some form. To say that a norm is something we cannot practically do without is a good reason to affirm it as true or "real."

In novels and in thought experiments, we see that our commitment to rationality is bound up with ideas about the good life. Take Huxley's novel *Brave New World.* The idea of a society where the populace is kept docile yet "happy" through the drug "soma" offends our values of free and rational persons, where happiness is not reducible to pleasurable states of mind. It does not fit our idea of "human cognitive flourishing."[47] Through such narratives, we realize what Iris Murdoch called the "sovereignty of good" – the role of our concept of the good in evaluating ideas of rationality, and evaluating ways of being.[48]

Putnam summarizes the holism of rationality, truth, goodness, and worldviews:

> The choice of a conceptual scheme *necessarily* reflects value judgments, and the choice of a conceptual scheme is what *cognitive* rationality is all about … One cannot choose a system that just "copies" the facts, because *no* conceptual scheme is a mere "copy" of the world. The notion of truth itself depends on our standards of rational acceptability, and these in turn rest on and presuppose our values … I am saying that theory of truth presupposes theory of rationality which in turn presupposes our theory of the good. Theory of the good … is itself dependent on assumptions about human nature, about society, about the universe. We have had to revise our theory of good (such as it is) again and again as our knowledge has increased and our world-view has changed … there is no such thing as a "foundation."[49]

47 Ibid., 134.
48 Murdoch, *The Sovereignty of Good,* especially chapter 3.
49 Putnam, *Reason, Truth and History,* 212, 215.

These profound considerations, whose complexity can induce intellectual vertigo at times, push us towards the idea of wide rationality. Some types of thinking and types of rationality are narrow. That is, they deal with specific problem areas and they can be formalized into a step-by-step method, a formal set of rules, or an algorithm. But over and above these specific applications there is a wide rationality that is humane, and has a human face. It is the basis upon which we evaluate narrow iterations of rationality and by which we evaluate accounts of the good life (fictional and otherwise). Recall those parts of your life where, in a difficult situation, you ran out of facts or "reasons" and had to judge wisely and widely, balancing a plurality of general values. Philosophy itself is an exercise in wide rationality and sense-making.

Imperfectionist Epistemology

What follows, epistemically, from these ideas? What does it say about truth, justification, and objectivity? The main implication is an epistemology that I call imperfectionism. Pragmatic philosophy, from Charles Peirce, William James, and John Dewey to Hilary Putnam, Willard V.O. Quine, and Richard Rorty, provides seminal ideas for imperfectionism.[50] The pragmatic philosophical mind is naturalistic, social, open to the future, attuned to contingency, and suspicious of both absolutism and subjectivism.

Imperfectionism, as a whole, is a pragmatic realism where, starting from our place in the natural world, we recognize the scheme-dependence of not only our beliefs, but of our norms themselves. Yet this epistemic relativism is not extreme. It does not deny the reality of the world, nor dismiss the validity of ordinary experience for a "higher reality." It does not claim that any scheme is as good as any other.

The tenets of imperfectionism are fallibilism, experimentalism, and conceptual relativity. All adhere to holism and reject dualistic epistemology and the craving for certainty. Fallibilism claims that none of our interpretations are immune to revision; experimentalism encourages invention in thinking; conceptual relativity holds that we think with holistic, internally complex, conceptual schemes.

FALLIBILISM

Objectivity is the evaluation of fallible interpretations and claims. We do not evaluate interpretations by asking if they achieve absolute truth. Fallibilism is the view that there are no "metaphysical guarantees to be had

50 For a review of this philosophical tradition, see Albrecht, *Reconstructing Individualism.*

that even our most firmly-held beliefs will never need revision."[51] Humans are imperfect inquirers. Their beliefs are fallible and never certain. The complexity of the world resists perfect results. Moreover, the cognitive capacity of humans is flawed by bias and other infelicities. Fallibilism regards beliefs as hypotheses concerning the best way to understand a phenomenon, or proposals about the best way to regulate conduct.

Fallibilism is not extreme skepticism. It does not require us to doubt *everything*. It only requires us to be ready to doubt anything – if good reasons to do so arise. One can be, as I am, a fallibilist about most beliefs. Or one can be a fallibilist about one type of belief. For example, one might regard the principles of mathematics as infallible and objective, yet regard ethical principles as fallible and subjective.

EXPERIMENTALISM

Fallibilism encourages us to be experimentalists and pioneers. If beliefs are fallible, they can be improved by new experiences and by discourse with others. We are psychologically open to new ideas. Even large social patterns, such as democracy, are what Mill called "experiments in living."[52] Experimentalism supports the widest possible exploration, and the freedom to engage in it.

Progress in thought and in society is often the result of experiments in living, through the invention of emergent conceptual schemes that disagree with existing schemes. Social and technological changes bring forward new practices, priorities, and values. The new practices become an emergent, alternate methodology; the new values become an emergent, alternate ethic. Journalism ethics today is a prime example of emergent ethics. It is a zone of contestation between new and old values. Before the digital revolution, professional practitioners came to think of their ethics as stable and settled. Disagreement or uncertainty were negative signs, indicating some weakness in the accepted ethics. Experimentalism takes a contrary position: emergence, disagreement, and uncertainty is part of inquiry and ethics.

Fallibilists see risk and trust as correlative aspects of constructing interpretations and acting on them. Things may turn out badly. Believing is analogous to making a "bet" that this belief will be reliable. We *gradually* trust beliefs, the way we dip a toe in the water to check its temperature. We extend to the stranger an initial, limited trust and see what happens. If they act as promised, we extend them more trust, until we regard a person as

51 Putnam, *Pragmatism*, 21.

52 Mill, *On Liberty and the Subjection of Women*, 65.

trustworthy. When it comes to beliefs we initially extend some trust to the belief as true, and act on it. We are like bankers who gradually extend greater and greater credit to a customer as they prove to be reliable in paying back loans. Beliefs and evaluations are validated retroactively; that is, after we have acted and consider how things turned out.[53]

CONCEPTUAL RELATIVITY

All statements, even matters of observation, contain some element of conceptualization, theorizing, and evaluation. All cognitions about the world, or at least all cognitions of interest to objectivity, are interpretations. We never reach statements with *no* conceptualization or theorizing, although we have experiences without conceptualization, such as reflex responses to stimuli. We arrive at a form of conceptual relativity: the view that our cognitions of the world, and our objective evaluations of them, are both based on a conceptual scheme. The scheme is one of several possible schemes. This relativism applies to descriptions of experiences and objects, observations of fact, interpretations of art, perceptions, and scientific theories. Different schemes produce a pluralism of truth. For any topic or domain of inquiry, we have rival or different views, and different claims to truth and fact. Interpreting and evaluating is dependent on, or shaped by, internally complex conceptual schemes.

PRAGMATIC REALISM

How does my conceptual relativity, with its emphasis on concepts, fit with my pragmatic naturalism, with its emphasis on nature? Can I *really* be a realist and a conceptual relativist?

In recent years, these questions have been debated intensely, ever since conceptual relativism was espoused by leading philosophers. Two criticisms of conceptual relativism are that (1) conceptual relativism entails idealism in metaphysics (i.e., what exists is mental or mind-dependent); and that (2) conceptual relativism entails relativism in epistemology (i.e., truth and "fact" are relative to conceptual scheme). The conclusion drawn is that conceptual relativism is incompatible with realism.

I disagree. There is a form of conceptual relativism that is compatible with a form of realism: pragmatic realism. Understanding how they are compatible requires reflection on the recent history of realism.

53 Rescher, *Rationality*, 53.

Origins of Conceptual Relativity

William James is the "grandfather" of conceptual relativity. In the early 1900s, James argued controversially that the plurality of theories in modern times, from alternate geometries of space to different forms of physics, undermined (absolute) realism in philosophy and science. What is realism, for James? It is the idea that there is exactly one true and complete description of, or truth about, "the way the world is," a description not dependent or relative to human theorizing or interests. Truth is mind independent. The world makes things true, in a determinate manner; not the mind and its schemes. Moreover, due to the many schemes, "the notion that even the truest formula may be a human device and not a literal transcript has dawned upon us." Truth is not singular or absolute. Truth is not a copying of reality which "stands ready-made and complete."[54] For James, human interests and perspectives colour our cognizing.

In 1981, Putnam, in *Reason, Truth and History*, reignited debate by making conceptual relativity the key to his "internal realism." Putnam was not advancing internal realism against common-sense realism – our ordinary view of the world. His target was the absolute or "metaphysical" realism of philosophy. Putnam's realism was "internal" because it argued that notions of truth and rationality were "grounded in," "based on," or "dependent on" a background conceptual scheme. He defined metaphysical realism as such:

> On this perspective, the world consists of some fixed totality of mind-independent objects. There is exactly one true and complete description of "the way the world is." Truth involves some sort of correspondence relation between words or thought-signs and external things or sets of things. I shall call this perspective the *externalist* perspective, because its favorite point of view is a God's Eye point of view.[55]

How to achieve a God's Eye view? We imagine getting "outside" of our conceptual schemes and determining if our ideas accurately describe objects as they exist in themselves. "The whole content of Realism lies in the claim that it makes sense to think of a God's Eye View (or better a view from nowhere)."[56] Lest one think that Putnam was tilting at a realism that does not exist, I note the long history of absolute realism and unsituated objectivity reviewed earlier. Also, realists today define their position in terms of

54 James, *The Meaning of Truth*, 123.
55 Putnam, *Reason, Truth and History*, 49.
56 Putnam, *Realism with a Human Face*, 23.

mind-independence. Searle talks about realism as the common-sense belief in an external world, apart from our psychological experiences, feelings, representations, and desires.[57] A second formulation is provided by Alston: "For the realist, there exists an independent, external world containing an immense number of objects, properties, relations, facts, and law-like behavior which await correct description."[58] Truth and objective knowledge is reality discernment. We describe the way the world is in itself.

Putnam objected to metaphysical realism on two counts – its portrait of how we know, and its negative consequences for our worldview. With regard to the first objection, Putnam believed, along with the constructionists discussed in chapter 2, that humans have no direct contract with reality. As Kant thought, the world is always the world as represented by us, through a conceptual scheme. There is no view from nowhere. There is no cognitive mechanism that can check if our conceptual understandings are in sync with the world as it is. Metaphysical realism is impossible. With regard to the second objection, Putnam accused metaphysical realism of denigrating common-sense realism in favour of a "superior" realism, such as scientific materialism. Sellars, for example, thought the manifest image of the world – the world according to common sense – was *false*. We may think tables are solid matter but physics tells us the table is mostly empty space.[59] Since Galileo, the denigration of lived experience has been expressed by the aforementioned dualism of primary and secondary properties. The primary properties of science are in the world; the secondary properties of ordinary experience are in the mind. Metaphysical realism, Putnam says, saddled our culture with the dualism of internal idea and external object. The dualism produced the unsolvable problem of representation, and other philosophical conundrums. What we need is an internal realism that acknowledges common-sense realism while rejecting a relativism where anything goes.

For some time, Putnam's conceptual relativity grew bolder, reinterpreting notions of fact and our very idea of an object. Consider these statements on objects: "It is characteristic of this view (internal realism) to show that *what objects does the world consist of?* is a question that only makes sense to ask *within* a theory or description."[60] Putnam also says: "'Objects' do not exist independently of conceptual schemes." He argued that we cannot even decide how many objects are in a room without presuming some prior scheme of counting objects, writing: "According to me, how many objects there are in the world (and even whether certain objects … exist at all as

57 Searle, *The Construction of Social Reality*, 150.

58 Alston, *A Realist Conception of Truth*, 5–6.

59 See Sellars, *Science, Perception, and Reality*.

60 Putnam, *Reason, Truth and History*, 49.

individual 'particulars') is relative to the choice of a conceptual scheme."[61] In a later work, he says: "In my picture, objects are theory-dependent in the sense that theories with incompatible ontologies can both be right."[62]

Facts received much the same treatment. "There are 'external facts' and we can ***say what they are***. What we ***cannot*** say – because it makes no sense – is what the facts are ***independent of all conceptual choices***."[63] Even our "experiential inputs" from the world, which restrain theorizing, "are shaped in some way by our concepts."[64] Meanwhile, fellow pragmatist Quine made conceptual schemes the vehicle for expressing truths within science. In a famous passage, Quine wrote: "Within our own total evolving doctrine, we can judge truth as earnestly and absolutely as can be; subject to correction, but that goes without saying."[65] Note that truth occurs "within" our evolving doctrine. Quine made objects, such as physical objects or classes, a posit required by our conceptual scheme. He defended ontological relativity. Our ontology is relative to a background theory: phenomenalism, physicalism, or idealism. Further, we cannot explain what the objects of our ontology *are* without translating them into some other ontology; for example, we explain physical objects as sets of sensations.[66]

Conceptual relativity appeared to be expansive, and triumphant.

However, criticisms mounted. Putnam amended conceptual relativity and internal realism.[67] By 1987, Putnam regretted using the word "internal" because it appeared to fall back on the old inner-outer dualism, and it smacked of idealism. He said he regretted having spoken of "mind-dependence" in *Reason, Truth and History*.[68] Putnam now said he should have called his view "pragmatic realism." In 1994, he discussed at length how he erred and what he now took to be pragmatic realism.[69]

Putnam's reform of realism encountered the same resistance that met James's definition of pragmatic truth. In letters, James complained bitterly about how people thought he had denied that our thoughts have to fit

61 See Putnam's discussion of "mereological sums": objects that are the sum of two or more objects, or the sum of parts of objects. Putnam, *The Many Faces of Realism*, 32.

62 Putnam, *Realism with a Human Face*, 114.

63 Putnam, *Reason, Truth and History*, 52; *The Many Faces of Realism*, 33. Italics and bold in Putnam's text.

64 Putnam, *Reason, Truth and History*, 54.

65 Quine, *Word and Object*, 25.

66 Quine, "Ontological Relativity," 54–5.

67 Critics portrayed Putnam's internal realism as idealism, anti-realism, relativism about truth, or an implausible epistemic realism. See Alston, *A Realist Conception of Truth*, 162, and 188–230.

68 Putnam, "Sense, Non-Sense and the Senses," 446n8.

69 Putnam, *The Many Faces of Realism*, 17; "Sense, Non-sense and the Senses."

reality to be true, or that he denied the existence of external objects. But both James and Putnam, in their strong statements about objects and facts, were partly to blame for the misunderstanding. Had James not said, carelessly, that a reality independent of human thinking seems to be "a thing very hard to find" and that "we create the subjects of our true as well as our false propositions"?[70]

Developing Pragmatic Realism

My conceptual relativity attempts to skate clear of these misunderstandings by developing Putnam's pragmatic realism.

Let us go back to our philosophical starting point at the opening of this chapter. The question was: What overall conception of inquiry helps us to understand objectivity *in situ*? I began with a broad ontological thesis: that an external world exists and that it is a natural world, as explained by our best natural knowledge. Inquiry is part of this natural world, the cognition of human organisms. I used a pre-existing view of the world to take up a perspective on human cognition and inquiry.

My naturalism contains three kinds of realism: global realism, substantive realism, and pragmatic realism. Under global realism, I affirm a belief in the external world that exists, at least in large part, independently of the human mind. Truths are beliefs that fit the world. This is realism at its highest level of abstractness. Like Alston's realism, it is a "thin" or "minimalist" realism that simply affirms a world about which we try to make true statements, without presupposing any specific theory of truth or what the world is like.[71] We cannot remain, philosophically, at this global level. We need to articulate a substantive realism or "metaphysic" about what this world is like. That is why I add my thesis of naturalism. However, a theory of inquiry also cannot remain at the substantive level. It needs to characterize how humans and their inquiry (and cognitions) fit into this natural world. Hence, I add my imperfectionism, which leads to pragmatic realism. I see pragmatic realism as a realism that deals specifically with human inquiry. Now, although I stressed holistic interpretation in defining inquiry, I never *forgot* my realist starting point. I was describing conceptual schemes as events in the natural world, as properties of human agents.

Pragmatic realism holds that the world does exist independent of mind, but *how* we understand what exists is dependent on mind. How we describe it is a plural, interpretive, and holistic process of situated cognition. I

70 James, *Pragmatism and Four Essays from The Meaning of Truth*, 162, 165.

71 On how principles can be minimalist and why they are necessary, see my *Radical Media Ethics*, chapter 6.

maintain the view of global realism that we are responsible for making our interpretations somehow fit reality. Yet my conceptual relativism warns that our descriptions will never be about the world "as it is" without human perspective. The best we can do is test our interpretations for how they match up with the world – how they cohere, follow logic, agree with existing fact, agree with our best naturalistic theories, and follow from other truths.

Pragmatic realism does not require a God's Eye view of unadulterated reality. Nor does it reduce the world or truth to whatever we happen to think. We can believe in a real world and the ubiquity of our interpretations at the same time. The real question is *what* cognitive norms and practices are best for interpreting the world. But if schemes are so important, why not eliminate reference to truth and fact? Because we need such concepts to act as regulatory notions for inquiry. They remind us that the purpose is to inquire into the ways of the world. We need these notions to avoid the "incredible shrinking world" phenomena in philosophy: philosophers start with naturalistic reflection on inquiry and, before you know it, ideas are *all* that matter. As I said earlier, philosophers "betray" the world as lived.

Also, pragmatic realism's commitment to the world avoids subjective idealism and Nelson Goodman's "irrealism." Irrealism claims that the world dissolves into versions of worlds. Humans make worlds, or versions of worlds, in science, art, philosophy, and elsewhere. In his "constructivist" philosophy, Goodman rejects metaphysical realism. Goodman says he is not talking about different possible versions of one and the same actual world, but "of multiple actual worlds" as versions.[72] Addressing the challenge that the versions must be of the real world, Goodman replies: "I insist that you tell me how it is (the world) apart from all frames, what can you say? We are confined to ways of describing whatever is described. Our universe, so to speak, consists of the ways rather than of a world or of worlds."[73] Irrealism undermines reductionism. How, for example, could we "reduce" Constable's or James Joyce's world view to physics? For Goodman, the idea of one, pregiven world, or a world as it is, is a world "well lost."[74]

I admire Goodman for courage in following where his ideas lead. His work validates the importance of sense-making outside of science, as in the arts. But I do not think that philosophy can eliminate our commitment to a common world. Alston, Lynch, and the later Putnam show how we can retain our idea of a world *and* recognize a pluralism of truths and conceptual schemes. Alston wonders why people think realism is necessarily

72 Goodman, *Ways of Worldmaking*, 2.
73 Ibid., 3.
74 Ibid., 4.

incompatible with Putnam's conceptual relativity. Why do we think that conceptual relativity means we "manufacture" facts? He writes:

> To be sure, what truths there are depends, at least in part, on what conceptual schemes we work with ... But within a given scheme why can't the truth of a proposition (statement, belief) amount simply to things being, in or relative to that scheme, as the proposition would have them be? ... The conceptual relativity comes in not to make the matter infinitely malleable *within a given scheme*, but only to affirm the multiplicity of acceptable schemes within which whatever facts there are obtain.[75]

Conceptual relativity and realism would be incompatible if we assert the metaphysical realist's view that truth is totally independent of conceptual activity. But why hold *that*?

Putnam considers that Kant may have been right to make the idea of a noumenal world a "limit thought." Perhaps, Putnam says, "we can't help thinking that there is somehow a mind-independent 'ground' of our experiences. A non-relative ground for our conceptual relativity."[76] Why presume that there is no common reality simply because we must describe it under some conceptual scheme? Putnam writes: "This does not mean that reality is hidden or noumenal; it simply means that you can't describe the world without describing it."[77]

Moreover, Putnam claims that the central error of metaphysical realism and scientific materialism is to think that our awareness of the world is always indirect, seen through the veil of internal ideas. Perception is seeing our sense data, not external objects. These ideas can be avoided by a pragmatic realism which argues that we not only make contact with the world in perception, we also act in that world.[78]

A Priority Problem?

Despite these comments, there still may be some epistemic discomfort in my choosing naturalism and pragmatism as a starting point. How, as a philosopher, can I simply "help myself" to such beliefs? Do I not have to first justify their adoption? First, I do not just help myself. The presumption of global realism is a reasoned adoption. Second, I do not need to "first" justify such choices. This worry is due to the continuing legacy of the belief

75 Alston, *A Realist Conception of Truth*, 179–80.
76 Putnam, *Reason, Truth and History*, 62.
77 Putnam, "Irrealism and Deconstruction," *Renewing Philosophy*, 122–3.
78 Putnam, "Sense, Non-sense and the Senses," especially 464–7.

that philosophy should be a First Philosophy. We do not have to choose between starting with "First" epistemology or starting with metaphysics (or ontology). In Quine's phrase, ontology and epistemology are "reciprocally contained."[79] We can say, at one and the same time, that, ontologically, there is an external world in which we think and which shapes our inquiries; *and* that, epistemically, we know these truths because they are justified by our best evidentiary standards. Our ontology informs our epistemology, and our epistemology shapes what we believe is true.

With pragmatic realism, the circularity of mind and world is acknowledged and we can work from world to mind, or from mind to world. This is a circularity that is not vicious and does not need to be explained away or avoided. Cognitively, we never get outside our circles of interpretation. But we are not solipsists, living within our minds. We are agents. It just so happens that our tools for understanding the world are conceptualized materials – beliefs, interpretations, and theories. We need to replace the duelling metaphors of realism and idealism: the mind makes the world, or the world makes our minds. Putnam provides a new metaphor: "If one must use metaphorical language, then let the metaphor be this: the mind and the world conjointly make up the mind and the world. (Or, to make the metaphor even more Hegelian, the Universe makes up the Universe – with minds – collectively – playing a special role in the making up.)"[80]

CONCLUSION

In this chapter, I explained objectivity with a human face. It starts from the agent's naturalistic attitude. The agent is a purpose-driven, mind-endowed organism who uses holistic interpretations to make sense, and holistic standards to evaluate interpretations. Experience, cognition, and rationality are wide and informal. Rationality is practical and value-laden. Objectivity with a human face employs an imperfectionist epistemology with its tenets of fallibilism, experimentalism, and conceptual relativity. Pragmatic realism overcomes problems surrounding conceptual relativity.

In the next chapter, I examine how objectivity with a human face is part of social engagement. I outline a specific theory of objectivity – pragmatic objectivity. I explain how pragmatic objectivity guides human engagement with the world, especially in ethics. Objectivity with a human face becomes objectivity for a community of moral agents.

79 Quine, "Epistemology Naturalized," 83. See also Gibson, "Translation, Physics and the Facts of the Matter," 147.

80 Putnam, *Reason, Truth and History*, xi.

6

Objectivity with a Human Face, Part 2: Objectivity in Engagement

Moral philosophy cannot avoid taking sides and would-be neutral philosophers merely take sides surreptitiously.

Iris Murdoch, *The Sovereignty of Good*, 76

When I compose, I find out who I am. I compose my identity, through my life and work.

Linda Catlin Smith, Canadian composer, "Composing Identity: What Is a Woman Composer?" Talk given at University of Victoria, 1 November 1997

In chapter 5, I explained objectivity with a human face. Objectivity *in situ* was portrayed as the imperfect, holistic evaluation of interpretations pragmatically rooted in agency.

This conception is still abstract. Chapter 5 did not say how agents conduct holistic evaluations in real life. Nor did it tell us how objectivity fits with human engagement with the world, through the advocacy of causes and ideals. It did not discuss how objectivity operates in ethics. In this chapter, I make objectivity with a human face more practical. Rather than regard objectivity and engagement as incompatible, I explain how the practice of objectivity can help us evaluate our commitments – especially in ethics.

ENGAGEMENT: AGENCY IN SOCIETY

The etymology of "engagement" revolves around three senses: being occupied with something, being committed, and finding something interesting or entertaining.

We are occupied when we perform a role or job. Teachers are engaged in classrooms; the police are engaged in directing traffic; seventeenth-century European explorers engaged in colonization. Being occupied can also mean being engrossed or absorbed in some activity, such as learning to paint watercolours or play chess. Engagement is commitment when we undertake some serious course of action, or pursue some complex, difficult-to-reach goal. One gets "involved" or entangled with someone or some process where withdrawal is difficult, for example, engaging in combat, getting married, devoting one's life to helping street people. One is occupied and committed. We are engaged with something as entertaining when something grabs our attention, such as when we say it was an engaging play.

What these senses have in common is intentional human agency, described in chapter 5. Engagement presupposes our capacity as agents to pursue and evaluate goals. In being engaged, we express our values and life plans. To be not engaged, or disengaged, means that one's agency is diminished or less active than in the past, or diminished relative to some goal. We are not taken up in the pursuit of a practical goal that demands a commitment.

This disengagement can take two forms, global and local. Global disengagement is an overall withdrawal from agency, often caused by a decline in interest in the world. One can take little interest in the plans of others or in the issues that roil social life. One can withdraw to one's study, become an ironic spectator on life's passing show, or become a hermit. Such disengagement also characterizes seriously depressed people. They experience a nihilism about the world and the value of acting in it. Local disengagement means that a person is not engaged in *this* issue, or *that* activity, or *these* groups, at *this* time. I may temporarily become detached from some of my usual engagements to find quiet time to develop a theory.

In this book, engagement means being an agent who is occupied and committed, through activity, with certain goals and values. Being engaged occurs on the agency side of our continuum of activities, discussed in chapter 5. Engagement involves a significant amount of activity, bodily agency, pursuit of goals, and adherence to practices. We can be engaged with theoretical problems and intellectual activities, that is, with activities on the "theory" side of our continuum. However, this engagement is not the focus of this chapter.

Engagement here refers primarily to actions and practices in society. People are engaged to maintain certain forms of community, including acting to reform society and its political structure. Engaged activity includes performing an important social practice, protesting government policy, being an activist for a new law, or acting an as official who, for example, protects the environment from corporate polluters. Depending on the cause, the people engaged, and the methods employed, engagement can have a positive or negative meaning for the public.

We have names for some of these engaged people. Some we call advocates; some we call activists; some we call partisans or ideologues. How close these terms are in meaning is shown by simply consulting dictionary entries for these terms. For example, a partisan is usually associated with a party – "A strong supporter of a party, cause, or person" – and is "prejudiced in favor of a particular cause." An advocate is defined as "a person who publicly supports or recommends a particular cause or policy." On this score, the difference between a partisan and an advocate is the former's allegiance to a party. Further, an activist is a person who uses "vigorous campaigning to bring about political or social change." Does the introduction of "campaigning" clearly distinguish the activist from partisan or advocate? Clearly not, since both the partisan and advocate may engage in vigorous campaigning.

We should not place too much pressure on these definitions. We should think of these social activities as differing in the degree of some property, like adherence to party or campaigning. They are different (yet similar) forms of political engagement. What these people have in common is a rejection of disengagement as a mode of being in society. They actively support some *thing* (person, party, idea, cause, law, reform). All are "partial" in preferring certain goals and activities. All are "ready to act" by voicing concerns, recruiting supporters, or marching in protests. They differ on what they support, the degree to which they are willing to act, and the methods they are prepared to use – as extremists, fanatics, moderates, or democrats.

I do not restrict "engaged citizen" to the familiar stereotypes of the protesting activist or the strong partisan. These are simply the examples that come most readily to mind when we talk of engagement. Judges too can be "activist" in changing outdated or unfair laws. Journalists can be advocates of democracy. There are many ways to be engaged.

In what follows I argue that engagement is not incompatible with objectivity. Therefore, I need to explain my notion of objectivity in more detail, which I call pragmatic objectivity. Then I will show how pragmatic objectivity is part of engaged citizenry in democracy.

PRAGMATIC OBJECTIVITY – A MODEL

Objectivity, as practice, is the evaluation of the interpretations that result from inquiry.[1] More precisely, objectivity is a fallible, situated, holistic *testing* of interpretations that are similarly fallible, situated, and holistically

1 For the full theory of pragmatic objectivity, see chapter 8 of my *The Invention of Journalism Ethics*. In recent years, scholarly work on a pragmatic philosophy of objectivity has grown. See *Pragmatism and Objectivity*, edited by Sami Pihlström.

constructed. Objectivity is "double" interpretation: an evaluative interpretation of an interpretation. Objectivity is second-order evaluation of first-order interpretations of the world; for example, theories, beliefs, artistic constructions, and claims to know. It is an epistemic interpretation of interpretations as valid, reasonable, and so on. Philosophy is "triple" interpretation: an evaluative interpretation of our modes of evaluating interpretations. Philosophy is, as Dewey said, a "generalized theory of criticism," a "criticism of criticisms."[2] All three levels evolve together as agents interact with the world and among themselves, and as our knowledge and methods change. Again, holism and history are king.

Among our types of interpretation, which ones are of most interest to this book? They are the interpretations we can call epistemic, for lack of a better term. Epistemic interpretations are those whose primary purpose is to interpret and explain some object in the world. These interpretations tend to be "literal" or descriptive, and data about the world is important. They are claims to knowledge about the world or some part of it, and notions of truth, evidence, rationality, and empirical fact take centre stage. The range of epistemic interpretation extends from perception, empirical generalizations, and historical narratives to theories in the natural and social sciences and claims to knowledge in the professions and other social practices.

Artistic interpretations, avant garde music, and works of imagination and fiction are not the central focus. This is not because their interpretations are subjective. It is not because their methods shed no light on interpretations elsewhere. To the contrary, the study of metaphor, depiction, and other forms of aesthetic representation help us to understand how we make sense in science, journalism, and other domains.[3] I set them aside to show how pragmatic objectivity operates in epistemic interpretations.

Pragmatic objectivity is my favoured theory of how to evaluate epistemic interpretations. It contains a stance that is applied to interpretations via a holistic set of standards. The standards are both generic to rational inquiry of any kind and domain specific – standards specific to particular practices. The capacity of humans to be objective is distilled into a set of practices, from checking on social facts statistically and testing a scientific hypothesis to subjecting testimony in court to cross-examination. Pragmatic objectivity describes how we should exercise this natural capacity for epistemic evaluation.

2 Dewey, *Experience and Nature*, xvi.

3 On the value of artistic criteria for other disciplines, see Goodman's *Languages of Art*.

The Objective Stance

Pragmatic objectivity is a stance that can be adopted by individuals, groups, and societies in their practices. The choice of this stance is pragmatic, judged by its overall contribution to inquiry, practice, and life. Objectivity begins with a willingness to adopt a certain stance – to subject one's beliefs to scrutiny and standards. Without this stance, the standards and methods of testing beliefs will not be applied. Someone must *care* about being objective.

Dictionaries define a stance or attitude as a "settled" opinion or way of thinking, or a cast of mind reflected in the person's conduct. The term originates in the "disposition" of a figure in sculpture or in painting – its bodily posture or pose. One can think of Mary's distraught face as she holds the dead body of Christ, in Michelangelo's sculpture, the Pieta. Stances are practical. They are mental dispositions that structure how we engage with people and the world. They motivate certain emotional responses and choices. Ideally, a stance brings beliefs and conduct into a unity that defines the person. For instance, many people never forget their encounter with a great teacher and their stance toward students and the world.

Objectivity is a complex, persistent psychological state, consisting of dispositions to respond in predictable ways over time to issues of inquiry and claims to knowledge. The dispositions include what Aristotle called the intellectual virtues.[4] There are at least four dispositions: a disposition towards open rationality, towards partial transcendence, towards disinterested truth, and towards intellectual integrity.

Objective inquirers display open rationality if they accept the burdens of rationality and judgment.[5] They are open to the demands of others to be logical, to face the facts squarely, and to give reasons that others can accept.[6] Rescher puts the point this way: "To proceed objectively is, in sum, to render oneself perspicuous to others by doing what any reasonable

4 Aristotle, *Ethics*, 203–25.

5 Rawls talks about the "burdens of judgement" when reasonable citizens propose principles to other reasonable citizens. Determining the correct judgment is difficult where evidence can conflict, and where citizens disagree about the importance of various considerations. Rawls, *Political Liberalism*, 54.

6 Philosopher Joseph Raz has defined objectivity in a way that is compatible with my dispositional analysis: "People are objective about certain matters if they are, in forming or holding opinions, judgments, and the like, properly sensitive to factors epistemically relevant to the truth or correctness of their opinions or judgments, that is, if they respond to these factors as they should." Raz, "Notes on Value and Objectivity," 195.

and normally constituted person would do in one's place, thereby rendering one's proceedings intelligible to anyone."[7]

Open rationality is related to the disposition towards partial transcendence. Open rationality assists the objective inquirer to partially transcend their epistemic situation. To transcend partially one's epistemic situation is to expand, enhance, and deepen one's current understanding of the issue in question. When our critical faculties encounter the experience of others, we enlarge our perspective or "fuse" our horizons.[8]

To practise open rationality and achieve partial transcendence requires support from another disposition – to be disinterested in the pursuit of truth. Disinterestedness means not allowing one's interests to subvert one's truth-seeking. One way to explain disinterestedness is to use the metaphors of space and distance. We step back, metaphorically, and put a critical distance between us and our beliefs. We can adopt a critical distance in a number of ways. In philosophy, we can practise skepticism and self-doubt. In literature, we can exhibit this distance by the way we write and present characters. We have seen how the early modern scientists displayed their disinterestedness by using plain language, avoiding heated rhetoric, and making modest claims about the philosophical implications of their experiments.

Unfortunately, disinterestedness is one of the most misunderstood and maligned of the intellectual virtues. Some people incorrectly think that disinterestedness entails complete emotional detachment. They confuse disinterest with lack of interest, or a lack of caring. To the contrary, disinterestedness is not radical detachment. It is an extension of our common and important ability to reflect on the grounds of our beliefs, apart from our partialities. Disinterestedness does not mean that the objective stance is without passion. Disinterestedness is the correct use of our passion for truth. A good deal of pseudo-inquiry is the reasoning of an inquirer who has a "prior and unbudgeable commitment to the proposition for which he tries to make a case."[9] Another variant of the pseudo-inquirer is what Harry Frankfurt called frankly the "bullshitter," a person indifferent to the truth of the proposition she advances so long as she impresses others.[10]

At the bottom of all these dispositions is the inquirer's intellectual integrity. This is a trait of character that disposes inquirers to reject wishful

7 Rescher, *Objectivity*, 8.

8 Gadamer, *Truth and Method*, 304, 336.

9 Haack, *Manifesto of a Passionate Moderate*, 9.

10 Frankfurt, "On Bullshit," 11–33.

thinking, to face up to the toughest questions, and, where necessary, to admit that their ideas are flawed.

Applying the Stance: Standards

One is not objective by dint of having a set of dispositions, or cognitive virtues. One has to put those dispositions to work in real inquiry and in concrete situations. One needs standards and methods. Good inquiry is objective if it is standard-guided thought, or disciplined rationality. In objectivity, the mind turns back on itself; it monitors and corrects its activity. We judge, epistemically, an interpretation to be objective if it has good support, according to the standards of a conceptual scheme. We determine "what is objective from the point of view of our best and most reflective practice."[11] Beliefs are objective insofar as they satisfy, to some degree, the best available epistemic standards, applied by a person who adopts the objective stance.

Pragmatic objectivity tests practices by adopting a stance that can apply two levels of standards: generic and domain-specific. Objectivity is generic when its uses general standards of rational inquiry and decision-making. We have already named a number of general standards, from coherence of ideas to the predictive power of a theory. Objectivity is domain-specific where we use, in addition to generic standards, the distinct standards of a discipline, developed to address the peculiar problems of that practice. Domains such as law, journalism, and the sciences interpret the general standards to suit their purposes. This adaptation of objectivity results in an additional set of distinct and detailed norms. Objectivity is "realized" in many ways.

A theory of objectivity, then, makes explicit our standards and considers their relative worth.

Generic Standards: A Framework

There are three types of generic standards. There are *empirical standards*, which test a belief's agreement with the world; *standards of coherence*, which evaluate how consistent a belief is with the rest of what we believe; and *standards of rational debate*, which test how fair we have been in representing the claims of others and to what degree we have opened our claims to the scrutiny of others.

11 Putnam, *Words and Life*, 177.

The empirical standards begin with the value that we place on observation, especially observation under good conditions, and on repeated perceptions by unbiased observers. The empirical standards of science take these informal standards and make them more formal, more precise. Experiments must satisfy standards and methods that are rigorous, controlled, quantifiable, replicable, and mathematically correct.

The generic standards of coherence include the rules of logic, such as principles of logical consistency and non-contradiction; the support that a belief receives from other beliefs; and the way a hypothesis fits with established knowledge.[12] Coherence standards include aesthetic values such as the simplicity or mathematical elegance of a theory. We use coherence standards every day, such as when we try to make sense of a surprising perception. As I drive down my street at sunset, I am surprised to see that my house appears to be pink when I believe it to be beige. Do I accept this perception as correct or objective? No, because the perception does not cohere with previous perceptions of my beige house. Also, this perception of pink does not cohere with my firm belief that I painted the house beige last summer. Furthermore, it is improbable that someone painted my house pink while I was at the office. A more likely explanation is that the pinkish colour is the result of the sunset, and I set about verifying that hypothesis by making further observations.

Second, standards of coherence are at work in assessments of theory. Suppose I am skeptical about a new book that claims that science can show that nature exhibits a mysterious sort of "intelligent design," perhaps by a deity. I am suspicious not only because of the logical implausibility of the theory and its lack of evidence but also because it does not cohere with my basic belief in design by natural selection. Take another example, from law. A jury refuses to believe that Jim murdered Mary because evidence shows that he was not at the murder scene at the time of the killing. The proposition that Jim is guilty does not cohere with a basic belief of logic – no one can have the property A and the property not-A at the same time. That is, Jim cannot be in two places at the same time. The case against Jim is logically incoherent. The same preference for coherence applies in theology. Coherence considerations are essential to constructing reasonable interpretations of conflicting passages in the Bible.

Third, standards of rational debate consist of the norms of rational deliberation and criticism among groups, disciplines, and societies. They include diversity, equality, and inclusiveness. For the attainment of objective

12 Many of these standards appear in the writings of William James, such as *The Meaning of Truth* and *Pragmatism*.

beliefs, it is important that all rational voices in the debate receive fair and respectful treatment, that the process of debate be inclusive, and that hierarchies of power do not distort deliberation. The process of deliberation should not block inquiry by preventing the formulation of hypotheses or criticisms. Our empirical and coherence standards must be applied in a social context of inquiry that is as open and democratic as possible. We support standards of rational debate not only because we want to be fair to participants, but because we want to ensure the presentation of a full range of facts, theories, perspectives, and objections during the objective evaluation of any claim.

A century and a half ago, John Stuart Mill, in *On Liberty*, recognized the importance of living in a society that encouraged the open criticism of beliefs. More recently, liberal philosophers have made standards of rational deliberation an essential part of the construction of acceptable ethical rules, fair principles of justice, and objective scientific theory. Putnam, following Dewey, has stressed that science "requires the democratization of inquiry."[13] Open and fair rational debate is just as vital for rational inquiry in science as it is for rational deliberation on public policy in democracies. Norms for rational deliberation are central to Rorty's theory of objectivity. Rorty defined objectivity as "agreement reached by free and open discussion of all available hypotheses."[14] The norms are central to Habermas's theory of communicative action and his "discourse ethics." For Habermas, communicative action is communication governed by the ideals of rational discourse – ideals that define discourse ethics. In communicative action, participants perform speech acts that presuppose such norms as sincerity, telling the truth, and asserting what reason warrants.[15] In discourse ethics, problems in moral argumentation cannot be "handled monologically but require a cooperative effort." Habermas states that people attempt, by entering into norm-governed moral discourse, to restore "a consensus that has been disrupted."[16]

Rational standards of debate support Rawls's appeal to "public reason." Public reason is the means by which a society fairly and openly discusses fundamental political issues. Rawls argues that citizens in a pluralistic democracy must agree on the sort of reasons that they will give each other when basic principles are at stake. If each group insists on the unique truths of its worldview, the issues are unsolvable. Rawls recommends that the groups debate according to public reason. They put forward reasons that

13 Putnam, *Words and Life*, 173.
14 Rorty, *Truth and Progress*, 7.
15 Habermas, *The Theory of Communicative Action*, 1:ix, 1:86, 1:94.
16 Habermas, "Discourse Ethics," 67.

are politically acceptable to all citizens as citizens. What reasons might those be? For Rawls, they include fundamental principles of justice. Through the exercise of public reason, the principles of justice attain some degree of objectivity.[17]

The three types of generic standards correspond with the three senses of objectivity in chapter 2. Empirical standards express the ontological sense of objective facts; they anchor an interpretation in experience and worldly facts. Coherence standards express the epistemic sense of careful, systematic method. They make sure that the interpretation is part of a meaningful and consistent conceptual system. Standards of rational debate express a moral objectivity, an intersubjective, discursive sense of objectivity and fair process. All three types of norms may come into play in the objective evaluation of a scientific theory. Thagard uses the notion of explanatory coherence to explain conceptual revolutions in science. According to Thagard, scientists throughout history have adopted a new theory, such as Darwin's natural selection or Lavoisier's oxygen, because it satisfies empirical and rational (coherence) standards better than rival theories. Thagard recognizes that there is a "data priority" in theory evaluation. Yet there is more to evaluation than collecting data: "Theories are enmeshed in conceptual systems, just as rationalists have argued, and such systems are not open to simple empirical challenges." To "data priority" we must add such norms as the explanatory breadth of a theory, the coherence of its propositions, and the simplicity of its assumptions. Acceptance of a theory is an inference to the best explanation – the one that satisfies multiple constraints.[18]

Under these three kinds of standards fall the following, more specific, norms:

- *Standard of empirical validity*: What is the empirical evidence for the interpretation? How strong is it, and what are the countervailing facts? Is the evidence complete? Does the belief have carefully obtained and collaborated evidence, and does it accurately present that data? Does it place the facts in context?
- *Standard of diverse and trusted sources*: What are the sources, and are there any conflicts of interest? Are all important sources taken into account and fairly assessed? Are fallacious arguments or manipulative persuasive techniques used to promote a view?

17 Rawls, *The Law of Peoples*, 132–3. Rawls limited public reason to the "public political forum," which included the discourse of senior judges and elected officials, and the public oratory of candidates for political office.

18 Thagard, *Conceptual Revolutions*, 251, 97.

- *Standard of clarity and coherence*: Do the beliefs and values of the interpretation cohere with other beliefs and values? Does the claim cohere with existing knowledge in the field? Is the interpretation logically consistent? Are the concepts clear?
- *Standard of implications and consequences*: Does the interpretation rigorously and fairly examine the implications for public policy, or the positive and negative consequences of acting on the belief or theory?
- *Standard of self-consciousness*: In forming our view or belief, are we conscious about the conceptual frame we use to understand it? Are there other frames? What is the effect of the language we use?
- *Standard of open, public scrutiny and discourse*: Have we shared our claims and views with other people – other journalists, experts, and citizens? Have we subjected our work to sustained public scrutiny?
- *Standard of moral aims*: Does our interpretation or decision promote, or is it at least consistent with, the public purposes of the practice? Is it part of responsible practice? Does it exemplify the practice at its moral best, or in its best light?
- *Standard of the public interest*: In the final analysis, does our practice promote the public good as the primary and most inclusive goal?
- *Standard of public moral reasoning*: Have we engaged, with others, in careful moral reasoning about the decision or action in question? Under what principles does it fall? Have moral goods, duties, and rights been thoroughly considered? Have we applied to moral reasoning the standards cited above – of empirical validity, implications, trusted sources, self-consciousness, clarity and coherence, and public scrutiny?
- *Standard of transparency and public accountability*: Are we transparent to our colleagues and to the public about the moral principles by which we can be held accountable, and about how we have followed our stated values in practice?

The standards of domain-specific objectivity are too numerous to summarize. I will discuss the standards for journalism in the next chapter. Meanwhile, a couple of examples may help. A study of the objective efficacy of a new drug requires health researchers to subject the drug to a multi-phased clinical trial. Researchers must, of course, act rationally. They adhere to the generic standards of objectivity. In addition, they follow standards and methods developed for their domain. The researchers must disprove the null hypothesis, construct a control group, apply triple-blind procedures, and evaluate results according to standards of statistical significance. Another example is the rule in law courts against hearsay evidence. It is a particular application of the general standard to consider only reliable empirical evidence.

In summary, an inquirer practices pragmatic objectivity if she evaluates interpretations and actions by adopting this stance and by consulting these standards.

Objectivity as Holistic

Pragmatic objectivity is multi-dimensional. It is plural in its standards, and holistic in those standards' application. Objectivity is not reducible to one standard, such as agreement with observations of fact. Evaluation involves a convergence of standards.

Objectivity is not an exception to fallibilism. Our standards are as fallible, in nature and application, as the beliefs that they attempt to govern. Pragmatic objectivity presumes neither absolute standards nor pure facts. They are not universal and unchanging, known by reason a priori. At the same time, we do not invent the standards of objectivity *ex nihilo*. The standards are used because they have been successful guides in past inquiry. By inquiry, we not only learn what exists, what is a fact. We learn what *works* in terms of methods and standards of evaluation. Together, our standards represent our best judgment about how to conduct and evaluate inquiry, given our experience. We learn how to learn.

Objectivity, therefore, is a complex property of people and their beliefs. To say that John is an objective person is a second-order evaluation of John's dispositions and conduct. He follows the stance and standards of objectivity. The judgment of objectivity is a matter of degree and comparative. The judgment says that interpretation *A* satisfies standards *x*, *y*, and *z*, to degree *d*. It says that interpretation *A* is more objective than interpretation *B*, given certain standards. The result of objective evaluation is a judgment that q is objective, where q can be a person's belief, theory, journalism report, or decision. Given the complexity of this judgment, appeals to brute fact rarely settle the objectivity of a claim. We cannot "perceive" directly that a claim is objective the way we perceive an object to be red. Rather we *cognitively apprehend* something as objective, given our holistic testing by standards.

PASSIONATE IMPARTIALITY

Meaning of Impartiality

In previous chapters, I underlined the misunderstandings that surround objectivity as just the facts. Here I turn to the misunderstandings that objectivity requires an inquirer who is strictly neutral and not influenced by emotions or interests – the assumption that objectivity resembles a value-free zone.

Neutrality is not the correct term for describing the practice of objectivity. Impartiality is the correct term. It is a certain type of impartiality – an impartiality that is engaged, and passionate. Impartiality is not value-free, emotion-free, or goal-free.

The confusion begins when we treat impartiality, neutrality, objectivity, detachment, and disinterestedness as near synonyms. We think they are all about detaching oneself from engagements and being steadfastly neutral about whatever issue is in question. Yet these terms are not synonymous. Reducing them to an arid neutrality is a parody of true objectivity, and treating them as synonyms leads to errors about what objectivity requires. Steadfast neutrality is only one way of standing back from one's beliefs.

The term "neutrality" derives from the idea that something belongs to neither of two things, or two opposites. Originally, neutrality's meaning was sexual, that is, to be neuter – neither masculine nor feminine. In chemistry, a neutral solution is neither acidic nor basic. In physics, a neutral particle is without electrical charge. When applied in social contexts, neutrality means that we do not belong to any side – a neutral party in a war between two nations does not assist either side in any manner. In everyday life, my car is in "neutral" when the driveshaft is not attached to any gear that moves the vehicle. When people studiously avoid taking any side in a dispute, there is a similar lack of direct action and engagement. In journalism, a neutral reporter does not take sides and reports only the facts.

Unfortunately, this demanding sense of neutrality is confused with impartiality. Impartiality does not require a strong neutrality. Impartiality is part of the stance of a person – professor, judge, journalist – who is active and often engaged. Impartiality does not mean that one has no partialities. It does not mean that one does not feel the tug of one's own biases and interests. It does not mean that one must withdraw from agency, detached like the neutral gear in my car. It does not require that one can never express a judgment, conclusion, or perspective. What impartiality demands is that a person is willing and capable of not letting their partialities unduly bias their judgment. In my view, the best way to ensure that one's partialities are not biasing one's thinking is to adopt the stance and standards of pragmatic objectivity.

Consider some examples of impartiality-in-action. Take the case of an impartial judge adjudicating a dispute. The judge does eventually "take" sides: she comes down on one side as having the better case in law. The judge judges. She issues conclusions that favour one side in the case. Impartial judging means that the judge does not prejudge the case. She adopts the stance and generic standards of pragmatic objectivity, and then applies the domain-specific standards of the law. Nor does impartiality require that a person or an agency "do nothing." The Red Cross is famous for its neutrality among warring sides. Yet I prefer to think of their neutrality as impartiality-in-action. The Red Cross is far from being detached from or uninterested in the warring sides. The Red Cross acts. It has goals. It enters war zones to help all injured combatants and distressed citizens. But it tries to not let the partialities of staff (or its organization) bias their treatment of one side in the dispute. Similarly, impartial UN officials may be asked to investigate whether a military leader violated human rights. Or, a team of investigative journalists, after extensive investigation into the facts of a case, may conclude that an official acted wrongly, and against the public interest.

Impartiality guides how we do something, how we are engaged. It guides how we judge and act. Impartiality is crucial for fair engagement, and should not be confused with a spineless avoidance of taking stands or expressing viewpoints. If this is so, then impartiality – not neutrality – is the correct norm for objectivity.

PASSIONATE IMPARTIALITY

A crude but widespread belief among objectivity's legion of critics is that impartiality and objectivity are not desirable or possible because they require that agents turn themselves into emotionless analysts, or cold-blooded spectators to the urgent issues of life. Why should this be so? Throughout history, passion has motivated impartial inquiry – a passion to know and learn, a passion to solve a riddle, a passion for wonder and awe, a passion for fairness. People who practice objectivity care very much for it. Pragmatic objectivity is a passionate commitment to dispassionate inquiry.

Genuine inquiry derives from an impartial search for the truth, "regardless of what the color of that truth may be."[19] Impartiality means caring so much for the honest truth that one does not allow personal interests to subvert inquiry or to prejudge the issue. When impartial people see bias and partiality twisting the public's understanding of some matter, or badly influencing conduct, they experience frustration, even anger. To be impartial is to prevent the passion for truth from succumbing to other interests. One *cares* so much about fairness and objective judgments that one submits to the discipline and undertakes the study needed to be objective.

19 Haack, *Manifesto of a Passionate Moderate*, 10.

Perhaps the classic portrait of the cold-blooded "rational" person is Thomas Gradgrind, the school board superintendent in Charles Dickens's novel *Hard Times.* Gradgrind treats all questions, including interactions with his children, in terms of numbers, facts, prosperity, and expected utility. Critics of bloodless objectivity then ask rhetorically: *Who* would support an attitude like that? The response is: No one should; and, luckily, no one has to. Impartiality does not require people to become a "logic machine" – a human Spock.[20] In ethics, appeals to compassion and empathy can and should be part of rational arguments about ethical decisions. Moreover, the best practices of objectivity often combine partiality and impartiality. In a trial, the partiality of the prosecutor and the defence attorney (and the parties they represent) occurs within a larger impartial context – a judge or jury that subjects partial arguments to the test of objective evidence and to the impartial rules of law. Ideally, what is fair and objective emerges from a sort of "trial by fire" – a trial where rival partialities make their case.

My talk of objectivity as passionate should not surprise. I have said from the beginning that objectivity is a natural desire or psychological impulse. It is a rational passion for objective knowledge and disinterested decisions. Objectivity involves our cognitive emotions – such as wonder, curiosity, and awe.[21] Objectivity is a love of truth impartially sought and obtained.

The "Repressed" Monarch

The idea of a passionless objectivity is sometimes said to require severe psychological repression. The neutral and objective person is required to completely repress any feelings of bias or favoritism. In the British television series *The Crown,* about the early years of the reign of Queen Elizabeth II, there is a scene where the inexperienced queen discusses the constitutional limits on her powers. The queen is troubled by demands from senior political officials that she ask Prime Minister Winston Churchill to step down as prime minister because of his seeming inability to respond to a poisonous smog that has descended on London and is killing citizens.[22] But she also knows that acting politically would violate her neutrality. The queen has this tense conversation with her aunt, Queen Mary:

20 Spock is the famous character from the TV science fiction series *Star Trek.* The non-human Spock was frequently baffled by the human insistence to bring emotions into decisions.

21 On the contribution of wonder to the progress of science, see Daston and Park's *Wonders and the Order of Nature.*

22 From episode 4 of the series, "Act of God." *The Crown* was created and written by Peter Morgan and produced by Left Bank Pictures and Sony Pictures Television for Netflix. The episode was first shown on Netflix on 4 November 2016. The poisonous fog lasted from 5 to 9 December 1952 and killed thousands of people.

Queen Elizabeth: It doesn't feel right, as head of state, to do nothing.

Queen Mary: It is exactly right.

Queen Elizabeth: Is it? But surely doing nothing is no job at all.

Queen Mary: To do nothing is the hardest job of all and it will take every ounce of energy that you have. To be impartial is not natural, not human. People will always want you to smile, or agree, or frown, and the minute to do, you will have declared a position, a point of view, and that is the one thing as sovereign that you are not entitled to do. The less you do, the less you say, or agree, or smile …

Queen Elizabeth: Or think, or feel, or breathe, or exist …

Queen Mary: … the better.

Queen Elizabeth: Well, that's fine for the sovereign but what about me?

The plaintive last phrase, "but what about me?," is the cry usually raised against not only neutrality but impartiality and objectivity – as too demanding for flesh-and-blood individuals. Objectivity seems to require a perfectly "empty" person, who presumably never feels the strong tug of their partialities – a dehumanized, rational robot.

No doubt there are some people who occupy very special roles, such as a British monarch, where neutrality is demanded by law and covers most of their public lives. But this model of neutrality, in its strictness, is rarely the impartiality we practise in society. It is not even practised by constitutional monarchs in all of their activity, but only in special cases. It is a caricature of our ordinary norms of impartiality. Or, it is a straw man argument that attacks a position not held by reasonable proponents of objectivity. The norms of objectivity were not constructed because its creators thought that most humans, when they judge, should be masters at repression. The norms were constructed *because* of an acute awareness of human bias, because it is evident. As shallow critics of objectivity never tire of saying: "We all have biases." Rather than conclude that objectivity is impossible because bias is universal, scientists, journalists, and others concluded the opposite: we biased humans need the discipline of objectivity to *reduce* the ineliminable presence of bias.

Objectivity with a human face does not require a rational robot. It requires only that a person is capable, *to some significant or satisfactory degree,* of disciplining their partialities. Impartiality requires discipline and effort, but not superhuman repression of all feeling.

Emotions as Cognitive Response

The idea that objectivity requires the fierce repression of emotion stems from a distorted view of emotions and their role in cognition and inquiry. Repression seems necessary because of the legacy of our cognitive dualisms. Like the dualism of fact and value, we erect an antagonistic dualism of emotion and cognition. We see emotions as non-cognitive in nature and a threat to correct cognition and evaluation.

Fortunately, recent work in the theory of emotion has challenged this implausible dualism. Martha Nussbaum, for example, promotes a "cognitive-evaluative" notion of emotion.[23] Nussbaum starts with our common-sense list of emotions – grief, fear, hatred, love, anger, envy, jealousy, and empathy. She distinguishes them from desires, "objectless" moods (e.g., feeling irritable), bodily states (e.g., hunger and thirst), and bodily sensations (e.g., shivering when afraid). Nussbaum then adopts a neo-Stoic "cognitivist" view of the emotions. It holds that the emotions as "intelligent" not because they always guide us rationally and wisely, but because they have an important cognitive element. She rejects the idea that emotions are unthinking energies that "simply push people around" and whose presumed opposition to rationality means they should be excluded from ethical deliberation. Rather, Nussbaum regards emotions as "intelligent responses to the perception of value." The cognitive content of emotions consists in how we understand and evaluate the object. All emotions involve (a) an intentional thought or perception directed at an object, and (b) some type of evaluative appraisal of the object's importance or salience. Emotional responses are judgments about an object; these emotional judgments are a subclass of value judgments.[24]

The difference between fearing and loving a person depends on cognition, that is, our beliefs about the person, and information about the world. The visceral pain of grieving a spouse "violently tears the fabric of attachment, hope, and expectation that we have built around that person."[25] That fabric is composed of beliefs, goals, interpretations, and other cognitive elements. Also, our emotional response to a piece of music involves a cognitive interpretation of the lyrics and musical phrases. Moreover, emotions are shaped by social norms and specific circumstances. Even biologically "given" emotions such as anger are expressed in different ways in different societies. Our emotional response to artistic productions, for example when Shylock asks for his "pound of flesh" in Shakespeare's *The Merchant of Venice*, is mediated by our norms, knowledge of history, and ways of interpreting the play.

Nussbaum thinks that the emotions are *eudaimonistic*, which means "concerned with one's flourishing." The value of an object is determined relative to a person's own values and goals. The objects of emotion are self-referential. They are "mine" and are valued because I believe they contribute

23 See Nussbaum's *Upheavals of Thought*, and *Political Emotions*.

24 Nussbaum, *Upheavals of Thought*, 24, 1, 30.

25 Nussbaum, *Political Emotions*, 400.

to my overall flourishing. Emotion for my dying mother is due to the fact that this mother is *mine* and is a valued object in my flourishing. "Emotions," Nussbaum writes, "view the world from the point of view of my own scheme of goals and projects, the things to which I attach value in a conception of what it is for me to live well."[26] Without some linkage to my flourishing, to my circle of concerns, an emotion is weak or fails to exist.

Goodman has provided further arguments for considering emotions to be much more than brute feelings. In *Languages of Art,* Goodman stresses the cognitive function of emotion in art. Goodman start his analysis as I have done: decrying the "domineering dichotomy" between the cognitive and the emotive. On the latter view, science is cognitive but art, and our responses to it, are matters of emotion that tell us much about our psychological profile but little that is objective about the work of art. Goodman complains that this dichotomy keeps us from seeing that, in aesthetic experience, "the *emotions function cognitively.*"[27] Emotional "numbness," he says, disables us as completely as blindness or deafness. Emotions provide access to, and call our attention to, aspects of objects, such as works of art, that we might otherwise not notice or appreciate. We don't use our "feelings" just to explore the emotional content of a work of art. We may "feel how a painting looks as we may see how it feels." Emotion in aesthetic experience "is a means of discerning what properties a work has and expresses." The cognitive use of emotions in art involves discriminating and relating felt emotions so as to grasp the work "and integrate it with the rest of our experience and the world."[28] Aesthetic experience is dynamic, not static. It includes making subtle discriminations and discerning subtle relationships, identifying symbolic systems and what characters within these systems denote or exemplify. It involves "interpreting works and reorganizing the world in terms of works and the works in terms of the world."[29]

In this experience, there is a holistic interaction between emotions, facts, the environment, perceived qualities such as colours, and the more abstract apprehension of how elements in the work of art are ordered. We have a wide experience.

Therefore, we must be careful *not* to exclude emotions from how we objectively apprehend the world around us, whether that is via science, journalism, or art. However, this does not mean that we do not need to be critically attentive to the emotions we have and how we use them. We need to know when certain types of emotion (and certain degrees of emotions)

26 Nussbaum, *Upheavals of Thought,* 49.

27 Goodman, *Languages of Art,* 248. Italics are in Goodman's text.

28 Ibid.

29 Ibid., 241.

are appropriate or inappropriate, and what sorts of emotions are conducive or not conducive to achieving personal and communal goals. Our capacity to have emotions, like our capacity to observe, to imagine, and to reason, need to be used wisely. As Aristotle thought, our emotions and our virtues are matters of habit and education. So it *is* true that emotions can lead us astray. We can overreact to events; we can be filled with anger or hatred; our emotional attachments can blind us to objective facts and make us deaf to calls for moderation or prudence. For example, as I have argued elsewhere, journalism and democratic society need to be attentive to the sort of political emotions that people embrace, such as the strong emotions that are part of patriotism and nationalism. We need a moderate, critical patriotism that reins in more extreme forms of patriotism.[30]

Yet to issue these warnings about emotion is not to return to the view that emotions are dangerous irrational forces. Rather, it is to remind us that we have a responsibility, individually and collectively, to develop healthy emotional habits, and to learn to use well our emotional "window" on the world, just as we must learn to use well our other faculties.

One final point on the emotions. They show that wide experience may use a multi-modal approach to understanding objects. Modalities transgress their assigned borders and mix with other ways of experiencing. As I said above, we "feel how a painting looks." The modalities of feeling and seeing mix, and create paradoxical expressions. Furthermore, we often come to apprehend more deeply when our neat system of categories breaks down, when our categories blur, mix, and create new hybrid categories. We understand aesthetic experience more deeply, for example, when we stop thinking of it as a relatively passive "looking" at works of art, and start thinking of it as a form of action, a "restless, searching, testing" of the work of art. As Goodman states, the aesthetic attitude, for both artists and art appreciators, is "less attitude than action: creation and re-creation."[31] By mixing our cognitive modalities and categories we not only produce richer experiences, but our interpretive powers are enhanced, taking us deeper into the nature of complex phenomena, such as a strikingly original film or painting. Here, the interpretation of things, and the evaluation of the interpretation, are sophisticated, fascinating forms of cognition.

30 Ward, "Patriotism and Journalism."
31 Goodman, *Languages of Art*, 241–2.

Objectivity and Engagement

It is time to explain how objectivity is compatible with being engaged. The answer is implicit in the remarks above, but I want to be explicit because this compatibility is an important feature of my theory of objectivity.

I defined engagement as the pursuit of goals: an agent who is strongly occupied with certain goals and in supporting certain values and activities. Engagement refers primarily to actions and practices in society and politics. I defined objectivity as a "method" in the most general sense: the holistic evaluation of the correctness of claims and interpretations about the world in science, ordinary life, and in the professions. The method consists of an open-minded stance and a set of appropriate standards, at the generic or domain-specific level.

These definitions indicate why objectivity and engagement are compatible. They are compatible because they are different aspects of agency. Engagement is about goals; objectivity is about method, a means to goals. Objectivity tests for reliability and cogency of belief and potential courses of action (means), whether those goals be highly practical (e.g., building a tunnel), or more conceptual (e.g., developing a theory about bipolar mental illness). Since goals and means are different things, objectivity and engagement are compatible. I can adopt the objective stance in the course of pursuing goals. I can be partial about goals – that is, I can prefer certain goals over others – while at the same time being impartial in how I seek to realize such goals. Scientists follow objective methods to create new technology to solve a problem. Judges follow the objective methods of law to pursue their goal of justice. The value of objectivity is that it helps us to be intelligently and fairly engaged.

One thinks engagement and objectivity are incompatible if one defines objectivity as a strong neutrality that precludes the person having an interest or perspective; or, if one thinks that objectivity precludes emotion and agency. But we have seen that these presumptions are neither plausible nor necessary. Objectivity can be defined as having a human face.

Yet, despite all I have said, I do not think this is a complete account of the role of objectivity. Why? Because it is still compatible with something my pragmatism rejects: the deeply entrenched notion from Hume that we can rationally evaluate our means, but not our ends.[32] But we *can* evaluate our ends, as long as we do not think of them as impulses or immediate

32 For documentation as to how entrenched this view is, see Searle, *Rationality in Action*, 11.

desires. Can I not evaluate, albeit imperfectly, the end of getting married, the end of curing cancer, the end of eliminating the Jewish population in Germany, the end of sending humans to Mars? All of these ends call for evaluation. Therefore, I think the compatibility of objectivity and engagement is twofold: we can adopt an objective stance towards both our ends and our means.

MORAL OBJECTIVITY

How does objectivity-within-engagement apply to ethics? What is moral objectivity?

When people ask about moral objectivity, or, for that matter, about ethics, they often make the topics sound abstract or arcane. But both topics are very familiar to us, if we stop and think about it. Ethics is lived, reflective engagement with the world. From the days of childhood, our lives have been immersed in talk of good and bad, right and wrong, fair and unfair, kind and cruel, virtuous and shameful, honest and corrupt. So much of what we experience is described in these ethical terms. As adults, we face decisions about the best course of action. We have learned ethical rules; formed ethical beliefs; debated issues ethically; and made ethical decisions. It is not the case that you pick up this book devoid of ethical experience and ask: What is this thing they call ethics and moral objectivity?

Ethics, as a learned, norm-guided response to life, is all around us. It is part of life. The study of ethics does not aim at learning completely new knowledge about a completely new object. Rather, it is the search for a clearer, deeper, and more consistent understanding of what we already know to some extent. To study ethics is to believe that we can improve our values, their justification, and their application to situations. The same holds for moral objectivity. It is a term that refers to something we have done all our lives.

Moral Evaluation: Holism

In chapter 3, we noted how, in the Enlightenment, philosophers defined moral objectivity as the adopting of an impartial perspective on any moral question – asking how an action would affect all parties, or taking up a "common" perspective (a view to the common good). These stances reduced partiality. This stress on the attitude of the moral reasoner links up with my notion of moral objectivity.

Moral objectivity is pragmatic objectivity applied to moral questions about what to do, and how to be engaged. It begins with *caring* about objective moral judgments, and being willing to adopt the objective stance.

The agent adopts the objective stance towards beliefs, proposed actions, and issues in the ethical sphere. The stance applies the four dispositions of pragmatic objectivity to the world of ethical decision-making. The moral reasoner adopts a disposition towards open rationality, towards partial transcendence, towards disinterested truth, and towards intellectual integrity.

Then, the moral reasoner applies the stance to cases by considering the latter in light of the best available standards. Part of these standards are the generic standards outlined above. The moral reasoner attempts to be well grounded in facts, coherent in ideas, and open to the scrutiny of others. The ethical stance also employs domain-specific standards – standards from morality. These standards appear in ethical theories, such as utilitarianism or Kantian deontic ethics. The standards are drawn from the three great areas of ethics: standards of what is good, standards of what is right, and standards of what is virtuous. In many cases, reasoners will weigh standards from all three areas. For example, under the standards of what is right, the reasoner may consider the fair distribution of goods. Under the standards of what is virtuous, he may consider the impact of action on one's character, such as lying about a sexual affair to his wife.

In other works, I have spelled out my own system of standards, having to do with balancing human rights with human flourishing.[33] I will not repeat the details. Nor, for grasping the idea of moral objectivity, is it necessary to do so. It is enough for the reader to understand that there is a pluralism of standards to consider when deciding how to act in a morally objective manner. In ethics, our judgments about what is the good or right thing to do is a matter of normative conceptual schemes. Moreover, the application is holistic, weighing considerations and standards.

Here is an example that calls for holistic moral reasoning of an objective form:

> Suppose that you live with your partner, Ellen, and your mother-in-law, Dorothy, in Vancouver, BC. Several years ago, you invited Dorothy to live with you because, at eighty-seven, she was frail and could not manage her large house. However, after moving in, Dorothy is diagnosed with Alzheimer's disease. As the months go by, Dorothy becomes progressively more difficult to live with, and constantly criticizes Ellen for whatever she does. Ellen starts to develop health problems from the pressure of caring for Dorothy. A physician strongly advises that Ellen, for health reasons, move Dorothy to a nursing home – a move that you and Ellen support. But Dorothy would strongly oppose it. What should you do?

33 Ward, *Global Journalism Ethics*, especially chapters 2 and 3.

Intuitively, most people recognize this as an ethical situation. They don't need a course in ethics to do so. Why? Because we have learned that some problems pose questions that are neither a matter of law nor a matter of self-interest. We realize that people, especially the vulnerable, have rights to be respected. We know we have duties to others. As the main caregivers for Dorothy, you and Ellen have a duty to take Dorothy's interests into account.

Most people would not say that, because this situation is complex, we should therefore not bother thinking it through – checking facts, reviewing options. We need to "do" ethics by balancing factors in a fair frame of mind. You have to balance the health issues (and interests) of Ellen and Dorothy. If ethics was as subjective as some people claim, thinking through the situation could be replaced by arbitrary or subjective methods such as rolling a dice, or acting on how we feel about things, without reasoning. But responsible people do not do this in real life. We assume that thinking ethically is necessary and we hope it can improve our decisions. Pragmatic objectivity in morality will assist us in systematically applying standards in a holistic manner.

Impartiality and Impartialism

It is important not to confuse an appeal to impartial considerations with the doctrine of impartialism in moral theory. In ethics, we are always dealing with partialities and interests. How should we regard our partialities? There are two erroneous views in moral theory on this issue: impartialism and partialism. Impartialism rejects incorporating, balancing, and evaluating partialities. Partialities are seen as sources of bias that should be excluded from fair and objective decision-making. In moral thinking, we should be impartial by rising above selfishness and prudential reasoning to consider what is best for all parties involved. We do not allow our partiality towards our personal interests or friends to prejudice, bias, and thereby taint our reasoning. The mayor of a city, in deciding the location of a new highway, should not choose a location because it directly benefits himself or his political supporters. A judge should not hear a case involving a business partner. Rules against conflicts of interest in government and in the professions is based on the fear that the partialities of officials and professionals may prejudice their judgments on public matters.

Strong partialism is the opposite thesis. It holds that it is not merely psychologically understandable but morally correct to favour one's own in all or most cases. The existence of unethical partialities refutes this generalization.

Yet strong impartialists are also incorrect to argue that the fact that some object is *mine* is not (or never) worthy of consideration.[34] Strong impartialism is a version of objectivity without a human face. It stumbles theoretically because there are many examples in which we *should* include partialities in moral reasoning. How could we exclude the parent's love of (and duty to) their child when we decide if a parent acted properly in saving their child and not others, when several children were drowning in a lake? Similarly, how can we dismiss, *carte blanche*, my patriotic duty to defend my nation from an unjust attack by an aggressive foreign power? Nor is it practically possible to exclude partialities because partialities are literally everywhere in life, creating ethical dilemmas. As Sartre famously put it: Should Pierre stay in France to look after his aging mother or join the Free French in England to fight for the liberation of his country? He must choose between two loyalties: filial loyalty and the preservation of his country.[35]

What ethics needs is not exclusion of the partial viewpoint, but systematic, morally objective evaluation of partialities such as love of family or country, because partialities may influence us for good or for ill, and because, in ethics, we must choose among contending partialities. We cannot rely entirely on "gut feelings" or act on whatever partiality is currently having the greatest emotional impact on us. Instead, we should rationally deliberate in a holistic manner, balancing rival values and principles. The overall task is to determine to what extent partialities should be incorporated into moral reasoning and decision-making.

In ethics we should not try to impose a dualism that separates the partial and impartial, the emotional and the rational. Many of our general principles are about partialities. The fourth biblical commandment to honour one's father and mother is both universal – asking all children to honour their parents – and partial – they should honour *their* parents because they are *their* parents. Also, we can feel an emotional attachment to principle, such as a universal respect for persons as human beings, or a human rights principle, such as a prohibition against torture. Moreover, our commitments to general principles, which restrain narrow partialities, are themselves partialities. A commitment to global equality and to the promotion of humanity at large is a partiality in the sphere of value. These commitments are distinct in being "wider" partialities, involving partialities towards groups that are larger than the citizens of one nation.

34 See Cottingham, "Favouritism and Morality," Singer, "Famine, Affluence, and Morality," and Singer, Cannold, and Kuhse, "William Godwin and the Defense of Impartialist Ethics."

35 Sartre, *Existentialism and Humanism*, 35–6.

Ultimately, the issue for ethics is not how a perfectly impartial attitude can negate a partial attitude. It is not partiality versus impartiality. Rather the issue is how to decide, through careful deliberation, what partialities should be primary in general, and in situations. We should seek ways to rationally incorporate partialities into our ethical thinking by finding ways to evaluate them for ethical weight.

Objectivity without Objects

Readers will note that my conception of moral objectivity does not talk about moral statements corresponding to external moral facts. This takes us to the front door of questions in meta-ethics about realism and anti-realism. I do not want to be deflected from explaining pragmatic objectivity by addressing such deep questions. But I do want to state my position.[36] Facts about the world are important parts of moral reasoning but I do not think that moral statements are descriptions of independently existing moral facts. Ethical judgments are not descriptions of the way the world is. They are proposals about what to do, about what principles should guide the interaction of people. We adopt the objective stance not to know a separate moral reality but to make reasonable practical decisions. Our values and standards refer to things we have found useful and reliable in the past. Our apprehension of value is not the apprehension of some external moral property. Even what we call moral universals – for example, the imperative not to kill – are not metaphysical universals. They are epistemic universals. We propose that a prohibition on killing be a basic rule in our ethical scheme for social interaction.

To call ethical principles "pragmatic proposals" is not to suggest that ethical values are unreal or subjective. As noted earlier, to say that some concept, value, or ontology is indispensable to how we think is a good reason to think of it as real. Putnam argued along these lines that we can have "objectivity without ontology" or without "objects." Beliefs of ethics and beliefs in other areas, such as mathematics, have an objectivity without being about "sublime or intangible" objects, such as "Platonic forms" or abstract entities. We employ many different kinds of discourses "subject to different standards and possessing different sorts of applications."[37]

Holistic evaluation "without objects" can be seen as the search for reflective equilibrium. Rawls thought we should justify principles of justice by finding a balance among beliefs about what is just at various levels, from

36 I have explained my pragmatic view of ethical statements at length in *Radical Media Ethics* and *Global Journalism Ethics*.

37 Putnam, *Ethics without Ontology*, 52–85.

general principles to specific maxims. In constructing a theory of justice, we seek reasonable principles that "match our considered judgments duly pruned and adjusted" and "at all levels of generality."[38] We ask whether the principles "match our considered convictions of justice or extend them in an acceptable way." Under reflective equilibrium, "no one level, say of abstract principle or that of particular judgments in particular cases, is viewed as foundational. They all may have an initial credibility."[39]

Applied to ethics in general, reflective equilibrium means we evaluate an ethical rule by asking a series of questions. Does it fit with our intuitions about these cases? Does the rule fit with basic ethical principles? Where there is a lack of fit, we alter our intuitions or principles until we achieve a new equilibrium in our ethical conceptual scheme. Ethical construction and evaluation is this activity of mutual adjustment of principles, rules, facts, and judgments. Any concept or rule is interpreted and evaluated holistically in terms of its overall fit with a conceptual scheme.[40]

Nussbaum notes that Rawls' ideas on justification are "holistic" and "internal."[41] Reflective equilibrium presumes that we are "starting in the middle" of an imperfect conceptual scheme with inevitable tensions between levels and with problems in the application of principles. The scheme provides "provisional fixed points," such as rejecting racial intolerance, for the start of reflection. There are judgments, concepts, and principles that we feel are basic and sound *at this point of time*. However, such convictions are fallible, and we would be prepared to change them if confronted with a strong counterargument.

Reflective equilibrium can be extended to describe the process by which we evaluate our conceptual systems at large. As Elgin states: "A system of considered judgments in reflective equilibrium is neither absolute nor arbitrary: not absolute, for it is fallible, revisable, revocable; not arbitrary, for it is tethered to antecedent commitments. Such a system neither is nor purports to be a distortion-free reflection of a mind-independent reality. Nor is it merely an expression of our beliefs. It is rather a tool for the advancement of our understanding."[42]

38 Rawls, *A Theory of Justice*, 19.

39 Rawls, *Political Liberalism*, 8n8.

40 Ibid., 8, 20, 89–90. Rawls advocated constructivism in ethical theory. He believed that, since humans cannot agree on a metaphysical basis for ethics, they must construct the most plausible set of ethical principles through impartial and reasonable deliberation. Valid ethical principles are the "outcome of a certain procedure of construction."

41 Nussbaum, *Frontiers of Justice*, 299–300.

42 Elgin, *Between the Absolute and the Arbitrary*, 198.

CONCLUSION: THIRTEEN THESES

After two chapters, we come to the end of my exposition of objectivity with a human face as an objectivity *in situ* and an objectivity within engagement. In the rest of the book, I show how these theories explain objectively engaged journalism.

Since we have traversed a lot of philosophical territory, here is a list of the main points – thirteen theses – made over the last two chapters.

Objectivity has a human face. There is no eliminating human factors from inquiry or the evaluation of inquiry.

Objectivity in situ *is grounded in a naturalistic and pragmatic worldview, as a starting point for theorizing. Evaluation is the capacity of an agent, where the key notions are pragmatic inquiry, engagement, and practice.*

Objectivity is a natural cognitive desire to evaluate beliefs and conduct, an evaluation shaped by human interests and conceptual schemes. Knowledge and objectivity reflect a partial, but never absolute, transcendence of one's existing beliefs and context. Partial transcendence is due to the fact that the mind is incarnate.

Objectivity is inherently social. Objectivity is not about going "my own way" in terms of belief and evaluation, but asking what other reasonable people would think in this circumstance.

Knowledge is an interpretive achievement due to the necessary mediation of conceptual schemes. There is no direct or metaphysically objective contact with Reality as it is.

Objectivity is not grounded in a narrow point of contact with the world. It is grounded in a complex cognitive access to the world. Cognition, experience, and rationality are "wide" and holistic. Holistic cognition defeats dualisms and reductionisms.

Rationality and objectivity are value-laden and humane, depending ultimately on a conception of the human good. Objectivity is a property of human agents, of being objective. Objectivity is a virtue: a matter of human will and character.

Pragmatic inquiry is based on an imperfectionist epistemology whose central notions are fallibilism, cognitive relativity, and pragmatic realism.

Pragmatic objectivity is the use of a holistic stance and set of standards to test interpretations that are themselves holistic constructions. Objectivity consists of generic and domain-specific standards for varied applications.

Objectivity and engagement are compatible because the former refers to methods and evaluative stances, while the latter refers to goals. Objectivity can evaluate both means and goals.

Ethics is a form of social engagement, using practical rationality.

Moral objectivity, like all objectivity, consists of the objective stance and the application of standards – epistemic and moral – to issues and situations. Moral objectivity is evaluation of judgments about what to do, in terms of standards about what is good, right, and virtuous.

Moral judgments can be objective without being about external objects or independently existing moral facts in nature.

7

Objectively Engaged Journalism

Accordingly, you are interpreters of interpreters?

Socrates to Ion, expositor of Homer, in Plato, *Ion*, 221 (535a)

The rest of this book applies concepts from previous chapters to journalism.

I use the philosophy of objective engagement to construct a philosophy of objectively engaged journalism. I argue that the aim of this journalism is engagement for global, egalitarian democracy and human flourishing. Its method is pragmatic objectivity. It tests journalism inquiry by adopting the objective stance and standards specific to journalism.

In this chapter I sketch the rise of news objectivity and explain its dualisms. I say why we should overcome traditional ways of doing journalism ethics. I describe objectively engaged journalism.

JOURNALISM ETHICS

Journalism ethics is a species of applied ethics, as defined in chapter 1. It examines the norms of a practice. Put simply, journalism ethics asks what journalists and news organizations should do, given their role in society. More particularly, journalism ethics is the study of principles which constitute codes of journalism ethics, worldwide. Traditionally, the general principles of journalism have included such familiar notions as impartiality (or objectivity), truth-telling, minimizing harm, promise-keeping, accuracy, verifying information, and serving the public. Under these principles fall a large number of specific norms and protocols for dealing with recurring situations, such as the use of deceptive techniques to obtain information. Traditionally, the main problem areas have included editorial independence, verification, anonymous sources, fabrication of sources, and the use of graphic or altered images. The problems of journalism ethics can be divided into "micro" and "macro" problems. Micro problems concern what individual journalists should do in particular situations, for example, whether to publish the name of a victim of sexual assault. Macro problems concern such issues as how well media systems inform the public and who owns the media.

A common misunderstanding needs to be avoided: Journalism ethics is not identical with the promotion of a free news media. That being said, despite its restraining rules, journalism ethics is not "against" media freedom either. Journalism ethics recognizes freedom of media as a central but not absolute (or sole) value. Journalism ethics begins when we concern ourselves with the *responsible* use of the freedom to publish, in any form or context. This involves, in specific situations, weighing freedom with other values such as minimizing harm and justice. Since journalism has a significant impact on persons and societies, journalists cannot escape responsibilities and the expectations of their publics.

However, what "responsible journalism" means varies. Among media cultures globally, the aims and principles of responsible practice both overlap and diverge. Some principles are shared, such as truth-seeking, and others are not, such as objectivity. Some cultures value an aggressive watchdog journalism to expose official wrongdoing; other cultures stress the role of media in maintaining social solidarity.

Ethical Frameworks

No matter what form of journalism is in question, its ethic is typically a framework of principles, norms, and specific protocols. Frameworks are moral systems. They exist because values travel in groups, even if they come into tension along the way. Humans do not usually live their lives by following one principle here and another principle there. They consider how the principles are related, and which principles are more important than others.

The history of ethics is populated by moral systems. There is the Bible's Ten Commandments, the morality of Buddhism, the values of ethical egoism, and the morality of utilitarianism. We use metaphors to explain these systems. We say the systems are moral "perspectives," using a term from perception where the position of the observer affects the way objects are seen. "Frameworks" is a metaphorical extension of the idea of a window frame. A window frame determines what you see and how you see it. Frameworks influence how we think about ethical issues; they shape our response to problems in the moral landscape.

There are advantages to doing ethics with frameworks. They remind us that there may be many values at stake in a situation. A framework suits ethics because ethical issues are not one-dimension situations where the question is simply whether a principle applies or not. If we do ethics by focusing on individual and separate values – say we focus only on freedom of expression – then we are likely to neglect other concerns, such as minimizing the harm caused by that freedom. Also, a framework encourages consistency. We employ similar methods and values across many situations.

Of course, having a framework does not mean that one has the best framework. Frameworks should be evaluated.[1] The rules of a framework may be outdated or articulated improperly. Frameworks can be internally inconsistent, marred by contradictions among principles. Frameworks may fail to say anything helpful about a range of new problems.

A framework is typically spelled out in a code of ethics. A framework for a practice like journalism consists of three components:

A moral interpretation of practice: A moral interpretation is a broad conception of the ethics of one's practice – its purposes, duties, and freedoms. To ethically interpret a practice is to explain the point of the practice in ideal terms. The point consists of the ethical and social aims of the practice, for example, the way that law aims at justice, and journalism aims at enabling a democratic public. As Dworking states: "A participant interpreting a social practice … proposes a value for the practice by describing some scheme of interests or goals or principles the practice can be taken to serve or express or exemplify."[2] The moral interpretation can be a "press" philosophy.[3] Press philosophies are usually associated with political and social views, such as the liberal democratic view of media or the Marxist (or socialist) theory of the press.[4]

A meta-ethic: Embedded in any journalism framework is a meta-ethic that transcends press philosophies or moral interpretations. A meta-ethic contains several things: (1) a conception of the human good – what constitutes a flourishing human existence; (2) a consistent social and political philosophy of what constitutes a good and just society; (3) a theory about the nature and purpose of ethics; and (4) epistemic presumptions about the nature of ethical claims, their truth, objectivity, and justification. This meta-ethic is not spelled out in a code of ethics.

A set of principles and norms for practice: A framework contains a network of ethical principles and norms, from the general to the particular, which promote the point of the practice. This structure of values is worked up with a concrete application in mind – to guide journalists in making daily editorial decisions. Frameworks are expressed in codes of ethics, such as the codes of the aforementioned Society of Professional Journalists and

1 I provide evaluative criteria in my *Global Journalism Ethics*, 69–72.

2 Dworkin, *Law's Empire*, 52.

3 See Siebert, *Four Theories of the Press.*

4 See Christians et al., *Normative Theories of the Media.*

the Canadian Association of Journalists (CAJ).[5] Codes are not as general as frameworks. A framework for journalism, for instance, can be expressed in various ways by codes for print, broadcast, and online journalism.

ORIGINS OF JOURNALISM ETHICS

Five Ethical Revolutions

The history of Western journalism can be divided into two parts: (1) a pre-digital, non-global journalism from the seventeeth century onward, whose modern form is professional mainstream journalism, and (2) a digital, global journalism, from the late twentieth century to today, which includes professional and non-professional journalism. The history of journalism ethics exhibits a similar division, between a pre-digital, non-global ethics for professional journalism, and an emerging, digital, global ethics for a news media that is professional and non-professional.

The history of journalism ethics has five stages.[6] The first stage was the invention of an ethical discourse for journalism as it emerged in Western Europe during the sixteenth and seventeenth centuries. Gutenberg's press in the mid-fifteenth century gave birth to printer-editors who created a periodic news press of "newssheets" and "newsbooks" under state control. Despite the primitive nature of newsgathering, and the partisan nature of their times, editors assured readers that they printed the impartial truth based on "matters of fact."

The second stage was the creation of a "public ethic" as the creed for the growing newspaper press of the Enlightenment public sphere. Journalists claimed to be tribunes of the public, protecting their liberty against government. They advocated reform and eventually revolution. By the end of the eighteenth century, the press was a socially recognized institution, a power to be praised or feared, with guarantees of freedom in the post-revolutionary constitutions of America and France. This public ethic was the basis for the idea of a Fourth Estate – the press as one of the governing institutions of society.

The third stage was the evolution of the idea of a Fourth Estate into the liberal theory of the press, which took place during the nineteenth century. Liberal theory began as a libertarianism with the premise that a free and

5 For the code of the Society of Professional Journalists, see https://www.spj.org/ethicscode.asp. For the code of the Canadian Association of Journalists (CAJ), see http://www.caj.ca/ethics-guidelines.

6 See Ward, *The Invention of Journalism.*

independent press was necessary for the protection of the liberties of the public and the promotion of liberal reform.

The fourth stage was the simultaneous development *and* criticism of this liberal doctrine, across the twentieth century. Both the development and the criticism were responses to deficiencies in the liberal model. The "developers" were journalists and ethicists who constructed a professional ethics of objective journalism. Developers thought that adherence to fact and impartiality would restrain a free press that was increasingly sensational (or "yellow") and dominated by business interests.[7] The "critics" were journalists who rejected the objective model and practised interpretive, investigative, and activist forms of journalism.[8] Meanwhile, communitarian ethics, with its stress on shared values, and feminist ethics, with its stress on care and emotion, provided new perspectives on the aims of journalism.[9] By the late 1900s, the objective professional model was under attack, despite improvements.

The fifth stage is the current state of journalism ethics caused by a media revolution – a decline in the professional objective model and a transition to an ethics for digital, global media.

Before Objectivity: Objectivism and Reformism

Across these stages, there have been two traditions of importance to objectivity in journalism. They are what I call objectivism and reformism.

Objectivism and reformism are moral interpretations of the point of journalism. For objectivism, the journalist is an observer of the world who values facts. On this view, journalism plays an important part in society – perhaps its greatest part – by chronicling events accurately and comprehensively. The news function of journalism is paramount for democracy. Decision-making, judging, and analyzing depends on a robust source of reliable information. Objectivism is not the professional doctrine of objectivity. Before professional objectivity there was objectivism, a non-dualistic, less strident form of objectivity, a "proto-objectivity."[10] Professional objectivity was a later development.

Reformism holds that journalism plays an important part in society – perhaps its greatest part – by interpreting events and advocating reform.

7 Baldasty, *The Commercialization of the News in the Nineteenth Century*; Campbell, *Yellow Journalism*.

8 Miraldi, *Muckraking and Objectivity*.

9 Gilligan, *In a Different Voice*.

10 As I showed in *The Invention of Journalism Ethics*, the roots of journalistic objectivity go back to the seventeeth century.

Sharp-minded political and social analysis is important. The journalist is an interpreter and actor in the world, who often becomes an opinion writer, or reformer. Journalism's function includes but is not limited to reporting what other people do or say. Journalists in the reformist tradition write on events from some perspective; they favour some interpretation of the issues; they argue that some line of reform is required; and they may join forces with other groups seeking reform. They are among the participants arguing, interpreting, and contending in the public sphere.

Today, we are accustomed to separating the functions of chronicling and reforming. But prior to the late 1800s, most journalists and newspapers did not see them as opposite sets of norms. Journalists were both chroniclers *and* interpreters. The purpose of searching for facts is to feed interpretation, and interpretation would lack purpose if it did not support some goal. One and the same journalist (and newsroom) can report and opine. As far back as the seventeeth-century news books, editors placed strong political commentary next to news items. News items contained interpretation and partisanship; and opinion pieces appealed to matters of fact. The "thundering" editorials of the *Times of London* in the eighteenth century, when the paper was the epitome of an elite liberal publication, relied on the paper's devotion to its reporting function, including foreign reporting.

In the late nineteenth century, a mass commercial press took up news reporting as its raison d'etre, and espoused a hearty empiricism when it came to reporting on events in the world. But this empiricism was still not news objectivity. How, then, did news objectivity arise, and how was it distinct from the prior objectivism and empiricism?

Emergence of a Professional Ethic

Before there was professional media ethics, there was professional journalism ethics. Journalists at newspapers and magazines, working in a pre-digital media era, created their own ethics in the form of rules for publication, varying from one newsroom to the next. Later, as other forms of media developed, "media ethics" was coined to refer collectively to the norms of professional media practice. Media ethics referred to the ethics of journalism, advertising, marketing, and public relations. Journalism ethics came to be a branch of media ethics.

A craft-wide journalism ethics began to appear as journalists in the US and elsewhere established professional associations.[11] The associations constructed codes of ethics with principles that are still familiar to us, such as

11 See ibid. for details of this emergence.

the principles of objectivity, truth-telling, and editorial independence. The new professional codes were intended to apply *across* different types of newsroom and journalism. In the US, state-wide codes of ethics were followed by national ones, first for newspaper journalists and then for broadcasters.

According to these codes, newsroom reporters were to apply the principle of objectivity in a strong and narrow manner, unlike the columnists and editorial writers who commented on the reporter's facts. It was news objectivity. Objectivity was more than one principle among many. It was the supreme principle of responsible journalism.

Why did this remarkable emergence of a craft-wide ethic occur? Journalists had started to work in the large newsrooms of the mass commercial press. They claimed professional status. Professionalism would raise the social status of journalists, whose members were increasingly well educated. But it was more than that. Professionalism was meant to assure a skeptical public that journalists would use their power to publish responsibly. Professionals, it was argued, had an overriding and distinct duty to serve the public. Serving the public interest trumped serving one's own interest and those of specific groups. The trades and crafts, it was assumed, had little public-interest rationale. Practitioners of the trades and crafts served the private needs of individuals, not society at large. The practitioners of trades and crafts entered into economic contracts with clients without reference to larger public concerns. In contrast, professional soldiers, doctors, and then journalists defined their duties in terms of public service. The professionalism of this era emphasized social responsibility and objectivity because, as it was increasingly recognized, these professionals receive sensitive information from clients and therefore could do great harm, if they were not ethical. Hence, licensing and mechanisms of self-regulation seemed appropriate for many professions.

In journalism, the stress on responsibility was due to the development of a powerful mass commercial press. This press came to enjoy a virtual monopoly on the provision of news, analysis, and advertising to the public. The public became passive consumers of information dependent on data provided by a professional class of journalists employed by large news organizations. In the early 1900s, and beyond, this dependency raised public concern about the reliability of this mediating class of news workers. Did the press really serve the public or did it advance its own interests? Did it tell the truth or was it biased? Amid this concern, governments threatened draconian press laws. Professional journalism ethics was a conscious attempt to assure the public and government that they could trust the press to serve the public first. It was hoped that a professional attitude among journalists would run counter to the growing power of the press and the worrisome influence of press barons, newspaper syndicates, and business on reporting.

Serving the public as information mediators required journalists to embrace a distinct set of principles. One was a professional duty to act as editorial gatekeepers of what should be published. Journalists should make sure their stories were accurate, and they should verify claims. They should be impartial of mind, independent in spirit, and objective in reporting. News should be separated from opinion. This self-imposed ethics, supported by accountability structures such as press councils and readers' ombudsmen, would constitute the self-regulation of journalism.

In this manner, journalism ethics became the professionally mandated ethics of an important social practice, rather than the personal and idiosyncratic values of individual journalists or their news outlets. Times had changed. In a society dependent informationally on journalism, many journalists accepted a collective responsibility and, together, endorsed the principles of truth-seeking, minimizing harm, objectivity, and accountability.

Articulating Objectivity

The rise of news agencies (sometimes called, anachronistically, "wire services") was instrumental in creating the genre of objective reporting. Since a given agency served multiple papers of different political persuasions, they had good reason to develop an objective reporting style.[12] In 1866, Lawrence Gobright of the Associated Press in Washington, DC, explained his factual news-agency style: "My business is merely to communicate facts. My instructions do not allow me to make any comments upon the facts which I communicate ... My dispatches are merely dry matters of fact and detail." This is an early and clear statement of strict news objectivity.

After the First World War, objectivity arrived as a principle. It occurred in numerous press codes, articles, and textbooks. One of its earliest known uses appears in Charles G. Ross's *The Writing of News*, published in 1911: "News writing is objective to the last degree in the sense that the writer is not allowed to 'editorialize.'" Ross told journalists to "keep yourself out of the story."

The formal recognition of objectivity as a fundamental principle goes back to the formulation of two major statements about ethics: the 1923 code of the American Society of News Editors (ASNE) and the 1926 code of Sigma Delta Chi, forerunner of the Society of Professional Journalists.

12 Citations for the quotes in this section can be found in ibid., chapters 6 and 7.

Both documents enshrined objectivity as a canon of journalism and drew the distinctions that define the professional framework. The ASNE's code – the first national code – stressed responsibility, freedom of the press, independence, truthfulness, impartiality, and decency. Anything less than an objective report was "subversive of a fundamental principle of the profession." Impartiality meant a "clear distinction between news reports and expressions of opinion." Objectivity was second only to truthfulness in the code of Sigma Delta Chi (1926). Its first two principles were: "Truth is our ultimate goal," and "Objectivity in reporting the news is another goal, which serves as a mark of an experienced professional. It is a standard of performance toward which we strive. We honour those who achieve it."

The principle of objectivity was so widespread in mainstream journalism by the 1930s that it played a role in labour disputes. Editors opposed unionization for journalists on the grounds that journalists could not be objective if they were members of trade unions. Philosophically, influential journalists such as Walter Lippmann argued that democracy needed professional journalists who provided objective information. Objectivity reached its zenith in the 1940s and 1950s. In 1949, Herbert Brucker, journalist and freedom of information advocate, saluted objective reporting as one of the "outstanding achievements" of the American newspaper."

What was new about the professional objective ethic?

The difference was the decision to introduce uncompromising dualisms at every turn in journalism ethics. As mentioned above, for most of journalism's history, there was no attempt to make an absolute distinction between reporting and commenting. So it was a curious but monumental development when, in the late 1800s and early 1900s, journalists turned the cooperating traditions of objectivism and reformism into polar opposites.

The objective framework required a stricter approach to reporting than objectivism and empiricism. It was stricter in requiring the reporter to suppress their penchant to judge, to adopt a studied neutrality. It was stricter by requiring reporters to report *only* the facts. It was stricter in requiring reporters to closely adhere to many rules for constructing stories. And it was stricter in drawing hard lines between activities that once were separated by soft and flexible lines: reporting versus interpretation; neutrality versus engagement; fact versus value; objectivity versus subjectivity. The reporting of the nineteenth century was a rough-and-ready empiricism, characterized by a "veneration of the fact."[13] Yet, for all its talk of fact, the journalism still contained healthy doses of "colour," sensationalism, and interpretation.

13 Stephens, *A History of the News*, 244.

Editors did talk about the need for reporters to restrain their partisanship. But for most of the century, impartiality had meant reducing, not eliminating, bias in political coverage. In contrast, the twentieth-century editors who enforced the professional model banned *all* comment or interpretation. To "editorialize" was the reporter's mortal sin. Objectivity was a policing action against the desire to interpret or campaign. News did not differ from opinion by having less interpretation or comment. It was different because it had *no* interpretation or opinion. Or so it was claimed. The nineteenth-century idea of a healthy independence of journalists from sources was ratcheted up to become the austere ideal of complete neutrality. The ideal was complete detachment from events, like Pythagoras's philosophical spectator at the Olympic Games. Everything in the newspaper that was not a news report lacked objectivity because it went beyond facts into the arena of opinion, values, and interests. Journalists transformed their informal nineteenth-century empiricism into a strict methodological empiricism based on dualisms of fact and value, fact and interpretation.

It took an impressive convergence of factors to encourage journalists to develop a strict method of reporting that drained stories of personal touches and interpretation, an objectivity without a human face. Did journalist invent this objectivity? No, they did not. The main ideas came from two areas: (1) objectivity of fact, especially positivism; and (2) the prevailing conception of professionalism. As explained in previous chapters, positivism had already popularized neutrality and the reporting of facts, explained in dualistic terms. The rising professionalism of the day contained a strong trace of positivism. Professionalism bequeathed to journalists, as they formulated their codes, the idea that a professional is disinterested, neutral, and bases judgments on facts; a professional's primary commitment is to serve the common good, rather than partisan interests. Together, positivism and professionalism provided the conceptual resources by which to construct objectivity for professional journalism. Ironically, news objectivity emerged at a time when journalists were never more active in their work – interpreting and investigating.

A KNOT OF DUALISMS

Such were the origins of journalism objectivity. It is time to switch from history to analysis, to explain in more detail the dualisms. Because we have already examined these dualisms in philosophy and culture, I can focus not on explaining the dualisms per se but on how they were interpreted in journalism. Sometimes, these dualisms strike me as the "antinomies" of journalism ethics, to echo Kant's famous description of the antinomies of pure reason.[14] Journalists, when discussing their ethics, display what Putnam called the "recoil" phenomenon – or shifting from one side of a dualism to the other side. For example, we reject objectivity only to end up with subjectivity.[15] However, I think the antinomies of journalistic thinking and the tendency to recoil can be avoided.

Four forms of cognitive dualism stand behind the codes of ethics shaped by the traditional professional framework, and they reflect the dualisms of logical positivism, discussed earlier. There is the overarching "master" dualism of objectivity and subjectivity. This dualism explains the difference between objective and the subjective journalism. The other three dualisms are sub-dualisms of the objective-subjective division. I call the sub-dualisms "domains of dualism" since each sub-dualism applies to an aspect or domain of journalism.

The domains are dualisms of (a) attitude, (b) faculty, and (c) content. The domain of attitude uses dualisms to describe the correct psychological attitude of the inquiring journalist toward the subject matter and sources of stories. The domain of faculty uses dualisms to describe the faculties and methods to use when doing journalism. The domain of content focuses on the "product" of inquiry, the stories themselves. It uses dualisms to describe what content is permissible, if a story is to be a work of objective journalism. Taken together, these conceptions form a dualistic epistemology for journalism.

Master Dualism: Objectivity-Subjectivity

The traditional professional framework views the objective-subjective distinction as an antagonistic dualism.

The only objective criteria for testing stories are empirical facts. The facts of the senses are the objective factor in journalistic cognition. Other factors are subjective. "Subjective" means not only that they originate in the subject who is doing the inquiry, but also that they may bias his thinking. Where journalists depart from facts, they expose their cognizing to the error-inducing and self-interested forces of desire, emotion, wishful thinking, and speculation. The journalistic inquirer is a psychological battleground between objective and subjective forces.

14 Kant, *Critique of Pure Reason*, 471–95. Kant believed that reason leads to certain types of contradiction when it tries to grasp reality as it is, e.g., is the universe infinite or bounded? Are human free or determined? The questions exceed experience. Reason is "stuck" between the terms of a dualism, both of which seem equally rational to believe.

15 Putnam, "Sense, Non-Sense and the Senses," 446.

This dualism should sound familiar to the reader, since it is an extension of the antagonistic dualisms of fact and interpretation, and fact and value. An everyday, useful distinction in journalism between reports that are more or less objective and subjective is turned into a philosophical dualism. To be objective in journalism is to privilege one form of inquiry and testing – fact-gathering and testing – and to exclude other forms, such as valuing the facts, responding emotionally to states of affairs, and interpreting the meaning of a phenomenon. This is the philosophy behind the famous slogans of the framework: reporters must "take themselves out of the story," "never editorialize," and report "just the facts."

Like all dualisms, journalism's master dualism recognizes no degrees of being objective. No continuum runs from strong subjectivity to strong subjectivity, from fact to value, from observing to interpreting. A belief or report is either objective or subjective, the way one is either alive or dead. The things that are objective and subjective fall cleanly into two separate categories. There is a dualistic gulf between objective and subjective reports.

Domain of Attitude: Neutrality

The master dualism contains a dualism of attitude. It is a dualism between being neutral and being engaged, as discussed in chapter 6. Neutrality, was, and is, an essential part of the journalism profession's culture, inculcated as one enters into practice.

Neutrality in journalism requires non-involvement with groups and a disengagement from advocacy. A journalist should restrain emotion and decline judgment. Neutrality is a psychological attitude that one uses to describe fact; it *promotes* a pure factual objectivity in reports. The reporter stands apart from the contending opinions of rival groups and relates what each group has to say. Journalistic neutrality is the unbiased recording of the biases of others. Objective reporting eliminates bias through the repression of the reporter's interpretation, perspectives, ideologies, interests, or values.

Journalists and citizens sometimes use the values of professional objective reporting (e.g., accuracy and fairness) to evaluate other forms of journalism, such as columns or political analysis. Media commentators are criticized for being overtly biased; they ignore contrary facts and misrepresent opposing interpretations. Their interpretations lack fairness or balance. These criticisms imply that there is such a thing as objective *journalism*, not only objective reporting.

This dualism of attitude had implications for the comportment of journalists when reporting to the public. Neutral reporters should act, talk, and report with the neutrality and sobriety of a contract mediator. Nothing in one's conduct – say, shedding tears or showing anger – should indicate the reporter's personal reaction. Only in rare cases are journalists "forgiven" for showing their emotions. When anchor Walter Cronkite choked up as he announced the assassination of John F. Kennedy in Dallas, or described his pride and joy at the American moon landing, the expression of emotion and partiality in an otherwise objective and neutral news anchor was considered understandable and appropriate. But such cases were to be exceptions to the rules of neutrality and objectivity in the television journalism of that era. In the 1900s, many newspapers and news agencies did not think reporters should get bylines on their stories because *who* wrote it was irrelevant to the news report. Facts about the reporter – his name or other details – never influenced the report, so why mention such details? Theoretically at least, the report could be written by any objective reporter, or affirmed as true and accurate by any objective person. Objectivity did not wear a human face.

This concern for the biasing influence of emotion, viewed as noncognitive responses to events, caused journalists to worry if they felt themselves identifying with story subjects, for instance by feeling empathy for a minority's plight in society. Today, journalism ethics textbooks still discuss a type of situation that challenges neutrality: situations where reporters are reporting on a human disaster and feel torn between reporting the suffering or helping the afflicted. It is called the problem of "report or help," and is a frequent topic for classes in photojournalism. Such a discussion would be not so prominent unless journalists assumed that neutrality was a norm for reporting.

Neutral reporters maintain editorial independence by keeping a "distance" from sources and story subjects who may seek to influence reporters through bribes and other benefits. There still are news organizations that admonish their journalists to accept literally *nothing* of value from sources, including a cup of coffee. In political coverage, the framework frowns on reporters who are members of the groups they report on, or who support the advocacy of groups by joining their marches or signing their petitions. Some journalists think that neutrality prevents them from voting in elections. Neutrality is an all-or-nothing affair.

Domain of Faculty

Dualism in the domain of faculty is a dualistic understanding of how we should use our faculties in understanding and acting in the world. In journalism, dualisms of faculty originated in the ambient culture. As explained earlier, dualisms between faculties are part and parcel of Western history. We find hierarchies, tensions, and oppositions between faculties in the long tradition of faculty psychology, which stretches from Plato and Locke to Gall and contemporary philosophers such as Jerry Fodor.[16] The dualisms of faculty that influenced journalism objectivity were the aforementioned dualisms of observation and interpretation (and theorizing), and factual describing and valuing.

Observation-Interpretation: Journalistic objectivity adopted the positivistic dualism between uninterpreted observation of fact and interpretations of fact. Facts in journalistic reports were to be scrubbed clean of the subjective acts of interpretation and theorizing. This presumes that we have a faculty of observation that is encapsulated and independent of other faculties.

According to the professional framework, objective journalists restrict themselves to the exercise of one, encapsulated faculty: the capacity to observe (and report) fact. The realm of observable fact in journalism includes: (a) directly perceived fact (e.g., observing an event, listening to a news conference, or recording what a spokesmen has to say); (b) official records and written documents (e.g., correspondence by a politician that shows his knowledge of a scandal); (c) claims verified carefully by using a number of reliable sources and factual documents; (d) scientific studies that establish certain things as facts (e.g., that vaccines are safe for young children, PTSD increases the likelihood of job burnout, and so on). Objective journalists stick close to the shoreline of facts. They do not venture out into the roiling sea of opinion.

Factual-Evaluative judgment: The second dualism of faculty amounts to the directive that journalists should avoid embellishing their factual reports with evaluations of the event covered and the views expressed by parties to the event. To include evaluations would violate neutrality, and it would incorporate a subjective element into reports. The good objective journalist follows the prescriptions of the dualisms of fact-interpretation and fact-value.

Domain of Content

The dualisms of attitude and faculty determine how journalists should view themselves and how they approach their work. But what about the results of such work? What do objective stories look like? What language do they use or avoid? Here, again, dualism is dominant. How do objective narratives display commitments to factuality, neutrality, observability, and avoidance

16 Fodor, *The Modularity of Mind*, 1. He defines faculty psychology as the view that we must postulate many discrete and separate kinds of psychological mechanisms to explain our mental life, from sensation, perception, learning, and remembering to volition, cognition, and language.

of value judgments? Practically, one honours those dualisms through *elimination* and *replacement.* The objective news reporter eliminates forms of expression that express a personal view, interpretation, or evaluative judgment. She replaces them with more neutral words.

How did this come about, historically? About a century ago, reporters for news agencies and the new "objective" newspapers constructed a genre for objective reporting. Rules and formats for constructing stories were introduced. For example, new agencies developed the "inverted pyramid" structure for conveying quickly the essential facts surrounding an event.[17] Story construction involved the avoidance of the use of the first-person pronoun by the reporter. Reporters should expunge the "I" in describing what they observed, never saying "I saw this" or "I think this." Also, reports must balance viewpoints, giving equal emphasis to opposing sides. Objective content required clear labelling of articles as opinion, and publishing opinion articles together in separate places in the newspaper, that is, the "opinion pages."

Cautious description was required. Opinions, of course, were to be attributed to others. But more than that, journalists were to be careful about attributing states of mind to people – since such attribution was difficult to prove from observable facts. Rather than say the prime minister *avoided* journalists by leaving through a side door, the objective report says the prime minister left the event *without meeting* with reporters; rather than say the police chief was *incensed* at the reporter's question about his expense account, the objective report says that the police chief *appeared to be upset* at the question. Rather than say the government's economic policy is a disaster, the objective report attributes that opinion to an expert.

In summary, the master dualism of objectivity-subjectivity was composed of the sub-dualisms of neutrality-engagement, fact and interpretation, and fact and value. This led to restrictive conventions on how to write reports. News objectivity favoured factual observation, neutrality, detachment, control of emotions, and a repression of personal attachments. News objectivity did not favour emotion, feeling, desiring and valuing, and claims based on personal insight, intuition, inspiration, or vision.

According to this view, what constitutes subjective journalism? Almost any story that goes beyond the strict limits laid down by the dualisms: interpretive and advocacy journalism, along with opinion-writing such as editorials and columns.

17 This structure placed the most important facts at the beginning of a story. Details came later.

Overcoming Dualism

I have provided evidence for the claim that the objective professional model was based on cognitive dualisms that define good practice. Today, in an era when many journalists dismiss objectivity, these dualisms continue to lurk below the surface of discussions. Critics of journalism presume that the dualisms are essential features of journalism objectivity, and therefore use it to reject objectivity per se. Replies to critics rely on the dualisms, citing neutrality or claiming that the reporting of facts is the quintessence of responsible journalism.

Moreover, when new issues arise, journalists return to the old dualistic categories to debate the way forward. For example, recent debates about "fakes news" in media, and how to cover populist leaders, have divided journalists into two camps. One camp says that current trends show the futility of sticking to a neutral, "facts only" journalism. Journalists should be activists and oppose these developments. A second camp says that current issues only show why journalists need to maintain, or return to, reporting facts, and exposing the misuse of facts by others. Both camps presume that the choice is between maintaining or abandoning a dualistic conception of journalism.

The trajectory of this book has been to argue that neither dualistic objectivity nor the rejection of objectivity is necessary, or desirable. Appealing to dualisms is a dubious way of trying to shore up objectivity. Instead, we overcome dualism by adopting a holistic view of journalist cognition and endorsing a different view of the role of journalists – different from that of the neutral stenographer of fact. I propose that we see the journalist as objectively engaged.

DEMOCRATICALLY ENGAGED JOURNALISM

Journalists as Engaged Interpreters

In chapter 6, I argued that we can coherently speak of impartiality and engagement as self-supportive aspects of good inquiry. This means thinking of journalism as objective engagement.

Journalists should not strive to be neutral. Even where journalists trumpet their neutrality, they deceive themselves. The idea that journalists lack goals or never pursue social causes is contradicted by practice. Competitions for journalism awards and many codes of ethics appeal to the social goals of journalism: to serve a public, to give voice to the powerless, to reveal wrongdoing and injustice, to unearth the truth about some person or agency that lies and conceals facts. Journalists, whether they realize it or not, are interpreters of events. They do not report only a predetermined set of facts. They interpret events according to their conceptual schemes. They use their notion of what constitutes a fact. Even basic news stories include some interpretation of the event. The reporter decides on the news angle and chooses the facts and sources for inclusion in the story.

Saving a Dualism?

There is a form of journalism, called "interpretive journalism," that historically has not sought to deny a dualism of fact and interpretation. Instead, it confines interpretation by making it part of a carefully controlled form of journalism, or a clear, identifiable part of a story. For example, journalists talk about places in a story where they use interpretation, inserting "interpretive passages" within a story. The passages explain the import of a new government policy or scientific discovery. But the report, as a whole, is not labelled an interpretation. In fact, talk of interpretive passages presumes dualism – that what the reporter is doing in the rest of the story is *not* interpreting, but fact-stating.

However, there is a stronger use of "interpretation" within the professional model. Journalists brand as interpretive journalism reports where interpretation is explicit and plays a major role in the story. The phrase "interpretive journalism" came into use in the early 1900s as reporters began to cover complex events, from the First and Second World War to the Great Depression. Many journalists felt that the public needed more than a dry inventory of official facts. They needed to be given the meaning of events. To give the meaning was to engage in interpretation: saying what might follow from an arms treaty, or the meaning behind an unscheduled meeting between the president of the United States and the prime minister of Canada. In 1923, Henry Luce established his American media empire by creating the interpretive news magazine *Time*. The secret of *Time*'s early success was not its objective reporting. In fact, at the start, *Time* did not employ reporters. Instead, editors wrote concise interpretations of news.[18]

The first major textbook on interpretive journalism was MacDougall's *Interpretive Reporting*. The history of the book, over many editions, traces the growing recognition among journalists that the "just the facts" professional model had to be supplemented by interpretation, which provided the context for facts. When it was first published in 1932, the book was titled *Reporting for Beginners*. But, in 1938, the book was renamed to address the growing interpretive trend in journalism. Between 1938 and 1987,

18 Ward, *The Invention of Journalism Ethics*, 256–7.

Interpretive Journalism went through nine editions. The book argues that successful modern journalists need to be capable of more than "routine coverage." They must be able to "intelligently interpret as well as simply report what is going on." An event is understood as part of a "chain of important events." To interpret well, journalists need to be acquainted with history, economics, science, and so on.[19]

MacDougall was not creating a rival framework for objective journalism ethics. His book, with its attention to basic news reporting, is intended to fit within the professional objective framework. Interpretation is put forward as part of good, factual reporting. However, the book does not appear cognizant of the epistemic tensions lurking between its covers, which can be indicated by a few simple questions: By interpreting, are reporters not going beyond or challenging the traditional notion of objectivity as the neutral reporting the facts? By what standards are interpretive reports to be measured for accuracy, plausibility, or truth? What happens if there are several rival interpretations? Nonetheless, MacDougall was on to something important: that a reporting of just the facts is not desirable for journalism. Journalists do, and should, add interpretation. Yet the view of interpretation is pinched and cautious. Interpretation is an "add on" to pure facts that are neutrally observed. The old dualism of fact and interpretation comes under strain from an interpretive journalism of this kind, but it does not break.

Today, many journalists continue to explain interpretive journalism by contrasting it with "facts only" reporting. An interpretation is still regarded as a special, possibly subjective, mental construction. An interpretation is a viewpoint the mind imposes on facts. The reporting-interpreting distinction is explained by the fact-interpretation dualism.

In my view, such strains and stresses in the idea of interpretive journalism only underline the need to give up the dualisms and state frankly that *all* journalism reports, of any complexity or significance, are interpretations, and facts are part of interpretation. The ethical concern is not to make sure that we are still reporting from neutrally discerned facts. Rather, the ethical concern is with the quality and evidence of the inescapable interpretations that we call news reports.

What Sort of Engagement?

Journalists can have many goals. They can be engaged in ways that are positive or negative, responsible or irresponsible. So we face a choice in

19 MacDougall and Reid, *Interpretive Journalism*, 17.

forms of engagement. In chapter 6, I defined engagement as being involved and being committed to certain types of society and social values. I also said that people can be engaged, without being a protester or a partisan. People are engaged when they occupy many roles in society, from teacher to environmental lawyer. In the same way, journalists can be engaged.

In the past, engaged journalism was more likely to be called advocacy or activist journalism. It could be a gay newspaper in Vancouver that advocates against discriminatory marriage laws. Or, it could be a website based in New York that supports the Jewish community. Activist journalism includes "adversarial journalism" where the journalists see themselves as watchdogs – and, in many cases, opponents – of government and other sources of power. Activist journalism gets a bad press in some quarters of journalism, particularly from the supporters of objective journalism. The latter complain that activists produce journalism that is overtly biased, that twists facts, and that can be used to unfairly attack other groups. That engagement may cause bias is evidently true. But so can many other things. The fear that having a goal or a social cause can lead to bias is too general a reason to reject engaged and activist journalism as a whole. Almost any form of journalism can be biased and misused. Moreover, every form of journalism, including objective journalism, has its limitations and drawbacks. The issue is what constitutes good and bad forms of each category of journalism.

I take the term "engaged journalism" to include activist and advocational journalism as traditionally understood. But I use the term to refer more broadly to a journalism that amounts to civic engagement with the community. It is a successor of the civic journalism movement of the 1990s, prior to the rise of online journalism.[20] More particularly, I regard civic engagement as promoting democracy.[21] In my view, engaged journalists should have, as their ultimate goal, the protection and advancement of democracy, globally, for the sake of human flourishing and social justice. I make democracy the general end of journalism since it is a necessary condition for free inquiry, equality, and human flourishing. We need an ethic for *a democratically engaged journalism* that makes possible an informed and participatory public.

Democratically engaged journalism is not support for just any sort of democracy. It should not support a populist democracy where demagogues use media to portray themselves as "strong" men of the people; and it should not support an elitist form of democracy. The democracy I have in

20 See Rosen, *Getting the Connections Right.*

21 This civic sense of engagement is different from a current and popular use of journalism engagement as an economic and audience-building concern – of how to attract readers to your online publication. See Batsell, *Engaged Journalism.*

mind is a representational, liberal democracy that is plural, egalitarian. It is open and participatory in impulse and structure, with constitutional protection for minorities from the tyranny of majorities. Plural, egalitarian democracy is grounded in the rule of law, division of powers, public-directed and transparent government, and core liberties for all. The process of plural democracy is robust, knowledge-based, respectful dialogue, a willingness to compromise for the common good, and a readiness to test (and modify) one's partial view of the world.[22]

Journalism is crucial to this process. Journalists are social advocates of a distinct kind. They are advocates for this form of democracy at home and abroad. They value a factual, impartial journalism of *method* for partial ends: democratic goals. The future of this pluralistic liberal democracy – the best polity for a global world of media-linked differences – is at stake. Journalists take note: the future of democratic journalism depends on the future of pluralistic democracy. This civic engagement is not identical with traditional forms of activist journalism. While it may work, broadly, for social justice and other liberal ideals, civically engaged journalism is not partisan or activist in a narrow manner. Engaged journalism is not restricted to writings for a particular group or minority. Civic engagement means that journalists drop their studied neutrality and become part of the conversation among civic groups. Engaged journalism is a *wide* reformist journalism whose overall goal is the improvement of democratic civic life.

Intolerant Voices

The emphasis on democracy for plural societies is extremely important today as we witness the emergence of populist leaders and intolerant right-wing groups using social media to pollute the public sphere with false facts to stir up racist or intolerant feelings among majorities.

To face this troubled public sphere, journalists could "double down" on reporting just the facts. Or, journalists could become partisan activists. I believe both options would be mistake. If journalists join the protesters, it will erode media credibility and contribute to an already partisan-soaked media sphere. Yet a journalism of just the facts is too passive and ripe for manipulation. In a partisan public sphere, what *is* a fact is up for debate, and requires active investigation. I propose that we think of journalism as lying between partisan advocacy and mincing neutrality. In such a climate,

22 I realize that this preference for egalitarian, participatory democracy would need, to be fully persuasive, an extended argument. This exceeds the boundaries of this book. I provide a detailed description of my conception of journalism and egalitarian democracy in *Global Journalism Ethics* and *Radical Media Ethics.*

a democratically engaged journalism must not be a neutral spectator or a channel of information that merely repeats people's alleged facts. Critical evaluation and informed interpretation motivated by a clear notion of the goal of democratic media is essential.

Democratically engaged journalists protect their values by honouring two duties: the duty to advance democratic dialogue across racial, ethnic, and economic divisions; and the duty to explain and defend pluralistic liberal democracy against its foes.

DUTY 1: DIALOGIC JOURNALISM

Journalists have a duty to convene public fora and provide channels of information that allow for frank but respectful dialogue across divisions. They should seek to mend the tears in the fabric of the body politic. They should work against, in an advocacy role, the trend that sees confrontation replace reasonable discussion, and fear of the "other" replace an openness to humanity. Dialogic journalism challenges racial and ethnic stereotypes and policies, such as by investigating the factual basis of new immigration (and other) laws. It means opposing the penchant to demonize. It means exposing the perpetrators and supporters of hate speech. Whether a dialogue occurs depends not only on the speakers but on the manner in which their encounter in the media is structured. A heavy ethical burden lies on the shoulders of media producers, editors, and hosts to design dialogic encounters. We are all too familiar with the provocative "journalists" who seek ratings through disrespectful ranting and heated confrontation with guests. But we also have good dialogic examples, such as public-issue shows on public television, where viewpoints are critiqued on the basis of facts, not on the basis of the ethnicity or personal details of the speaker.

DUTY 2: GO DEEP POLITICALLY

However, fostering the right sort of democracy-building conversations is not enough. Conversations need to be well informed. Here is where the second duty arises. Journalism needs to devote major resources to an explanatory journalism that delves deeply into the political values, processes, and institutions of egalitarian democracy, while challenging the myths and fears surrounding issues such as immigration, terrorism, and so on. There is a movement towards fact-checking web sites. It is a good idea but insufficient. It is not enough to know that a politician made an inaccurate statement. Many citizens need a reeducation in liberal democracy. They will be called on soon to judge issues that depend on civic knowledge. A democracy without a firm grasp on its principles is flying blind.

I suspect that calling journalists "social advocates" prompts objections. As seen, journalism ethics typically draws a hard line between journalists and activists. This is a simplistic, overreaching, and pejorative distinction. Simplistic because it ignores the long history of non-neutral journalism – satirical journalists, editorial cartoonists, and columnists. Overreaching because the distinction disqualifies important forms of reporting, such as non-neutral investigative journalism. Pejorative because it implies that advocacy journalism *must* be biased or untruthful.

Democratically engaged journalists are advocates because to protect and advance anything is, by definition, to advocate. It is to be engaged, not disengaged. But they practise an important advocacy of a certain kind. They are *objective advocates* of democracy as a whole. They practice an informed advocacy for the common good. Journalists are not stenographers of alleged fact but they are avid investigators into fact. This advocacy is different from the partisan advocacy for a group or ideology. It is radically opposed to an extreme partisanship that would use any manipulative means of persuasion.

Democratic journalists see their methods as instrumental to a larger political goal – that of providing accurate, verified, and well-evidenced interpretations of events and policies as the necessary informational base for democracy. Policies are factually and fairly evaluated in terms of their consistency with democratic principle, and whether they help or harm the democratic republic. Democratic journalists seek to be rational, reasonable, and objective public informers and dialogue generators *within* an overarching commitment to liberal democracy.

In these days, journalists need to clarify their political and social roles, to redefine their ethics from the bottom up. Many journalism conferences focus on practical "tool box" tips, such as how to use new technology; or, they focus on how to attract audiences through social media. But in the days ahead, the key issues of journalism ethics will be questions of political morality: the way a democracy ought to be organized, and the media's role in it. That debate is already flourishing. When a country enters an uncertain political period, journalists need to return to journalism ethics and bedrock political themes, just as such themes arose during the civil rights movement from the mid-1950s to the start of the 1970s. For many journalists and news organizations, the next several years will be a severe test of their political beliefs and journalistic ideals – and their will to defend them. It will also test whether they can creatively reconstruct their ethics for a new reality.

CONCLUSION

In this chapter, I explained how antagonistic dualisms were embedded in journalism over history. I listed the main dualisms of the professional objective ethic and advanced the model of democratically engaged journalism.

In the next and final chapter, I further develop this engaged model by explaining its aims and methods. I describe how the method of pragmatic objectivity applies to journalistic engagement, and how the aim of democratic journalism must now be a global democratic journalism.

8

Engagement: Methods and Aims

A signature mix of reporting and commentary.

Slogan for the *New Yorker*

The value of adopting the concept of democratically engaged journalism cannot be grasped abstractly. Its value resides in the applications to, and implications for, practice. This is a tenet of pragmatism. But in applying the concept we have to make further philosophical choices, such as the system of democracy we have in mind, and what is good for humans in society. Without these additional concepts, the idea of democratically engaged journalism remains an inert ideal that makes no significant difference in thinking or practice.

In this chapter, I provide these additional concepts by outlining the methods and aims of democratically engaged journalism. In the first section, I discuss how journalists should employ pragmatic objectivity as a method for responsible engagement. In the second, I argue that the political aim of engaged journalism should be an egalitarian democracy of a dialogic cast.

In the third section, I place this political goal within the comprehensive goal of human flourishing defined as the promotion of primary human goods within the bounds of justice and dialogic democracy.

PRAGMATIC OBJECTIVITY IN JOURNALISM

A Corrupted Sphere

Inquiry and evaluation in journalism occur in a corrupted, media-saturated infosphere, where self-interest and ideology propagate misinformation. These forces make truth-seeking in journalism a difficult, imperfect process.

Journalists have to deal with the same obstacles facing all inquirers in their search for truth: the cognitive opacity of the world, the plurality of limited perspectives, and the threat of bias. They face hindrances due to the nature of their craft. Often, they lack the specialized knowledge needed to inquire critically. They labour under deadlines, powerful publishers, and finite newsroom resources. Their investigations begin with a jumble of unconfirmed reports from which good journalists ferret out the most plausible accounts through a gradual accumulation of facts and verified claims. Even where facts are available, as in official reports, the journalist faces an abundance of interpretations. Many stories deal with matters where no consensus exists and where controversy, bias, and conflict surround the issues.

Journalists occupy a precarious epistemic position in the public sphere. Therefore, truth-seeking in journalism is the diligent application of fallible methods over time. That is why many journalists stress the *attempt* to discern truth. The principles of the *Washington Post,* drafted by Eugene Meyer in 1933, advocated "telling the truth as nearly as the truth may be ascertained."[1] The *Post*'s Carl Bernstein, of Watergate fame, described the reporting process as providing "the best obtainable version of the truth."[2]

As stressed in chapter 7, journalists are interpreters, not passive recorders of events. All good journalism, including reporting, is active inquiry. It consists of searching and interpreting, of verifying and testing, of balancing and judging, of describing and observing. Good journalists possess research skills that reveal reclusive and important facts. They have interpretive skills that explain complex events. The methods of journalism grow increasingly more sophisticated and powerful, such as using computers to discern patterns in large amounts of data. But journalism does not have a rigorous method of verification, compared to some natural sciences. Journalists cannot run verifying experiments, nor do they have special instruments, such as microscopes, to study their topics. Journalism is not science. It lives at the intersection of many fields, such as the humanities' love of language and interest in all things human, and the social sciences' focus on the political. In many cases, the "method" of an investigation is a non-systematic hodgepodge of common sense, skepticism about certain claims, intuitions about who is a trusted source, the ability to persuade people with sensitive knowledge to "go public," and procedures for finding official documentation. That truth in journalism is a work in progress is evident to foreign reporters. In war zones, the fog of war severely hampers journalists' search for truth. Obstacles include lack of access to conflict areas, a plethora of dubious atrocity stories, a dearth of hard evidence, and many well-orchestrated efforts to mislead the media.

When all goes well, the process of truth-seeking in journalism gradually strips away error, inaccuracy, or exaggeration from the initial descriptions

1 Meyer, "The Post's Principles," 7.
2 Quoted in Kovach and Rosenstiel, *The Elements of Journalism,* 44.

of events. The process of truth involves sifting out fact from innuendo, identifying spin, and refocusing on what is true and significant for the public. Journalists follow leads, add up probabilities, compare what they think they know with what others say, and receive feedback from the community. Journalism truth is a "protean thing which, like learning, grows as a stalagmite in a cave, drop by drop over time."[3]

Objective Evaluation in Journalism

Given their corrupted informational environment, journalists can contribute to a healthier public sphere by following the stance and standards of pragmatic objectivity. Pragmatic objectivity is consistent with the realism of journalism, discussed in chapter 2. Pragmatic objectivity is the appropriate epistemology of engaged journalism.[4]

Pragmatic objectivity is the epistemic evaluation of truth-seeking inquiry in journalism. It guides the difficult search for verified truths, and it restrains partiality. Journalists and their reports are objective to the degree that they satisfy two levels of objectivity. On the first level, reports must satisfy, to some tolerable degree, the requirements of objectivity in general. That is, reports must be constructed by an objective stance in accordance with generic standards. On the second level, reports must satisfy, to some tolerable degree, the standards and rules specific to journalism. The same applies when we consider the objectivity of journalists and news organizations. Journalists are objective to the degree that they adopt the objective stance and adhere to the two levels of objective standards in composing their stories.

Let us examine each level separately. On the first level, objective journalists have adopted the objective stance if they display the general dispositions of open rationality, partial transcendence, disinterested truth, and integrity. Objective journalists practise open rationality in their domain of inquiry by accepting the burdens of rationality – to listen to all sides, to learn from criticism, and to be accountable to the public for the content of their reports. Objective journalists seek partial transcendence by attempting to improve their current understanding of issues by engaging other viewpoints. They exhibit partial transcendence by putting aside their biases and parochial preferences. They practise partial transcendence by putting a critical distance between themselves and their beliefs and by approaching stories with a healthy skepticism. Journalists display their objectivity by their professional attitude and the carefulness of their reporting. Objective journalists

3 Kovach and Rosenstiel, *The Elements of Journalism*, 44.

4 See my "Epistemologies of Journalism."

are disposed towards disinterested truth if they refuse to prejudge a story and follow the facts to the truth, wherever the facts lead. Disinterested journalists do not allow personal interests to overwhelm passion for truth. They are willing to correct errors and to admit that a story idea is wrongheaded and should not be published. Objective journalists let integrity guide their work.

Journalists are not objective simply by dint of having a set of dispositions; objective journalists put these general dispositions to work. They evaluate their reports for their overall fit with the generic objective standards for all inquiry, discussed in chapter 6. They should base any report on sufficient evidence derived from reliable observations and, where possible, from solid empirical studies. A report should not contain logical inconsistencies, manipulative rhetoric, or fallacies. If claims violate well-known facts and established knowledge, the objective journalist investigates this incoherence.

Pragmatic objectivity also requires reports to satisfy, to a tolerable degree, standards that are domain-specific to journalism, in the same way that health researchers apply specific standards to drug trials. These rules and standards interpret the meaning of objectivity for the domain of journalism. Many of them exist as informal rules of practice in newsrooms or occur in journalism codes of ethics. In newsrooms, specific empirical standards take form in editors' directives to reporters to gather accounts from eyewitnesses, or to go observe events themselves. The journalist should check claims against available facts and sources.

Accuracy, verification, and completeness are prime empirical standards in journalism. *Accuracy* calls for accurate quotations and paraphrases of statements and correct numbers. It forbids manipulation of news images and the use of misleading dramatizations and "reconstructions" of events. *Verification* calls on reporters to cross-check claims of potential whistleblowers against original documents. Its standards include rules on the number (and quality) of anonymous sources. The standard of *completeness* means that stories should be substantially complete by including the essential facts, main consequences, and major viewpoints. Good newsrooms have empirical standards for types of recurring stories, such as the reporting of opinion polls. The standards demand that reporters check the poll sponsors, the polling agency, the sample size, the margin of error, the wording of questions, the dates when the poll was taken, and other information. Good newsrooms support these reporting standards with a layer of tough editing standards that take nothing for granted and challenge assertions.

Codes of ethics for journalism do not spell out standards of coherence. They do not contain directives to "be logical" or "test your claim against other beliefs." But quality journalism tests for coherence at every turn. Any journalist who has tried to construct a complex story knows that the coherence of evidence from many sources is a prime consideration. Any journalist who has tried to report on an alleged scientific breakthrough knows how important it is to evaluate the claim by appeal to other experts and existing scientific knowledge. Coherence considerations take centre stage when journalists attempt to weigh diverse perspectives on a controversial issue.

Journalists cannot avoid selecting and evaluating viewpoints. They must ask questions such as: How does this viewpoint fit prevailing knowledge in the field in question? Is it credible? Does it fit with previous, similar studies? This is Thagard's "explanatory coherence" at work in journalism. Some degree of subjectivity and uncertainty will surround such selections. What is the "appropriate" number of diverse views? Who is a bonafide expert? Is there an authoritative consensus on this issue? Might today's "fringe" viewpoint be tomorrow's majority opinion? Despite these difficulties, the responsible, objective journalist makes every effort to reach a fair judgment on the credibility of viewpoints.

Objective journalists adhere to the standards of rational debate in their work. This includes a diversity of views in their reports. They are careful to represent fairly the views of all groups. Some newsrooms have rules that reduce or eliminate stereotyping by race, gender, age, and religion. The code of ethics for the Society of Professional Journalists, under its principle to seek the truth, urges journalists to "tell the story of the diversity and magnitude of the human experience." In recent years, journalists have interpreted the standard of rational debate to mean that reporters should make a special effort to represent the voices of the less powerful and the marginalized.

In real-world journalism, the ethical evaluation of what to do is a holistic balancing of values similar to ethical evaluation in other walks of life. For example, consider this situation:

Suppose you are a political reporter in Ottawa, Ontario. You are covering a hotly contested federal election for Parliament. Someone tells you at a social event that there are allegations that John Jones, the Conservative Party leader, has sexually harassed women on his office staff. That someone is Bill, a senior official for the Liberal Party.

Bill mentions that a woman in Jones's office, Martha, has told fellow workers about his actions. You contact Martha by telephone. She confirms that Jones sexually harassed her. She hints there may be other victims, but refuses to go into detail. "Please don't use my name," she asks.

You feel uncertain about your next step. Should you report this allegation?

Why are you feeling uncomfortable when this is a great story? What should you do?

Most journalists would recognize this as an ethical situation, not simply a question of what can be legally published or what serves the reporter's self-interest. Again, questions of what is good, right, or dutiful take centre stage. But this time they are joined by the journalistic values of verification, truth, serving the public, and exposing wrongdoing. These additional norms make the situation a case for journalism ethics.

Values conflict. Journalists feel a duty to expose wrongdoing such as sexual harassment, especially when the person accused is powerful and running for public office. Yet, journalists also worry about accuracy and verification. Does the reporter have a duty to contact Martha? To seek confirmation of harassment from other women in the office? What if Martha and others will only speak if you grant them anonymity? Moreover, the desire to expose wrongdoing is balanced against the rights of people accused of wrongdoing, especially where such allegations start from an opposing political party and would affect the election. The Conservative leader has the right to not have his reputation and election prospects damaged by an allegation from an anonymous source. Like the case of Dorothy in chapter 6, we know we need to "do" ethics before we publish, that is, to balance factors in a fair frame of mind. We do not roll the dice or consult only our feelings.

In summary, a report is objective to the degree that it derives from an objective stance and satisfies generic and domain-specific standards. In some cases, the standards will collide, making objective judgment difficult. For example, a journalist may find that, by some empirical standards, a new scientific study appears valid and important. Yet the study goes against existing knowledge and the opinion of most experts. Empirical and coherence standards appear to clash. The best that the objective journalist can do in such a circumstance is to weigh the standards and evidence against each other and include any uncertainty in the report.

Implications

At least two questions arise about pragmatic objectivity in application to journalism. First, does pragmatic objectivity, by stressing holistic evaluation, undermine the role of facts in journalism? Second, what are the roles of emotion and attachment, according to pragmatic objectivity?

FACTS IN CONTEXT

Pragmatic objectivity in journalism does not dismiss the importance of fact. To the contrary, it recognizes, for instance, the importance of facts to investigative journalists in their efforts to expose government corruption. Facts provide a vital test of interpretations, from the simplest of news reports to the most complex stories about foreign affairs. Pragmatic objectivity does not share the postmodern skepticism that there are no facts.[5]

However, pragmatic objectivity places important qualifications on the appeal to facts. It regards the appeal to facts as part of the inquirer's conceptual scheme and epistemic norms. That is, pragmatic objectivity operates with a *holistic and scheme-dependent notion* of what a fact is, a notion that precludes a foundational belief in pure fact, or a reduction of objectivity to "just the facts." Pragmatic objectivity denies that there are pure facts, a "given" in experience or in journalism. Facts are creatures of interpretation and conceptual schemes; they are only one (albeit one important) test of truth and objectivity. Facts are part of the many things we consider when evaluating interpretations, such as journalism stories. Odd or contentious facts may be overridden or doubted by other considerations, such as coherence with existing knowledge.

Even where we appeal to facts, the appeal may be a complex matter, requiring us to properly interpret the meaning of facts. As noted earlier, facts need context, and context is a matter of interpretation. For instance, government statistics about the rate of unemployment and police "facts" about how well they are fighting crime in their community cannot be accepted (or reported) at face value. Journalists should use statistical (and other) methods to interpret the data. In health reporting, journalists should compare the cancer rate of a group in a clinical trial with background levels of cancer in the general population. In political reporting, the "facts" of opinion polls are worthless unless they are correctly interpreted. Often, getting the correct interpretation of the facts is as important as knowing the "bare" facts. We need to select facts for relevance and importance, organize them into coherent statistical patterns, and place them in their proper context. Nevertheless, empirical facts anchor our conceptual systems in experience. They force interpretations to face an external world.

There is perhaps no more succinct debunking of the idea that isolated facts have a special power by themselves than John Dewey's introduction to *The Public and Its Problems.*[6] In a few pages, Dewey throws cold water on the idea that facts "carry their meaning along on themselves on their face." There may be disagreement on the facts or on what they mean. There may be insufficient facts to establish a claim. The same facts may support rival

5 Skepticism towards facts became so prevalent that in 1997 the Annenberg Public Policy Center of the University of Pennsylvania held a conference on "The Future of Fact." Leading scholars claimed that there are no "facts out there" independent of some conception of how the world really is. Another theme was that "facts follow interpretation." See Strange, *The Future of Fact.*

6 Dewey, *The Public and Its Problems*, 3–8.

interpretations. Purported facts may be false or manipulated. Dewey points out that a few recalcitrant facts need never force a person to accept or abandon a particular theory about what the facts mean. As we have seen, Quine argued that facts never "prove" an empirical theory. There is always the possibility of an equally good, rival theory. Just as facts underdetermine scientific theory, so they underdetermine our news reports.

VALUES, ATTACHMENTS, EMOTIONS

In previous chapters I have supported the view, against Hume and others, that the values and ends of action are desires that cannot be rationally evaluated, only "liked or disliked," valued or not valued.

It is fortunate that we *can* conceive of ways to assess statements that contain more than fact, because journalism is replete with value judgments. The daily news is full of implicit or explicit value judgments – tales of winners and losers, good guys and bad guys. Reporters cannot avoid evaluative language in reporting on unfair bosses, brutal massacres, vicious murders, notorious pedophiles, and dangerous terrorists. Journalists employ evaluations in selecting credible sources or displaying skepticism towards a new scientific theory. To enter journalism is to enter a value-laden craft. New journalists learn more than the skills of writing news and gathering information. They acculturate into a realm of reporting routines, news values, and peer attitudes. Thus a theory of objectivity must provide standards by which to assess these value-laden activities.

Pragmatic objectivity in general, and in journalism, evaluates values by asking questions such as: Do the facts of the case support the value judgment? Does the value judgment cohere with my other values and goals? Have I come to my judgment with a sufficient degree of critical distance? Do I provide reasons for pursuing such goals that are acceptable, or at least understandable, to other rational agents? Valuations and interpretations can be objective to varying degrees, depending on how well they satisfy the stance and standards of pragmatic objectivity. A report is not subjective just because it contains evaluative language. What matters is whether such elements have an objective basis.

But what about journalistic attachments to groups? If the claim is only that journalists have attachments to groups, then pragmatic objectivity agrees. But there is a stronger claim: that journalists *should* be attached to groups in their work. Activist and advocacy journalists support this stronger premise. What does pragmatic objectivity say about this? I have indicated in previous chapters what my answer would be. I have acknowledged that all journalists have values and goals. Everything depends on *how* they define those goals and *how* they seek them. I then supported democratically engaged journalism, where the journalist impartially promotes, and is attached to, democratic publics. In this view, advocacy or activist journalism is ethically proper so long as the journalists report on their favoured groups and causes using the method of pragmatic objectivity. Democratically engaged journalism thinks such forms of engaged journalism are a natural and often useful form of analysis and commentary in the public sphere. The question is whether they use pragmatic objectivity to advance egalitarian, dialogic democracy and forms of journalism.

When it comes to engagement, pragmatic objectivity has a serious reservation having to do with the ranking of attachments. Democratically engaged journalism requires that journalists of all kinds make their attachment to democratic publics *primary*. It regulates and trumps their attachments to more specific groups. There is, in attached journalism, the constant danger that bias towards one's specific group may override one's fundamental duty to inform the general public. Partisan and extreme activist journalists may be willing to depart from the standards of pragmatic objectivity where it advances their specific cause or group. Where serving a particular group clashes with serving the public, the latter must prevail. If it is in the public interest to inform society about problems within a minority or marginalized group, pragmatic objectivity insists that it is the ethical duty of any journalist – even if "committed" to helping this group – to report these facts. For example, activist journalists attempting to protect the environment or to advance the rights of gay people may favour advocatory articles over mainstream objective reports. Moreover, if the advocacy takes on the form of cheap rhetoric, blatant bias, partisan propaganda, or the denial of inconvenient facts, then it violates pragmatic objectivity. Positive talk about attachments, combined with emotional appeals to justice, can rationalize an unbalanced journalism of ideology, of faction, and of prejudgment. At its worst, attached journalism is irresponsible, non-credible journalism. However, when well practised, attached journalism provides evidence, sharp arguments, and new perspectives.

Pragmatic objectivity, then, is not so flexible as to sanction all forms of journalism. As citizens, it is natural for journalists to have a large number of attachments, ranging from one's ethnic group and religion to local school board. But to act as a responsible journalist, professional or non-professional, is to assume other duties, other attachments, and other priorities. A journalist is a special communicator to the public, for the public. *That* attachment trumps personal attachment to factions and special causes. Journalists have a stake in the fate of their society. They are not bemused, neutral bystanders who watch the passing political drama. Yet the engagement of journalists who adhere to pragmatic objectivity is different from the engagement of advocate or partisan journalists. Objective journalists are engaged in public life as agents who inform the public from an independent perspective. Pragmatic objectivity does have an "agenda" – that of an open public sphere. It is an engaged objectivity, in service to a democratic public.

Meanwhile, democratically engaged journalism has a more positive view of emotions in journalism than the traditional professional model. It incorporates the view of emotions in chapter 6. Emotions are important forms of access to the world, with cognitive functions. They help us know the world and pay attention to aspects we might ignore. Feelings of injustice can motivate courageous journalism, and empathy can prompt journalists to pay attention to people in distress. The issue, as I have said, is to be attentive to the emotions we have as journalists and develop healthy habits of emotions. There should be no call to repress emotions in general. Better discussions of emotion are much needed in journalism ethics. With its abstract codes and misleading notions of cool objectivity, journalism ethics can appear to be the logical exercise of applying rational principles to situations, without emotions.

The best journalism is a judicious blend of two fundamental impulses: the emotion-laden romantic impulse and the logic-directed objective impulse. The romantic impulse consists of the passion for interesting stories and substantial revelations. It is the impulse to seek out stories that give the journalist an opportunity for creative writing, interpretation, and self-expression. The objective impulse is the concern to verify what the romantic impulse finds.

POLITICAL AIM: LEVELS OF DEMOCRACY

When we turn to the general aims of engaged journalism there is no escaping political aims. It is inescapable because the political structure of our societies are crucial contributors to, or detractors from, our individual and social well-being. It is also inescapable because journalism is intrinsically bound up with this political structure. Journalists not only report on politics, their freedom (or lack of it) depends on a nation's political values.

When I said in the previous chapter that egalitarian democracy is the goal of engaged journalism, I quickly added, "but, not just any democracy." This is because they are many levels of democracy, from a barely functioning nation that allows elections, to a robust democracy where liberties are fully protected and citizens enjoy meaningful participation in defining the common good. Journalism can help societies make the often-difficult assent to better forms of democracy. Or, journalism can be part of negative social forces that send a democracy into a downward spiral to dictatorship or a nation directed by intolerant, populist majorities.

Let me explore this important area in a bit more detail.

There are three levels of ascent: Level 1 is a minimal democracy whose denizens can consider themselves citizens and not just "subjects" of a king, tyrant, or military junta. Citizens have limited rights to free speech, association, and political participation. The list of rights is meagre and the list of duties and restrictive laws is long. Inequalities are obvious and entrenched, and institutions often unjust, tainted by power and conflicts of interest. Such nations have citizens but the citizens do not form a public.

Level 2 is a further development of democracy. The list of liberties is longer and better protected, including constitutional protections for both the liberties and rights of minorities. Inequalities are less evident and reforms seek to bring about egalitarian society. Institutions are more independent and seek to honour principles of justice. In such a democracy, citizens can be called a public (or a plurality of publics) since they are effective, to a significant extent, in holding government accountable and, through their interactions, influencing decisions. Level 2 refers to democracies where the electoral control of power is evident. A democracy, by definition, is government by the "demos" through free and fair elections. Beyond elections, government by the people means political control in terms of how decisions are made between elections and whose interests prevail. Rawls defined a "well-ordered" democracy in these terms:

> The government is effectively under their [the public's] political and electoral control, and … it answers to and protects their fundamental interests as specified in a written or unwritten constitution and its interpretation. The regime is not an autonomous agency pursuing its own bureaucratic ambitions. Moreover, it is not directed by the interests of large corporations of private economic and corporate power veiled from public knowledge and almost entirely free from accountability.[7]

At its best, Level 2 democracy is a participatory democracy where citizens, as individuals and as groups, can speak out publicly and take common action. It is often, and mistakenly, thought that participatory democracy is the best form of democracy. For example, the rise of the internet, at least in its formative years, prompted people to think of it as positive, powerful tool for participatory democracy. Democracy was equated with having voices online. This equation failed to recognize, as noted previously, that *how* members of the public express their views to one another – for example, reasonably or by ranting – is crucial.

This leads to the idea of a third level of democracy: a robust egalitarian democracy that is dialogic. Such a country enjoys participatory democracy,

7 Rawls, *The Law of Peoples*, 24.

but, in addition, much of the participation is tolerant, reasonable, and cooperative. They use dialogue and compromise to civically (and civilly) define the common good. Elections are fair and inclusive, and citizens have substantial political control. In addition, the society exemplifies democratic community. Institutions and groups within society are organized around the democratic principles of inclusivity, transparency, and equal participation. As Dewey argued, democracy is a precondition for the richest kind of communal life and human flourishing.[8] Cohen has written that democracy is a "political society of equals, in which the justification of institutions – as well as laws and policies addressed to consequential problems – involves public argument based on the common reason of members, who regard one another as equals."[9]

Therefore, I call a democracy that governs itself to a substantial degree through reasonable dialogue a dialogic democracy. The aim is dialogue, informed analysis, and a fair sharing of views, not quiet deliberation, which happens too infrequently in society and in media. The goal is reasonable discourse. Dialogue is not about reaching unanimous, "watered down" consensus, or "liking" your interlocutor, or avoiding tough topics. Rather, dialogue can be a method for discussions across great differences in culture and economic status, especially when global issues are debated. For dialogic democracy, a public dialogue is a cooperative inquiry into a topic from different standpoints, where we partially transcend our situations to listen and strike a critical distance (if temporarily) from our beliefs. The aim is not simply to express my view; it is not to portray those who disagree with me as unpatriotic enemies who must be crushed. This is not a winner-takes-all affair. Dialogue is not a monologue. It is about listening, learning. It expects robust disagreement, but it also seeks areas of compromise and new solutions. It promotes what Rawls called a "reasonable pluralism" – a reasonable discourse among groups with different values and philosophies of life.[10]

In recent years, especially in the United States, there have been many calls for politicians, journalists, and advocacy groups to overcoming the fragmentation of politics by avoiding non-dialogic communication. Makau and Marty argue that substantial harm has been done to the US body politic – and the country's ability to respond to urgent issues – because of a simplistic individualism that creates an intolerant, non-listening "argument culture." They propose a number of techniques and methods to strengthen dialogue and deliberation in politics. Canadian philosopher Mark Kingwell has

8 Dewey, *Democracy and Education*, 16.

9 Cohen, *The Arc of the Moral Universe and Other Essays*, 1.

10 Rawls, *Political Liberalism*, 4.

summarized nicely why civility and dialogue are important for democracy. It is not just about being "nice" to others. When taken to extremes, incivility is "a creeping nihilism here, a disregard for the very idea of reason."[11]

Chronologically, countries must create Level 1 and Level 2 before they can aspire to Level 3. Most democracies in the world exist somewhere between Level 1 and Level 2, and move toward or away from Level 1 and Level 2 over time. Every day, people around the world fight to be members of minimal democratic publics. Achieving a democratic public is a matter of degree, and a constant struggle.

How does journalism help democratic publics exist? It does so by influencing the flow and quality of communication in a democracy's public sphere. Publics, those creatures of democracy, are created and maintained in large part through a public sphere. Journalism is an essential part of that public sphere.

But not all forms of journalism contribute to democracy, or contribute in equal measure. Dialogic democracy suggest the following criteria of evaluation: *A democracy should regard most highly those forms of journalism that create, maintain, and promote dialogic democracy. Forms of journalism should be judged by the extent to which they meet the crucial media needs of a robust democratic public.*

The most general standard is *having significant democratic value*, defined as meeting the important media needs of a dialogic democracy. This standard recognizes the following as valid forms: reporting and investigative journalism, explanatory journalism, participatory journalism, and dialogic journalism. Principled pluralism excludes unethical applications of these major forms of journalism, such as inaccurate reporting, uninformed explanatory journalism, and a disrespectful opinion journalism that maligns other views. The dialogic approach distinguishes between valuable opinion journalism and non-valuable opinion journalism, when we consider the needs of democracy. This is important at a time of increasingly partisan and intolerant journalism. Dialogic theory believes that the most valuable form of opinion journalism is a *moderate* opinion journalism that brings forward a diversity of positions for reasonable public scrutiny.

POLITICAL AIM: HUMAN FLOURISHING

Political aims are important but they are not our ultimate values. They are part of, and are justified by, some theory of the human good. I propose that the ethics of a democratically engaged journalism should be based on

11 Kingwell, *Unruly Voices*, 13.

the general principle that *all humans are equally valuable moral agents of a single humanity, and all deserve a full and flourishing life.*[12] Through this idea we affirm humanity, or express our love of humanity. Human flourishing is an all-encompassing human good. It is the ultimate aim for ethics in general and media ethics in particular. It calls on us to accept the "claim of humanity." Other people, as humans, make moral claims upon us.

A conception of human flourishing must be more than a hazy love for the brotherhood of mankind. The first step is spell out the idea of the human good. The human good is not one single type of good, but a composite of goods that together define a morally good and dignified form of life. To identify such goods, we need to think about what all humans have in common. What are the common needs to be met and capacities to be developed that (a) establish the basis for a decent human life, and, after that, (b) lead, hopefully, to a flourishing life? These goods are called "primary goods" because they allow us to pursue other goods.

All of us can think of some primary goods: physical security, shelter, food and drink, education, health, sufficient wealth and freedom to pursue one's plans. In *Global Journalism Ethics,* I presented a theory of human flourishing which consisted of four types of primary goods. I argued that journalism should promote the goods on all four levels. Here is a summary of the main ideas.

Flourishing means the exercise of one's intellectual, emotional, and other capacities to a high degree in a supportive social context. Ideally, flourishing is the fullest expression of human development under favorable conditions. In reality, humans flourish in varying degrees. Few people flourish fully. Life often goes badly; many live in desperate conditions where flourishing is a remote ideal. Nevertheless, the ideal of flourishing is important for evaluating social and political systems.

The concept of flourishing in ethics is not the concept of individuals maximizing their self-interests and goods in just any manner. We can pursue our goods unethically, at the expense of the good of others. Any capacity, virtue, emotion, or talent – from the capacity for rational thought to the virtue of loyalty – can be misused or employed for dubious purposes. We do not want people to develop their capacities for cruelty, hatred, and warmongering. These capacities should not be part of an ethical notion of flourishing. We need to develop capacities in ways that support our sense

12 For my full theory of human flourishing, see chapters 3 and 5 of *Global Journalism Ethics.*

of the ethically good life. When we ethically flourish, we enjoy such goods as trust, friendship, and right relations with others.

Four Levels

Ethical flourishing is the development of four levels of primary goods common to all humans – individual, social, political, and ethical goods. To achieve the goods of each level is to achieve a corresponding form of human dignity: individual, social, political, and ethical dignity.

By individual goods, I mean the goods that come from the development of each individual's capacities. This level includes the "physical" goods that allow physical dignity. All persons need food, shelter, and security to live a normal length of life in health. This level also contains the rational and moral goods that allow physical capacity to flower into distinct human traits. A person enjoys the rational and moral goods when she develops her capacities to observe and think as a critical individual, and to carry out a rational plan of life. Such a person is able to form emotional attachments, and to use their imagination to produce (or enjoy) creative and intellectual works. Also, the person is able to be a moral agent. She is able to empathize with others and to form a sense of justice. She is able to deliberate about the good of others. She has the dignity of an individual person.

The social goods arise when we use our rational and moral capacities to participate in society. Human reality is "social" not just because, instrumentally, humans need society to develop language and culture. Humans come to value participating in common projects as a good-in-itself. Among the social goods are the freedom to enter into and benefit from economic association, the goods of love and friendship; the need for mutual recognition and respect. In this manner, we achieve social dignity.

By political goods, I mean the goods that accrue to us as citizens living in a just political association. The latter is a participatory, dialogic democracy. These goods include the basic liberties, such as freedom of speech, combined with the opportunity and resources to exercise these freedoms. Citizens are able to participate in political life, to hold office, and to influence decisions. The primary means to these public goods are constitutional protections, the rule of law, barriers against undue coercion, and means for the peaceful resolution of disputes. A citizen who enjoys these goods has political dignity, through self-government.

By ethical goods, I mean the goods that come from living among persons and institutions of ethical character. We can rely on the latter to act ethically. We need to live not only in a society of rational people – that is, people motivated to pursue their own interests. A society motivated only by purely self-interested rational agents would be a terrifying "private" (or extremely individualistic) society. To flourish, we need to live among people who are disposed to be what Rawls calls morally "reasonable."[13] Reasonable citizens are motivated to consider the interests of others and the greater public good. They contribute to dialogue.

Congruence

These are the four levels of the human good. How should the levels be related?

The goods of each level should be developed simultaneously. I do not pick out one good (or one level) as sufficient to define the human good, such as pleasure, or utility. The human good is a composite of basic goods, none of which is reducible or eliminable. The satisfaction of one type of good allows another to exist. To be sure, we need to secure the physical goods before we can move on to other goods, but that doesn't make the other levels less important. In many countries, unstable political structures – that is, the lack of political goods – interfere with attempts to provide physical and social goods to citizens.

The proper relationship between the levels is governed by the fundamental moral principle that we pursue these goods within the bounds of justice. What we owe to others, and our duty to act justly, is prior and should not be overridden by our desire to enlarge our goods. The pursuit of the good needs to be restrained by justice because of the ever-present danger that people will act selfishly, violating the cosmopolitan principle that all people are of equal moral value, and therefore should enjoy the right to flourish as much as any other person.

The aim of ethics, then, is affirming humanity by aiming at ethical flourishing, understood as the promotion of the four levels for dignity, and where there is a congruence of the good and the just. The aim is global. It is not the promotion of flourishing only in Canada or China. The goal is flourishing across all borders. The individual, social, political, and ethical dignity that we seek for citizens in our society, we seek for humanity at large.

In terms of political structure, the best chance for a reasonable congruence of the good and the right is in a liberal, egalitarian democracy. In this historically contingent entity called democracy, humans have created a political structure whose principles come closer to capturing the idea of human flourishing than any other structure. Ideally, democracy means core liberties and the freedom to develop the capacities of citizens. It

13 Rawls, *Political Liberalism*, 48.

means equality of opportunity and rights, justice, and equality under the law. Therefore, we can include the promotion of democracy as part of the ethics of humanity in two ways: strengthening individual democracies and promoting international agencies that support democratic governance of global problems.

In the final analysis, the ethics of humanity provides two ultimate aims for journalism in a global age: to promote global human flourishing and, as a sub-component, to promote global democracy. These two aims help us to redefine our normative interpretation of journalism from a domestic serving of citizens to a global serving of humanity. This global normative interpretation integrates the various forms of journalism under one unifying theme: human flourishing. This is global journalism seen in its best light.

APPLYING HUMAN FLOURISHING

My fourfold theory of the human good can be used to turn journalism ethics into a global journalism ethics, by redefining the aims and principles of journalism. If journalists were to adopt the varieties of ethical flourishing as primary concepts, it would begin a chain of reinterpretations of primary concepts and revisions of codes of ethics. I indicate the scope of these changes in what follows in three ways. First, I discuss the idea of globalism in journalism ethics, and consider changes in the self-conception of journalists. Second, I indicate how journalists can promote the four levels of human flourishing. Third, I show how adopting a global ethics based on flourishing would call for changes in journalistic concepts and practices.

Thesis of Moral Globalism

What does it mean to be parochial or global in one's values?[14]

For many of us, our value systems are a mix of global and parochial values. But most of the time, parochialism is our default setting. The original meaning of "parochial" is what belongs to the parish, what is close to us. Therefore, a parochial value is an attachment to something or someone because it is "near, dear, and familiar." The parochial is, typically, associated with the people, places, and values of my upbringing. It forms part of my current identity and daily life. Parochial values display an extraordinary variety. My parochial values include an attachment to 1960s rock music and the seafaring traditions of Atlantic Canada where I was born. One form of parochialism is of importance for journalism ethics: group parochialism.

14 See Ward, "The Moral Priority of Globalism in a Digital World."

This is the love of groups to which I belong or with which I identify. Typically, these groups are my family, my kin, my close friends and colleagues, my ethnic group. It can extend to something as large and abstract as my nation. Yet, psychologically, the strength of my attachment tends to decline the larger the group is, the more different its members are from me, and the further it is from my daily life. Psychologically, geographical and cultural differences matter. For many people, it is a challenge to identify with strangers, and foreigners. People who are not members of my favoured groups are outsiders, and my attitude to them may be one of indifference, suspicion, or hostility. Parochialism, in large part, is a loyalty to groups that are mine, and this loyalty affects my decisions and what I am prepared to do. These parochial values have formed the basis of theories from political realism to ethical relativism and nationalism.

Globalism, then, is a deliberate attempt to develop a value scheme *not* based on parochialism – not based on my attachments to specific things and groups. Globalism finds value in things and in people for reasons other than the fact that they are "mine" or belong to my favoured group. The principles of globalism do not derive their normative force from the contingencies of where anyone was born and what groups populate their social environment. Global values are universal in not being values specific to any one group. They apply to all people as people, and therefore transcend parochial boundaries.

What sort of values are those? They are those things that promote the development and flourishing of the most inclusive group of all: humanity. A globalist cares about humans of all kinds, and their fate, as a whole. This attachment has expressed itself in ethical principles scattered across centuries of religious, ethical, and philosophical thought, not to mention social movements. Take, for example, the value of human rights, that is, the attribution of rights to people simply because they are human, regardless of their group, religion, race, or nationality. Globalism is on view in the UN's *Universal Declaration of Human Rights.* Or consider the Christian doctrine that one should love all humans because they are made in the image of God. This idea receives a secular interpretation in Kant's notion of the overwhelming dignity and worth of humans.[15] There is also the cosmopolitan principle that all of us are moral equals and therefore we have strong duties to strangers.[16] One can also detect the global spirit in art, music, and the humanities. In pop music, there is the enduring popularity of John Lennon's "Imagine"; in classical music, there is Beethoven's sublime "Ode

15 Kant, *Groundwork of the Metaphysics of Morals,* 42–3.
16 See Appiah, *Cosmopolitanism.*

to Joy." We can sense the workings of globalism in moral theories that require us to adopt impartial perspectives when dealing with others, or to work for global social justice. Globalism does not ask humans to deny their parochial values, but to restrain and transcend them when they conflict with global principles.

Therefore, we face a choice in how we rank our values. We can adopt what I call the thesis of *moral parochialism*, the thesis that it is not only possible but morally correct to make parochial values the basis of my ethical conceptual scheme. Or, we can adopt what I call the thesis of *moral globalism*, the thesis that it is not only possible but morally correct to make global values the basis of my ethical conceptual scheme. The same choice faces journalism ethics. Journalists can make moral parochialism or moral globalism their moral starting point when defining their duties. We can express the choice in terms of group loyalties. Journalists can adopt the parochial view that their ultimate loyalty is to the group to which they belong, typically their nation or ethnic group. Or, journalists can pledge their ultimate loyalty to a much larger group: humanity at large. They adopt the viewpoint of globalism.

What are the implications of adopting moral globalism in journalism?

Self-Consciousness

If journalists adopted moral globalism, they would alter their self-identity and alter their notion of who they serve. They would embrace three imperatives:

Act as Global Agents: Journalists should see themselves as agents of a global public sphere. The goal of their collective actions is a well-informed, diverse, and tolerant global "info-sphere" that challenges the distortions of tyrants, the abuse of human rights, and the manipulation of information by special interests.

Serve the Citizens of the World: The global journalist's primary loyalty is to the information needs of world citizens. Journalists should refuse to define themselves as attached primarily to factions, regions, or even countries. Serving the public means serving more than one's local readership or audience, or even the public of one's country.

Promote Non-parochial Understandings: The global journalist frames issues broadly and uses a diversity of sources and perspectives to promote a nuanced understanding of issues from an international perspective. Journalism should work against a narrow ethnocentrism or patriotism.

These imperatives, by themselves, are worthy of exploration. Yet even without a detailed exposition of the directives, we sense their revolutionary import. Human flourishing as ultimate aim changes journalists' self-conception from that of a citizen of one country to that of a global citizen serving humanity. It makes the serving of humanity the primary allegiance of journalists. Journalists owe credible journalism to all potential readers of a global public sphere. Loyalty to humanity trumps other loyalties, where they conflict.

This cosmopolitan definition of who is a journalist flies in the face of the dominant form of journalists' self-conception. Journalists have defined themselves non-globally and parochially, as serving local, regional, and national audiences. This loyalty to one's co-nationals is primary and trumps talk of serving foreigners or citizens in other countries.

Promoting the Four Levels

This change in identity is further specified by adding the aim of promoting the four levels of primary goods. Journalists, as global citizens, seek individual, social, political, and ethical dignity for humanity at large. But, practically speaking, how can global journalism promote something as abstract as levels of primary goods? We need to specify how media can promote each level.

INDIVIDUAL GOODS

Journalism can promote the individual goods by monitoring basic levels of physical and rational dignity in their own country and around the world. Journalism can promote individual goods in at least three ways:

1 Provide information on (and an analysis of) world events and trends. Journalism should be occupied with providing timely, accurate, and contextual information on political, social, and economic developments, from reports on new legislation and political instability to news of global trends in business and environment. This information is the basis for the deliberation of autonomous citizens in any nation.
2 Monitor basic levels of physical, individual, and social dignity. Physical dignity: journalism has a duty to help citizens be aware of the ability of their society and other societies to provide for citizens a decent level of physical goods such as food, shelter, health, wealth, a reasonable length of life, and physical security through effective laws (and regulatory agencies) to protect the vulnerable. Journalism has a duty to provide the same scrutiny of the ability of citizens in the development of their rational and moral capacities. This duty requires journalistic inquiry into the educational system's effectiveness in developing rational and imaginative citizens, the capacity of the social fabric to develop citizens' emotional capacity through supportive communities, and the capacity of the public sphere to develop citizens' rational capacities through opportunities for philosophical, scientific, and cultural engagement.

Journalism has a duty to bring forward for debate the fairness of existing physical, social, and educational opportunities within countries and also globally. By using a variety of metrics and by making cross-cultural comparisons, journalism can contribute to progress in these areas.

3 Investigate inequality. Journalism has a duty to conduct in-depth investigative stories on people and groups who have been denied physical, rational, and moral dignity, and by supporting global institutions that seek redress of these inequalities. Global journalism should reveal whether gender, ethnicity, and other differences account for inequalities. By exploring below the surface of society and our global economic systems, journalism promotes citizens' awareness of how egalitarian their society is, and the impact of policies on human development and dignity.

SOCIAL GOODS

Journalism can promote the social goods by taking up its duty to report on, analyze, and critique the ways in which citizens interact and create associations so as to enjoy the goods of social cooperation. Journalism should promote social goods in at least five ways:

1 Report critically on economic associations. Journalism has a duty to report on and analyze how a society allows citizens to participate and benefit from its various forms of economic association, including fair economic competition. It needs to monitor society's use of economic power and its effect on egalitarian democracy and the principles of justice.
2 Assess the quality of social life. Journalism should report on the types of social life, social and technological trends, and social possibilities available for citizens. It should inquire into whether such trends nurture caring relationships, meaningful collective activity, and flourishing communities.
3 Assist social bridging. In a pluralistic world, journalism has a duty to act as a bridge between diverse classes, ethnic groups, religions, and cultures within and among countries. Journalism has a twofold task to make visible, for consideration and critique, both the commonalities and the differences among citizens, and to encourage tolerant but frank cross-cultural discussion of issues.
4 Assist media literacy and the evaluation of media. Journalists have a duty to inquire into the impact of journalism, media, and communication technology on the global public sphere and on their society; and how new communication technology and new forms of journalism can be used to advance ethical flourishing and the social goods.

5 Use global comparisons. Journalism has a duty to evaluate the level of human and social goods among countries and to investigative different approaches to major social problems. In this way, journalism is a force for progressive ideas and "experiments in living."

POLITICAL GOODS

Journalism can promote the political and ethical goods by helping to nurture morally reasonable citizens willing to discuss essential issues objectively and fairly, and to nurture a society where the pursuit of the rational side of life is kept in check by firm and effective principles of justice. Journalism can promote the political goods in at least four ways:

1 Critique the basic structure. Journalism of the public good has a duty to inquire into and to encourage deliberation upon fundamental justice from a global perspective. Journalism should report on the basic institutional structures of societies and how well the principles of justice and international law are embodied by institutions, political processes, and legal systems.
2 Monitor the basic liberties. Journalism has a duty to promote and defend basic liberties around the world and to ask to what extent citizens are able to enjoy the full value of basic liberties, such as freedom of speech, freedom of association, freedom from discrimination, and other constitutional protections. Are citizens able to exercise these freedoms for the purpose of self-development and to enjoy the goods on the other three levels?
3 Encourage participation. Journalism needs to monitor (and help to make possible) citizens' participation in public life and their ability to have a meaningful influence on debate about government decisions. Journalism should engage in various forms of "civic" journalism that enhance public involvement in basic social issues and discourage public cynicism about civic engagement.
4 Report on diversity and representation. Journalism has a duty to insist on, and to help make possible, a diverse public forum within and across borders, with adequate representation of non-dominant groups. Journalism must be self-conscious about how groups can use language to manipulate, stereotype, and persuade citizens unethically. Through the media, powerful groups can dominate the public sphere.

ETHICAL GOODS

Journalism contributes to the ethical goods by helping to produce citizens who value ethical flourishing (including the public good). Journalism can promote the ethical goods as follows:

1 Take the public good perspective. When covering public issues or public events, such as elections, media should focus on how the public good is served or not served by proposals, promises, and actions. They should examine critically any claims by public officials, large private corporations, and any other agency to be acting for the public good.
2 Highlight those who enhance the public good. Cover individuals and groups who enhance society through courageous and public-minded actions.
3 Support the exercise of public reason through dialogic media. As discussed in previous chapters, how citizens speak to each other is almost as important as what they say. At the core of the global media system should be deliberative spaces where reasonable citizens can robustly but respectfully exchange views and evaluate proposals.

Altered Norms

These aims require a sea change in media ethics' basic concepts and ways of practice.

To get a sense of the change needed, consider the idea of journalism's social contract. In a global public sphere, if global journalism has a social contract, it is not with a particular public or society; instead, it seems to be something much more diffuse – a multi-society contract. The cosmopolitan journalist is a transnational public communicator who seeks the trust and credence of a global audience. Also, the ideal of objectivity in news coverage takes on an international sense. Traditionally, news objectivity asks journalists to avoid bias toward groups within one's own country. Global objectivity would discourage allowing bias toward one's country as a whole to distort reports on international issues. The ideas of accuracy and balance become enlarged to include reports with international sources and cross-cultural perspectives. Global media ethics asks journalists to be more conscious of how they frame major stories, how they set the international news agenda, and how they can spark violence in tense societies.

Adopting a global media ethics also requires a major change in serving the public. What happens when the journalist's commitment to informing their country conflicts with informing the world as global citizens? Global media ethics holds that transnational principles of human rights and social justice take precedence over personal interests and national interests, when they conflict. This emphasis on what is ethically prior provides some direction to journalists caught in the ethical maze of international events. When my country embarks on an unjust war against another country, I, as a journalist (or citizen), should say so. If I am a Canadian journalist and I learn that Canada is engaged in trading practices that condemn citizens of an African country to continuing, abject poverty, I should not hesitate to report the injustice. It is not a violation of any reasonable form of patriotism or citizenship to hold one's country to higher standards.

A globally minded media would alter how journalists approach covering international events such as a conference on climate change or talks on a new global trade agreement. A parochial journalism ethics would not object to journalists serving the public of their nations by reporting a climate change conference mainly from the perspective of their co-patriots. With regard to the climate conference, parochial journalists would tend to ask: What is in it for their country? What strategies will serve the national interests of their fellow citizens? As for global trade, parochial journalists would focus on how changes to a global trade agreement could open up markets for their country's farmers or oil producers.

A global attitude would oppose such narrow, nationalistic reporting. It would require that journalists approach such events from the perspective of the global public good. What is the global problem concerning climate change, and how should all countries cooperate to reach a fair and effective agreement? Globally minded journalists from the West would report the legitimate complaints that developing nations have against the environmental policy of their own country. They would question a global trade proposal made by their country if it advances their national interests while impoverishing developing nations. Global media ethics directs journalists to make issues of global justice a major part of their reporting and analysis.

A global ethics attitude limits parochial attachments in journalism by drawing a ring of broader ethical principles around them. When there is no conflict with global principles, journalists can report in ways that support local and national communities. They can practise their craft parochially.

Finally, a global media ethics rethinks the role of patriotism, as noted above when we discussed emotions. In a global world, patriotism should play a decreasing role in ethical reasoning about media issues. At best, nation-based forms of patriotism remain ethically permissible if they do not conflict with the demands of a global ethical flourishing. Global media ethics requires that journalists commit themselves only to a moderate patriotism, subjecting the easily inflamed emotion of love of country to rational and ethical restraint. A moderate patriotism means that one has a special affection for one's country and that one is willing to help it flourish and pursue its goals. But this special affection, based either on a love of the culture or respect for its laws, does not make one's country superior to other countries. A loyalty to one's country does not justify an aggressive national posture on the world stage whereby one's country pursues its goals at the expense of other countries. Where patriotism is extreme, and it asks journalists to ignore global justice and violations of human rights, such patriotic claims are to be denied.

Moderate patriotism, therefore, rejects all forms of extreme nationalism and patriotism based on race or superiority of culture. It rejects xenophobic portrayals of other cultures. A globally minded media should not participate in demonizing other groups, especially in times of tension. The duty of journalism in periods of looming conflict or war is not to follow a patriotism of blind allegiance or muted criticism of the actions of one's country. In such times, journalists serve their countries – that is, are patriotic – by continuing to provide independent news and analysis. It is not a violation of any reasonable form of patriotism or citizenship to hold one's country to higher standards.

Global journalism ethics does not entail that news organizations should ignore local issues or regional audiences. It does not mean that every story requires a cosmopolitan attitude. However, there are situations, such as military intervention in a foreign country, climate change, and the establishment of a fair world trading system, where we need to assess actions from the perspective of global justice and reasonableness. What is at issue is a gradual widening of basic editorial attitudes and standards – a widening of journalists' vision of their responsibilities. It asks them to consider their society's actions, policies, and values from a larger perspective.

CONCLUSION

This chapter has articulated the implications of democratically engaged journalism for a digital and global media world.

Methodologically, democratically engaged journalism follows pragmatic objectivity. Journalists adopt the objective stance and apply generic and domain-specific standards in holistically evaluating their reports, regarded as holistic interpretations of events.

The political aim of democratically engaged journalism is dialogic, egalitarian democracy. Dialogic democracy was identified as the highest form of democracy and therefore the proper aim of ethical journalism. The ultimate aim is human flourishing, the advancement of the four levels of the human good *within* the bounds of justice. Put all together, the aim is this: to advance human flourishing by advancing the four levels of human good, justice, and dialogic democracy, globally and within nations.

EPILOGUE

Benefits of Objective Engagement

Every question possessed a power that was lost in the answer.

Elie Wiesel, *Night*, 5

Objectivity and impartiality are attitudes that are easily undervalued in today's age of global media and partisan opinion. These virtues can be mocked as "neutering" oneself, a cowardly refusal to take a position. Or impartiality is said to require an impossible "view from nowhere."

We have seen how objectivity with a human face replies to these erroneous portraits of objectivity and its relationship with engagement. I ask critics to consider why we need objectivity in our lives in the first place, especially as a society.

WHY OBJECTIVITY?

Objectivity in society exists because the public sphere features a clash of subjective views and interests, advanced by people or groups that have little interest in meeting the criteria of pragmatic objectivity. The sphere of the partial in society is always larger than the sphere of the non-partial. Rightly or wrongly, impartiality has little significance for car salesmen, political lobbyists, right-wing advocates, writers of commercial ads for TV, and "hot talk" radio announcers. Impartiality is a crucial tool for discussing and evaluating the claims of these partisan people. As a society, we are in danger of no longer understanding why there needs to be, in a democracy, *self-imposed* limits to our partisanship and methods of persuasion.

Moreover, apart from strong partisanship, we need impartial professionals and officials every day in society to fairly adjudicate and peacefully resolve disputes between partial people, with their conflicting ideas about what actions, or reforms, are needed in a situation. Objectivity is valuable not only where there is fierce, potentially violent, conflict. It is valuable where we simply need a calm, fair evaluation and where there is an orderly competition for a benefit. The teacher needs to be impartial and fair when evaluating a student's test. An awards committee needs to be impartial when deciding on the recipient of a scholarship or a prize.

Without impartiality, bias seeps into the decision-making process. The demand for impartiality lies behind the rules for avoiding conflicts of interest in the professions, since conflicts impair impartial judgment. Also, impartiality supports the integrity of the decision process. Public perception of any process where adjudicators lack impartiality can undermine acceptance of their decision.

Objectivity and impartiality are not applicable everywhere. No one cares about objectivity when they cheer for their hockey team on Saturday night. But everyone cares if a judge is impartial in hearing a court case that involves their interests. We should care that mediators in labour disputes act impartially. Also, we should care if certain basic liberties and rights are applied equally to all citizens, no matter their race or religion.

Further, the notion of pragmatic objectivity has positive consequences for the debate over objectivity itself. It brings arid, acrimonious debates over objectivity down to earth. It shifts the debate away from irresolvable, abstract disputes about the theoretical possibility of a perfect objectivity to more concrete questions about the degree of objectivity of a specific report, relative to other reports on the same event. Pragmatic objectivity turns metaphysical questions about whether a report "mirrors" reality into more manageable epistemic questions about whether it meets certain basic tests in a specific context. Pragmatic objectivity clarifies what objectivity really requires, dispelling confusions that have been a persistent source of debate. Pragmatic objectivity replies that objectivity is a matter of good practice, available to ordinary humans. An objective stance is not too onerous a thing to demand of citizens with public duties, such as journalists.

CHOOSING OBJECTIVITY

In the end, we need to see rationality and objectivity as intrinsically related to issues of individual and social "will," character, and motivation. It not just about facts. It is about the extent to which people are *willing* to adopt the objective stance where it matters the most – in debates that affect the rights of citizens and minorities, and in debates over the direction of one's nation. To what extent are journalists willing to encourage objective public reason in the public sphere?

Hence, the future of objectivity depends upon more than the education and knowledge of citizens. It also depends on their moral character, their political virtues, and their sense of justice when they engage in public life.

Whether they have such a will to be objective will depend on whether they have grown up in a society that encourages objective modes of thinking and respect for plural democracy. Hence, democracy and democratic media have a major role sustaining and promoting dialogic democracy.

The decision to adopt the objective stance in dealing with social and political issues is one of the most important choices that we can make, as individuals and as a society. The decision is not restricted to a group of scientists or professionals. The decision involves all citizens. In the future, how many of us will care about thinking, acting, and valuing in a rational and coherent manner? Objectivity, properly understood, is a bulwark against authoritarianism in belief and practice. It is a defence against an obscurantism that allows the clever to manipulate the naïve or vulnerable. The attitude of objectivity stands squarely against the many forms of obscurantism in our culture, propagating themselves through the media. It opposes irrationalism, emotionalism, extreme religious fundamentalism, occultism, and fraudulent mysticism. For all the faults attributed to a detached, "cool" objectivity, I fear more a mindless emotionalism and an inability to assess critically beliefs inculcated by a media-saturated world.

The objective stance is part of that noble phenomenon called the liberal mind – a mind that is autonomous and critical and respects the autonomy of other minds. An objective disposition is a manifestation of rational, liberal agency at work. Citizens with objective dispositions, with their sense of fairness, insistence on evidence, and intellectual honesty, help public deliberation. The disposition to give reasons supports a peaceful resolution of disputes. Objectivity encourages respect for the views of others. Objectivity and impartiality help us to be clear about the strengths and weakness of different views and to treat each side equally and without prejudice. To be objective is to give reasons for and against views, rather than attacking the person or his or her class. To adopt the objective stance is to incur a responsibility to communicate freely, clearly, and rationally. To become suspicious of reason and argument is in effect to lose a measure of respect for humans and the process of sharing ideas. To follow objective standards and to practise objectivity's virtues are to express one's rational autonomy and to respect the rational autonomy of others.

The use of reason to dismiss reason and its commitment to truth and objectivity is a socially dangerous, insidious attitude. It uses logic and rationality to eat away at the basis of our commitment to rationality. It blurs the distinctions between reason and cause, rational persuasion and propaganda.

Few people would care to live in a society that had no respect for the concept of objectivity, that saw no virtue in adopting the objective stance, and that refused to guide inquiry by the best available objective standards. Few critics of objectivity would want journalism to abandon objectivity *tout court.* It is one thing to cavil in academia about the myth of objectivity; it is quite another to live in a society that lacks the ideal.

A NEW TYRANNY?

We now live in a global, media-linked world where the public sphere is being polluted, or corrupted, by intolerant people and powerful groups who spread misinformation and attempt to disrupt or influence democratic elections. Now, more than ever, we need a moral compass in journalism and media, generally. That compass, in my view, is provided by the aims and standards of objective engagement. It is a compass that can be used to educate not only journalists but citizens who consume and use media.

I conclude by returning one last time to the skeptical query: Why hang on to objectivity in journalism? My reply is: Because in the end so much depends on how we think. The discipline of mind that these values call for is what lies between reason and unreason, between seeking evidence and wishful thinking; between being informed and simply *having* an opinion; between being open to revision and being dogmatically self-satisfied; between seeking dialogue and rejecting compromise as a weakness; between the hard road of constructing well-evidenced positions and the easy pleasures of ranting; between welcoming dissent and seeing people with different views as traitors; between communication aimed at richer understandings and communication aimed at victory through any means.

When we ask journalists to step back from their own beliefs, to verify claims, and to fairly represent viewpoints, we ask them to practise their craft in a manner essential to tolerant, plural democracies. And, now, such an attitude is essential to correcting a corrupted public sphere where it seems that the force of personality and intolerant certainty is all, an illusionary and masochistic sign of strength.

If *this* mindset prevails, it will surely be the death of democracy and the rise of a new tyranny.

Bibliography

Albrecht, James M. *Reconstructing Individualism: A Pragmatic Tradition from Emerson to Ellison.* New York: Fordham University Press, 2012.

Alston, William P. *A Realist Conception of Truth.* Ithaca: Cornell University Press, 1996.

Appiah, Kwame A. *Cosmopolitanism: Ethics in a World of Strangers.* New York: Norton, 2006.

Aquila, Richard E. *Intentionality: A Study of Mental Acts.* London: Pennsylvania State University Press, 1977.

Aristotle. *The Ethics.* Translated by J.A.K. Thomson. London: Penguin, 1976.

– *On Interpretation,* in *The Basic Works of Aristotle,* edited by Richard McKeon, 40–61. New York: The Modern Library, 2001.

Arendt, Hannah. *Between Past and Future.* New York: Penguin, 1993.

Armstrong, Donald M. *Belief, Truth and Knowledge.* Cambridge: Cambridge University Press, 1973.

Ayer, Alfred J. *Language, Truth and Logic.* 2nd ed. New York: Dover Books, 1952 (1936).

– *Logical Positivism.* New York: The Free Press, 1959.

Bacon, Francis. *The Essays.* Edited by John Pitcher. New York: Penguin Books, 1985 (1597).

– *The New Organon.* Cambridge: Cambridge University Press, 2000 (1620).

Bakewell, Sarah. *How to Live: A Life of Montaigne.* London: Vintage, 2011.

Baldasty, Gerald. *The Commercialization of the News in the Nineteenth Century.* Madison: University of Wisconsin, 1992.

Batsell, Jake. *Engaged Journalism: Connecting with Digitally Empowered News Audiences.* New York: Columbia University Press, 2015.

Bayle, Pierre. *Dictionary Historical and Critical.* 2nd ed. London: Routledge, 1997 (1737).

Beiser, Frederick. *The Sovereignty of Reason: The Defence of Rationality in the Early English Enlightenment.* Princeton: Princeton University Press, 1996.

Berkeley, George. *Principles of Human Knowledge.* Edited by Colin M. Turbayne. New York: Bobbs-Merrill, 1970 (1710).

Berlin, Isaiah. "Two Concepts of Liberty." In *Four Essays on Liberty.* Oxford: Oxford University Press, 1969.

Blackburn, Simon. *Ruling Passions.* Oxford: Clarendon University Press, 1998.

Bloom, Paul. *Against Empathy: The Case for Rational Compassion.* New York: HarperCollins Books, 2016.

Boardman, John, Griffin, Jasper, and Oswyn Murray, eds. *The Oxford History of Greece and the Hellenistic World.* Oxford: Oxford University Press, 1991.

Bradley, Francis. *Appearance and Reality.* 2nd rev. edition. Oxford: Oxford University Press, 1969 (1893).

– *Essays on Truth and Reality.* Oxford: Clarendon Press, 1914.

Briggs, Asa, and Peter Burke. *A Social History of the Media: From Gutenberg to the Internet.* Cambridge: Polity Press, 2002.

Brucker, Herbert. *Freedom of Information.* New York: Macmillan, 1949.

Bruner, Jerome. *Beyond the Information Given.* Edited by Jeremy M. Anglin. New York: Norton, 1973.

Burke, Peter. *A Social History of Knowledge.* Cambridge: Polity Press, 2000.

Burtt, Edwin A. *The Metaphysical Foundations of Modern Science.* Garden City: Doubleday, 1954.

Butterfield, Herbert. *The Origins of Modern Science, 1300–1800.* Rev. ed. Toronto: Clarke, Irwin and Co., 1968.

Buxton, Richard G. *Persuasion in Greek Tragedy.* New York: Cambridge University Press, 1982.

Cain, Susan. *Quiet.* New York: Random House, 2012.

Campbell, W. Joseph. *Yellow Journalism: Puncturing the Myths, Defining the Legacies.* Westport: Praeger, 2001.

Camus, Albert. *The Myth of Sisyphus.* London: Penguin Books, 2000.

Carnap, Rudolf. *An Introduction to the Philosophy of Science.* Mineola: Dover Books, 1995.

– *The Logical Structure of the World and Pseudoproblems in Philosophy.* 2nd ed. Translated by Rolf A. George. Berkeley, CA: University of California Press, 1967.

– *The Unity of Science.* New York: Routledge, 2011. First published in English in 1934.

Chang, Le, and Doris Tsao. "The Code for Facial Identity in the Primate Brain." *Cell* 169, no. 6 (June 2017): 1013–28.

Christians, Clifford G., Theodore L. Glasser, Denis McQuail, Kaarle Nordenstreng, and Robert A. White. *Normative Theories of the Media: Journalism in Democratic Societies.* Urbana: University of Illinois Press, 2009.

Clavelin, Maurice. *The Natural Philosophy of Galileo.* Translated by A.J. Pomerans. Cambridge, MA: MIT Press, 1974.

Cohen, Joshua. *The Arc of the Moral Universe and Other Essays*. Cambridge, MA: Harvard University Press, 2010.

Cottingham, John. "Favouritism and Morality." *Philosophical Quarterly* 36, no. 144 (1986): 357–73.

Crombie, Alistair C. *Science in the Middle Ages*. Vol. 1 of *Medieval and Early Modern Science*. Garden City: Doubleday, 1959.

Daston, Lorraine. "Baconian Facts, Academic Civility and the Prehistory of Objectivity." In *Rethinking Objectivity*, edited by Allan Megill, 37–63. London: Duke University Press, 1994.

– "Fear and Loathing of the Imagination in Science." *Daedalus* 127, no. 1 (Winter 1998): 73–95.

– "Objectivity and the Escape from Perspective." *Social Studies of Science* 22, no. 4 (November 1992).

Daston, Lorraine, and Peter Galison. "The Image of Objectivity." *Representations* 40 (Fall 1992): 81–127.

– *Objectivity*. New York: Zone Books, 2007.

Daston, Lorraine, and Katharine Park. *Wonders and the Order of Nature*. New York: Zone Books, 2001.

Davidson, Donald. *Inquiries into Truth and Interpretation*. New York: Oxford University Press, 1984.

Descartes, René. "Discourse on Method." In *The Philosophical Works of Descartes*, vol. 1, 81–130. Cambridge: Cambridge University Press, 1986.

– "Meditations on First Philosophy." In *The Philosophical Works of Descartes*, vol. 1, 131–99. Cambridge: Cambridge University Press, 1986.

– *Rules for the Direction of the Mind*. In *The Philosophical Works of Descartes*, vol. 1, 1–77. Cambridge: Cambridge University Press, 1986.

Dewey, John. *Democracy and Education*. Radford: Wilder Publications, 2005.

– *Experience and Nature*. New York: Dover Publications, 1958.

– "The Need for Reform in Philosophy." In *The Essential Writings of John Dewey*, edited by David Sidorski, 29–46. New York: Harper Torchbooks, 1977.

– *The Public and Its Problems*. New York: Henry Holt, 1927.

– *Reconstruction in Philosophy*. Mineola: Dover Publications, 2004 (1948).

Dicken, Paul. *A Critical Introduction to Scientific Realism*. London: Bloomsbury, 2016.

Dworkin, Ronald. *Justice for Hedgehogs*. Cambridge, MA: Harvard University Press, 2011.

– *Law's Empire*. Cambridge, MA: Harvard University Press, 1986.

– *Sovereign Virtue: The Theory and Practice of Equality*. Cambridge, MA: Harvard University Press, 2000.

Eisenstein, Elizabeth L. *The Printing Press as an Agent of Change*. Cambridge: Cambridge University Press, 1979.

Eksteins, Modris. *Rites of Spring*. Toronto: Lester and Orpen Dennys, 1986.

Elgin, Catherine Z. *Between the Absolute and the Arbitrary*. Ithaca: Cornell University Press, 1997 (1983).

Fodor, Jerry A. *The Modularity of Mind*. Cambridge, MA: MIT Press, 1983.

Foucault, Michel. *The Archaeology of Knowledge*. Translated by Allan Sheridan. New York: Harper and Row, 1972.

Frankfort, Henry, et al. *Before Philosophy*. Baltimore, MD: Penguin, 1971.

Frankfurt, Harry G. "On Bullshit." In *The Importance of What We Care About: Philosophical Essays*, 117–33. Cambridge: Cambridge University Press, 1988.

Gadamer, Hans-Georg. *Truth and Method*. 2nd revised ed. New York: Continuum, 2004.

Gardner, Howard. *The Mind's New Science: A History of the Cognitive Revolution*. New York: Basic Books, 1987.

Gibson, Roger F. "Translation, Physics and the Facts of the Matter." In *The Philosophy of W.V. Quine*, edited by Edwin Hahn and Paul Schlipp, 139–57. LaSalle: Open Court, 1986.

Gigerenzer, Gerd, et al. *The Empire of Chance: How Probability Changed Science and Everyday Life*. Cambridge: Cambridge University Press, 1989.

Gilligan, Carol. *In a Different Voice: Psychological Theory and Women's Development*. Cambridge, MA: Harvard University Press, 1982.

Glass, Anthony L., Keith J. Holyoak, and John L. Santa. *Cognition*. Reading: Addison Wesley, 1979.

Goodman, Nelson. *Languages of Art*. Indianapolis: Hackett, 1976.

– *Ways of Worldmaking*. Indianapolis: Hackett, 1978.

Gopnik, Alison. "Artificial Intelligence Helps in Learning How Children Learn." *Scientific American* 316, no. 6 (June 2017): 6–10.

Gottlieb, Anthony. *The Dream of Reason*. New York: Norton, 2000.

Graves, Robert. *The Greek Myths*. London: Penguin, 1992.

Greene, Joshua. *Moral Tribes: Emotion, Reason and the Gap between Us and Them*. New York: Penguin Books, 2014.

Gregory, Richard L., ed. *The Oxford Companion to the Mind*. Oxford: Oxford University Press, 1978.

Guthrie, William K.C. *The Fifth Century Enlightenment*. Vol. 3 of *A History of Greek Philosophy*. Cambridge: Cambridge University Press, 1969.

Haack, Susan. *Manifesto of a Passionate Moderate: Unfashionable Essays*. Chicago: University of Chicago Press, 1998.

Habermas, Jurgen. "Discourse Ethics: Notes on a Program of Philosophical Justification." In *Moral Consciousness and Communicative Action*, translated by Christian Lenhardt and Shierry Weber Nicholsen, 43–115. Cambridge, MA: MIT Press, 2001.

– *The Theory of Communicative Action: Reason and the Rationalization of Society*. Vol. 1. Translated by Thomas McCarthy. Cambridge: Blackwell, 1991.

Hacking, Ian. "Natural Kinds." In *Perspectives on Quine*, edited by Robert Barrett and Roger Gibson, 129–41. Cambridge, MA: Basil Blackwell, 1990.

– *Representing and Intervening*. Cambridge: Cambridge University Press, 1983.

– *Rewriting the Soul*. Princeton: Princeton University Press, 1995.

– *The Taming of Chance*. Cambridge: Cambridge University Press, 1990.

Haidt, Jonathan. *The Righteous Mind: Why Good People Are Divided by Politics and Religion*. New York: Pantheon, 2012.

Hare, Richard. *The Language of Morals*. Oxford: Clarendon Press, 2003.

Hartley, David. *Observations on Man*. London: S. Richardson, 1749.

Hempel, Carl. "The Empiricist Criterion of Meaning." In *Logical Positivism*, edited by A.J. Ayer, 108–29. New York: The Free Press, 1959.

Hobbes, Thomas. *Leviathan*. London: Penguin, 1985 (1651).

Honderich, Ted, ed. *The Oxford Guide to Philosophy*. Oxford: Oxford University Press, 2005.

Hume, David. *Essays: Moral, Political and Literary*. Indianapolis: Liberty Fund, 1987.

– *A Treatise of Human Nature*. 2nd ed. Oxford: Clarendon Press, 1978 (1739).

Husserl, Edmund. *Cartesian Meditations: An Introduction to Phenomenology*. Translated by Dorion Cairns. The Hague: Martinus Nijhoff, 1973.

– *The Crisis of European Sciences and Transcendental Phenomenology*. Translated by David Carr. Evanston: Northwestern University Press, 1970.

– *Ideas: General Introduction to Pure Phenomenology*. Translated by W.R. Boyce Gibson. London: Collier Books, 1975.

James, William. *The Meaning of Truth and Pragmatism*. Cambridge, MA: Harvard University Press, 1978 (1910).

– *Pragmatism and Four Essays from The Meaning of Truth*. New York: Meridian, 1974.

Kahneman, Daniel. *Thinking Fast and Slow*. Toronto: Anchor Canada, 2013.

Kant, Immanuel. *Critique of Practical Reason*. Translated by Lewis White Beck. New York: Bobbs-Merrill, 1956 (1788).

– *Critique of Pure Reason*. Translated by Paul Guyer and Allen Wood. New York: St Martin's Press, 1998 (1781).

– *Groundwork of the Metaphysics of Morals*. Translated by Mary Gregor. Cambridge: Cambridge University Press, 2006 (1785).

Kierkegaard, Søren. "Becoming Subjective." In *Concluding Unscientific Postscript*, translated by David Swenson and Walter Lowrie, 15–167. Princeton: Princeton University Press, 1974 (1846).

Kingwell, Mark. *Unruly Voices: Essays on Democracy, Civility, and the Human Imagination*. Ottawa: Biblioasis, 2012.

Kirk, Geoffrey S., and John E. Raven. *The Presocratic Philosophers*. Cambridge: Cambridge University Press, 1966.

Kovach, Bill, and Tom Rosenstiel. *The Elements of Journalism*. New York: Crown Publishers, 2001.

Kraft, Victor. *The Vienna Circle: The Origin of Neo-Positivism.* New York: Greenwood, 1969 (1953).

Langan, Thomas. *Merleau-Ponty's Critique of Reason.* New Haven: Yale University Press, 1966.

Lewis, Clarence I. "The Given in Experience." In *Mind and the World Order.* New York: Dover, 1929.

Lloyd, Geoffrey E.R. *Magic, Reason and Experience: Studies in the Origin and Development of Greek Science.* London: Cambridge University Press, 1979.

Locke, John. *Essay Concerning Human Understanding.* New York: Dover, 1959 (1690).

Lord, Beth. *Spinoza's Ethics.* Edinburgh: Edinburgh University Press, 2010.

Losee, John. *A Historical Introduction to the Philosophy of Science.* Oxford: Oxford University Press, 1972.

Lowe, Edward J. "Action Theory and Ontology." In *A Companion to the Philosophy of Action,* edited by Timothy O'Connor and Constantine Sandis, 3–9. Malden: Wiley-Blackwell, 2013.

Lynch, Michael P. *Truth in Context: An Essay on Pluralism and Objectivity.* Cambridge, MA: MIT Press, 1998.

Lyotard, Jean-Francois. *Why Philosophize?* Translated by Corinne Enaudeau. Cambridge: Polity, 2013.

MacDougall, Curtis, and Robert D. Reid. *Interpretive Reporting.* 9th ed. New York: MacMillan, 1987 (1938).

Mach, Ernst. *The Analysis of Sensations and the Relation of the Physical to the Psychical.* Translated by C.M. Williams. New York: Dover, 1959 (1897).

– *The Science of Mechanics: A Critical and Historical Account of Its Development.* New York: Open Court, 1988 (1883).

MacIntyre, Alasdair. "Is Patriotism a Virtue?" The Lindley Lecture. Lawrence: University of Kansas Press, 1984.

Macmurray, John. *The Self as Agent.* London: Faber and Faber, 1957.

Makau, Josina M., and Debian L. Marty. *Dialogue and Deliberation.* Long Grove: Waveland Press, 2013.

McMullin, Ernan, ed. *The Concept of Matter in Greek and Medieval Philosophy.* Notre Dame: University of Notre Dame Press, 1965.

Megill, Allan. *Rethinking Objectivity.* London: Duke University Press, 1994.

Merleau-Ponty, Maurice. *Phenomenology of Perception.* Translated by Donald A. Landes. New York: Routledge, 2014.

Meyer, Eugene. "The Post's Principles." In *The Washington Post Deskbook on Style.* 2nd ed. New York: McGraw-Hill, 1989.

Mill, John Stuart. *An Examination of Sir William Hamilton's Philosophy.* Vol. 9 of *The Collected Works of John Stuart Mill,* edited by John M. Robson. Toronto: University of Toronto Press, 1969 (1865).

– *On Liberty and the Subjection of Women.* Edited by Alan Ryan. London: Penguin Books, 2006.
– *System of Logic (Part 2).* In *The Collected Works of John Stuart Mill,* vol. 8, edited by John R. Robson. Toronto: University of Toronto Press, 1974 (1843).
Miraldi, Robert. *Muckraking and Objectivity.* New York: Greenwood Press, 1990.
Montaigne, Michel de. *The Complete Works.* Translated and edited by D. Frame. London: Everyman, 2005.
Moore, George E. "The Refutation of Idealism." In *Selected Writings,* edited by Thomas Baldwin, 23–58. New York, Routledge, 1993 (1903).
Murdoch, Irish. *The Sovereignty of Good.* London: Routledge and Kegan Paul, 1971.
Nagel, Thomas. *The View from Nowhere.* New York: Oxford University Press, 1986.
Newell, R.W. *Objectivity, Empiricism and Truth.* London: Routledge and Kegan Paul, 1986.
Nietzsche, Friedrich. *Human, All Too Human: A Book for Free Spirits.* Translated by R.J. Hollingdale. Cambridge: Cambridge University Press, 1996 (1878).
– *Twilight of the Idols.* Translated by R.J. Hollingdale. London: Penguin Books, 2002.
– *The Will to Power.* Translated by Walter Kaufmann and R.J. Hollingdale. London: Weidenfeld and Nicholson, 1967.
Nussbaum, Martha C. *The Fragility of Goodness.* Cambridge: Cambridge University Press, 2001.
– *Frontiers of Justice.* Cambridge, MA: Harvard University Press, 2006.
– *Political Emotions: Why Love Matters for Justice.* Cambridge, MA: Harvard University Press, 2013.
– *Upheavals of Thought: The Intelligence of Emotions.* Cambridge: Cambridge University Press, 2001.
O'Connor, Timothy, and Constantine Sandis, eds. *A Companion to the Philosophy of Action.* Malden: Wiley-Blackwell, 2013.
Ortega y Gasset, Jose. *Meditations on Quixote.* Translated by Evelyn Rugg and Diego Marin. Urbana: University of Illinois Press, 2000.
Passmore, John. *A Hundred Years of Philosophy.* Harmondsworth: Penguin, 1966.
Pihlström, Sami, ed. *Pragmatism and Objectivity: Essays Sparked by the Work of Nicholas Rescher.* New York: Routledge, 2017.
Plato. "Ion." In *The Collected Dialogues of Plato,* edited by Edith Hamilton and Huntington Cairns, 937–49. Princeton: Princeton University Press, 1973.
– "Phaedrus." In *The Collected Dialogues of Plato,* edited by Edith Hamilton and Huntington Cairns, 475–525. Princeton: Princeton University Press, 1973.
Polanyi, Michael. *Personal Knowledge: Towards a Post-Critical Philosophy.* London: Routledge, 2002.
Poovey, Mary. *A History of the Modern Fact: Problems of Knowledge in the Sciences of Wealth and Society.* London: University of Chicago, 1998.

Popper, Karl. "Epistemology without a Knowing Subject." In *Objective Knowledge*, 106–52. Oxford: Clarendon Press, 1972.

– *The Open Society and Its Enemies*. 5th ed. Princeton: Princeton University Press, 1966.

Porter, Theodore M. *Trust in Numbers: The Pursuit of Objectivity in Science and Public Life*. Princeton: Princeton University Press, 1995.

Proctor, Robert. *Value-Free Science?* Cambridge, MA: Harvard University Press, 1991.

Proust, Marcel. *Remembrance of Things Past, Volume 1: Swann's Way and Within a Budding Grove*. New York: Vintage, 1982.

Putnam, Hilary. *The Collapse of the Fact/Value Dichotomy and Other Essays*. Cambridge, UK: Harvard University Press, 2002.

– "The Craving for Objectivity." In *Realism with a Human Face*, edited by James Conant, 120–31. Cambridge, MA: Harvard University Press, 1990.

– *Ethics without Ontology*. Cambridge, MA: Harvard University Press, 2004.

– "Irrealism and Deconstruction." In *Renewing Philosophy*, 108–33. Cambridge, MA: Harvard University Press, 1992.

– *The Many Faces of Realism*. LaSalle: Open Court, 1987.

– "Peirce the Logician." In *Realism with a Human Face*, edited by James Conant, 252–60. Cambridge, MA: Harvard University Press, 1990.

– *Realism with a Human Face*. Edited by James Conant. Cambridge, MA: Harvard University Press, 1990.

– *Reason, Truth and History*. Cambridge, UK: Cambridge University Press, 1981.

– "Sense, Non-sense, and the Senses: An Inquiry into the Powers of the Mind." *The Journal of Philosophy* 91, no. 9 (September 1994): 445–517.

– *Words and Life*. Edited by James Conant. Cambridge, MA: Harvard University Press, 1994.

Quine, Willard V. "Epistemology Naturalized." In *Ontological Relativity and Other Essays*, 69–90. New York: Columbia University Press, 1969.

– "Ontological Relativity." In *Ontological Relativity and Other Essays*, 26–68. New York: Columbia University Press, 1969.

– "Two Dogmas of Empiricism." In *From a Logical Point of View*, 20–46. New York: Harper Torchbooks, 1953.

– *Word and Object*. Cambridge, MA: MIT Press, 1960.

Ramsey, Frank. "Philosophy." In *Philosophical Papers*, edited by D.H. Mellor, 1–7. Cambridge: Cambridge University Press, 1929.

Rawls, John. *The Law of Peoples*. Cambridge, MA: Harvard University Press, 2004.

– *Political Liberalism*. New York: Columbia University Press, 1993.

– *A Theory of Justice (1972)*. Oxford: Oxford University Press, 1992.

Raz, Joseph. "Notes on Value and Objectivity." In *Objectivity in Law and Morals*, edited by Brian Leiter, 194–233. Cambridge: Cambridge University Press, 2001.

Reichenbach, Hans. "The Nature of Ethics." In *The Rise of Scientific Philosophy*. Berkeley: University of California Press, 1951.

Reid, Thomas. *Essays on the Intellectual Powers* of *Man*. University Park: Penn State University Press, 2001.

Rescher, Nicholas. *Objectivity: The Obligations of Impersonal Reason*. Notre Dame: University of Notre Dame Press, 1997.

– *Rationality*. Oxford: Oxford University Press, 1988.

Richardson, Alan. *Carnap's Construction of the World: The Aufbau and the Emergence of Logical Empiricism*. Cambridge: Cambridge University Press, 1998.

Rorty, Richard. *Philosophy and the Mirror of Nature*. Princeton: Princeton University Press, 1979.

– *Truth and Progress*. Cambridge: Cambridge University Press, 1998.

Rosen, Jay. *Getting the Connections Right: Public Journalism and the Troubles in the Press*. New York: Twentieth Century Fund Press, 1996.

Russell, Bertrand. *A History of Western Philosophy*. London: George Allen and Unwin, 1946.

– *An Inquiry into Meaning and Truth*. Harmondsworth: Pelican, 1969.

– "Logical Atomism." In *Logical Positivism*, edited by A.J. Ayer, 31–50. New York: The Free Press, 1959.

– "On Denoting." *Mind* 14 (October 1905), 479–93.

– "The Philosophy of Logical Atomism." In *Logic and Knowledge: Essays 1901–1950*, edited by Robert C. Marsh, 175–281. New York: Capricorn Books, 1971.

– *The Problems of Philosophy*. Oxford: Oxford University Press, 1974 (1912).

Sartre, Jean-Paul. *Existentialism and Humanism*. London: Methuen, 1973.

Schlick, Moritz. "A New Philosophy of Experience." Stockton: Publications in Philosophy of the College of the Pacific, 1932.

– "The Turning Point in Philosophy." In *Logical Positivism*, edited by A.J. Ayer, 53–9. New York: The Free Press, 1959.

Searle, John. *The Construction of Social Reality*. New York: Simon and Schuster, 1995.

– *Making the Social World: The Structure of Human Civilization*. Oxford: Oxford University Press, 2010.

– *Rationality in Action*. Cambridge, MA: MIT Press, 2001.

Sellars, Wilfred. "Philosophy and the Scientific Image of Man." In *Empiricism and the Philosophy of Mind*, 1–40. London: Routledge and Kegan Paul, 1963.

– *Science, Perception, and Reality*. Atlantic Highlands: Humanities Press, 1963.

Sen, Amartya. *The Idea of Justice*. Cambridge: Harvard University Press, 2009.

Shafer-Landau, Russ. *Moral Realism: A Defence*. Oxford: Oxford University Press, 2005.

Shapin, Steven, and Simon Schaffer. Leviathan and the Air-Pump. Princeton, NJ: Princeton University Press, 1985.

Shapiro, Barbara. *A Culture of Fact*. Ithaca: Cornell University Press, 2000.

– *Probability and Certainty in Seventeenth-Century England.* Princeton, NJ: Princeton University Press, 1983.

Siebert, Fred S., et al., eds. *Four Theories of the Press.* Urbana: University of Illinois Press, 1956.

Simon, Herbert A. "Theories of Bounded Rationality." In *Decisions and Organization,* edited by C.B. McGuire and R. Radner, 161–76. Amsterdam: North-Holland Publishing, 1972.

Sinclair, William A. *The Traditional Formal Logic.* 5th ed. London: Methuen, 1951.

Singer, Peter. "Famine, Affluence, and Morality." *Philosophy and Public Affairs* 1 (1972): 229–43.

Singer, Peter, Cannold Leonard, and Herman Kuhse. "William Godwin and the Defense of Impartialist Ethics." In *Unsanctifying Human Life,* edited by Helga Kuhse, 157–77. Malden: Blackwell, 2002.

Smith, Adam. *The Theory of Moral Sentiments.* Amherst: Prometheus Books, 2000 (1759).

Stephens, Mitchell. *A History of the News.* New York: Viking, 1988.

Stevenson, Charles. *Ethics and Language.* New Haven: Yale University Press, 1960.

Stigler, Stephen M. *The History of Statistics: The Measurement of Uncertainty to 1900.* Cambridge, MA: Harvard University Press, 1986.

Stokes, Philip. *Philosophy: 100 Essential Thinkers.* London: Arcturus Publishing, 2012.

Strange, Jeffrey, ed. *The Future of Fact: An Annenberg Scholars Conference.* Philadelphia: Annenberg Public Policy Center, 1997.

Strawson, Peter. *Analysis and Metaphysics.* Oxford: Oxford University Press, 1992.

Strayer, Joseph R. *On the Medieval Origins of the Modern State.* Princeton: Princeton University Press, 1998 (1970).

Thagard, Paul. *Conceptual Revolutions.* Princeton: Princeton University Press, 1992.

Thom, Paul. *Making Sense: A Theory of Interpretation.* Lanham: Rowman and Littlefield, 2000.

Walsh, Vivian. "Philosophy and Economics." In *The New Palgrave: A Dictionary of Economics,* vol. 3, edited by J. Eatwell, M. Milgte, and P. Newman. London: Macmillan, 1987.

Ward, Stephen J.A. "Classical Liberal Theory in a Digital World." In *The Handbook of Media and Mass Communication Theory,* vol. 1, edited by Robert S. Fortner and P. Mark Fackler, 3–21. Malden: Wiley, 2014.

– *Disrupting Journalism Ethics.* London: Routledge, 2019.

– "Epistemologies of Journalism." In *Handbook of Communication Science,* vol. 19, edited by Tim P. Vos, 75–93. Frankfurt, Germany: Mouton de Gruyter, 2019.

– *Ethical Journalism in a Populist Age.* Lanham, MD: Rowman and Littlefield, 2019.
– *Ethics and the Media: An Introduction.* Cambridge: Cambridge University Press, 2011.
– *The Invention of Journalism Ethics: The Path to Objectivity and Beyond.* 2nd ed. Montreal: McGill-Queen's University Press, 2015.
– *Global Journalism Ethics.* Montreal: McGill-Queen's University Press, 2010.
– "The Moral Priority of Globalism in a Digital World." In *Media Ethics and Justice in the Age of Globalization*, edited by Herman Wasserman and Shakuntala Rao, 23–42. Houndmills: Palgrave Macmillan, 2015.
– "Patriotism and Journalism." In *Handbook of Patriotism*, edited by Mitja Sardoc, 1–23. Amsterdam: Springer International Publishing AG, 2017.
– *Radical Media Ethics: A Global Approach.* Malden: Wiley, 2015.
– "Thomas Hobbes: The Ethics of Social Order." In *Ethical Communication: Moral Stances in Human Dialogue*, edited by Clifford Christians and John Merrill, 158–64. Columbia and London: University of Missouri Press, 2009.
Weber, Max. "Objectivity in Social Science and Social Policy." In *Methodology of Social Sciences*, translated by Edward A. Shils and Henry A. Finch, 49–112. London: Transaction Publishers, 2011.
Wiesel, Elie. *Night.* New York: Hill and Wang, 2006.
Williams, Bernard. *Descartes: The Project of Pure Inquiry.* Abington: Routledge, 2005.
– *Truth and Truthfulness.* Princeton: Princeton University Press, 2002.
Wisdom, John. "Logical Constructions." *Mind* 40, no. 158 (1931): 188–216.
Wittgenstein, Ludwig. *Philosophical Investigations.* 3rd ed. Translated by G.E.M. Anscombe. New York: The MacMillan Company, 1970 (1958).
– *On Certainty.* Edited by G.E.M. Anscombe and G.H. von Wright. Translated by Denis Paul and G.E.M. Anscombe. New York: Harper Torchbooks, 1972.
– *Remarks on the Foundations of Mathematics.* Edited by G.H. von Wright, R. Rhees, and G.E.M. Anscombe. Oxford: Basil Blackwell, 1956.
– *Tractatus Logico-Philosophicus.* Mineola: Dover Publications, 1999 (1922).
Wong, David. *Natural Moralities: A Defence of Pluralistic Relativism.* Oxford: Oxford University Press, 2006.

Index